ELECTING A MEGA-M/

Toronto 2014

Electing a Mega-Mayor represents the first-ever comprehensive, survey-based examination of a Canadian mayoral race and provides a unique, detailed account of the 2014 mayoral election in Toronto. After making the case that local elections deserve more attention from scholars of political behaviour, this book offers readers an understanding of Toronto politics at the time of the 2014 election and presents relevant background on the major candidates. It considers the importance that Torontonians attached to policy concerns and identifies the bases of support for the outgoing, scandal-ridden mayor, Rob Ford, and his brother Doug.

In the penultimate chapter, the authors examine how Torontonians viewed their elected officials, and the city's performance, two years after the election. McGregor, Moore, and Stephenson conclude with a reflection on what the analysis of the Toronto 2014 election says about voters in large cities in general and provide a short epilogue addressing the 2018 election results. Written in an accessible style, this is the first book on the politics of Toronto during the Ford era that focuses on the perspective of the voter.

R. MICHAEL MCGREGOR is an assistant professor in the Department of Politics and Public Administration at Ryerson University.

AARON A. MOORE is an associate professor in the Department of Political Science at the University of Winnipeg.

LAURA B. STEPHENSON is a professor in the Department of Political Science at the University of Western Ontario.

Electing a Mega-Mayor

Toronto 2014

R. MICHAEL McGREGOR, AARON A. MOORE, AND LAURA B. STEPHENSON

UNIVERSITY OF TORONTO PRESS
Toronto Buffalo London

ISBN 978-1-4875-0963-7 (cloth)   ISBN 978-1-4875-0966-8 (EPUB)
ISBN 978-1-4875-0964-4 (paper)   ISBN 978-1-4875-0965-1 (PDF)

Library and Archives Canada Cataloguing in Publication

Title: Electing a mega-mayor : Toronto 2014 / R. Michael McGregor,
    Aaron A. Moore, and Laura B. Stephenson.
Other titles: Toronto 2014
Names: McGregor, R. Michael, author. | Moore, Aaron A., 1979–, author. |
    Stephenson, Laura Beth, 1976–, author.
Description: Includes bibliographical references and index.
Identifiers: Canadiana (print) 2021015621X | Canadiana (ebook)
    2021015649X | ISBN 9781487509644 (paper) | ISBN 9781487509637
    (cloth) | ISBN 9781487509668 (EPUB) | ISBN 9781487509651 (PDF)
Subjects: LCSH: Mayors – Ontario – Toronto – Election. | LCSH: Local
    elections – Ontario – Toronto. | LCSH: Political candidates – Ontario –
    Toronto. | LCSH: Political campaigns – Ontario – Toronto. | LCSH: Voting –
    Ontario – Toronto. | LCSH: Toronto (Ont.) – Politics and government –
    21st century.
Classification: LCC JS1789.73 .M34 2021 | DDC 324.9713/541 – dc23

University of Toronto Press acknowledges the financial assistance to its
publishing program of the Canada Council for the Arts and the Ontario Arts
Council, an agency of the Government of Ontario.

Canada Council   Conseil des Arts
for the Arts   du Canada

ONTARIO ARTS COUNCIL
CONSEIL DES ARTS DE L'ONTARIO
an Ontario government agency
un organisme du gouvernement de l'Ontario

Funded by the   Financé par le
Government   gouvernement
of Canada   du Canada

Canadä

Contents

Figures

Tables

Acknowledgments

Projects like this depend upon many factors – a compelling real-world situation, academic interest, funding, and teamwork. We are fortunate to have had all of the necessary parts come together to produce this work. We thank scholars at the University of Western Ontario for sparking our interest in municipal politics and the Social Sciences and Humanities Research Council of Canada for funding (Insight Development grant #430-2014-00700). We also benefited from the help of able research assistants, most notably Carla Caruana. Finally, we must also recognize one other crucial element that is needed for any academic project to come to fruition – family support. We are forever grateful for the support that our families have provided, for this work and always.

This work is dedicated to our favourite co-authors: Morri, Bridget, and Jason.

ELECTING A MEGA-MAYOR

Toronto 2014

Chapter 1

The Study of Local Elections

The 27th of October, 2014, marked the end of a tumultuous and unprecedented era in Toronto city politics. Although the incumbent mayor, Rob Ford, would formally continue in the role until the end of 2014, John Tory's victory effectively and abruptly ended Ford's tenure and disrupted a potential Ford municipal dynasty. Though Tory won with less support than his predecessor, his 40.3 per cent of the popular vote was, nonetheless, a clear win over Rob's brother Doug (33.7 per cent) and Olivia Chow (23.2 per cent) (City of Toronto, 2014). The headline of an article in the *National Post* on election night summarized the feelings of many Torontonians: "Ford circus folds its tent as John Tory victory offers Toronto some needed calm" (McParland, 2014, 27 October). The 2014 mayoral race (and the period leading up to it) had captured the attention of Torontonians and the world, a fact reflected not only in the large volume of press coverage devoted to the contest but also in the relatively high voter turnout (54.9 per cent).

Tory's victory ended one of the most extraordinary elections in Canada's recent history. During the campaign, which had begun almost a year earlier in January, the incumbent mayor reluctantly took time off to seek treatment for drug and alcohol abuse. In the meantime, over a few months in the summer that largely corresponded with Rob Ford's time away from City Council, the Province of Ontario held its own election, the results of which coincided with a sharp fall in support for the early front-runner for the mayoral race, Olivia Chow, and the rise of John Tory, whom polls had suggested was the third-place candidate up until that point. Outside of Toronto, however, the press had little interest in any candidate other than Ford: it focused largely on the antics of the city's "crack-smoking mayor" – though notably, Jon Stewart of *The Daily Show* fame would endorse Chow (Semley, 2014, 9 September).

That the news media focused disproportionately on the more salacious aspects of the campaign is not surprising. After all, Rob Ford regularly disrupted his mayoralty with his scandals and unusual antics. Ford had been elected mayor in 2010 with 47 per cent of the vote, a clear sign of strong support for an anti-establishment candidate who promised to do things "differently" at City Hall. His closest competitor, George Smitherman, a former provincial cabinet minister, received less than 36 per cent support. Prior to his mayoral run, Rob served as a city councillor (from 2000 to 2010), during which time he established himself as a polarizing personality, one who was known for public drunkenness, inappropriate comments to and about others, and accusations of domestic assault (Doolittle, 2014). In May 2013, more than two years into his first (and last) term as mayor, the *Toronto Star*, Toronto's largest newspaper and a vociferous opponent of the mayor, reported that there was a video of Rob Ford smoking crack cocaine. Ford denied the charge, but after months of investigation, which included the police finding video evidence of his substance abuse, he admitted to drug use in November of that year. Nonetheless, he remained defiant, refusing to relinquish his position as mayor. In response, City Council stripped him of much of his mayoral authority, such as his ability to place items on the council's agenda, and moved much of his budget and staff to the deputy mayor, turning him largely into a figurehead (Mendleson & Edwards, 2013, 18 November). Enraged by Council's action, Ford vowed to seek re-election, becoming the first major candidate to enter the race, in January 2014. Torontonians were highly polarized by this decision, as was demonstrated by the sizable number of both Ford supporters and protesters who descended on the first mayoral debate, which took place not long after he left a rehabilitation facility (Mehta, 2014, 16 July).

Despite his foibles, many Torontonians continued to be attracted to Ford's small-c conservative promises, such as to cut city staff, contract out services, reduce taxes, and hire more police officers (Rider, 2010, 26 October), and, perhaps more importantly, to his populism, which appealed to anti-elite sentiment. More often than not, when opponents showed up to protest the mayor, they would find his equally vociferous supporters. In many ways, Ford's populism and continued support despite his behaviour mirrored that of the first mayor of a major North American city caught smoking crack during his time in office: Marion Barry, the former mayor of Washington, D.C. Though they had competing political ideologies and very different backgrounds, both were able to connect with sections of the public that felt largely disenfranchised, including visible minorities and the poor (Gilmour, 2012, 23 November; Loeb, 1998, 22 May). Where Ford diverged most from Barry was in his failure to deliver improved services to his marginalized constituents. Nevertheless, Ford's continued popularity, despite his admissions of drug use and increasingly erratic behaviour, closely resembled that of Barry, who after a stint in jail for crack possession triumphantly returned to politics and was eventually re-elected as mayor. Barry's success suggested that fears (or hopes) of Ford's re-election, despite the tumult of his first term of mayor, were not unfounded.

On many fronts, Ford's tenure as mayor was eventful. Beyond revelations of alcohol and drug abuse, he and his brother fought a conflict-of-interest lawsuit, and reports emerged of domestic assault (Hui, 2013, 22 November). His behaviour made headlines around the world, making him fodder for American late-night talk show jokes. He received so much media coverage in the United States that *The Globe and Mail* called his "saga" the "biggest Canadian story in [the] U.S. this century" (Panetta, 2013, 4 December). *The Guardian*, *The Irish Times*, *Le Monde*, *Der Spiegel*, and *Al Jazeera* also all carried stories about the mayor and his antics. Heading into the 2014 election, the eyes of the world were on Toronto politics, awaiting the fate of the city's scandal-plagued mayor.

As it turned out, the fervour surrounding the threat (or promise) of a Rob Ford re-election was for naught. The incumbent withdrew from the mayoral race on the candidate nomination deadline, after doctors diagnosed him with cancer. He chose to run instead for his old City Council seat in Ward 2. The mayor's brother Doug, Rob's campaign manager and a city councillor, took his place on the mayoral ballot, setting up the possibility of a Ford dynasty. Known for largely sharing his brother's political views, if not his populist appeal, Doug Ford took on the unusual role of pseudo-incumbent – someone who was very similar to the real incumbent and who represented continuity but was not the actual person who had held that office.

Doug's main challengers were themselves well-known politicians. Olivia Chow was a former Toronto city councillor and Member of Parliament for the left-wing New Democratic Party of Canada. Chow was part of a Toronto political dynasty herself, along with her husband Jack Layton, a former city councillor and leader of the federal NDP, and her stepson Mike Layton, a member of Toronto City Council. John Tory was the other major challenger, known to the city from his previous (unsuccessful) bid for mayor in 2003 and his time as leader of the Ontario Progressive Conservative Party. A former CEO of Rogers Communications, he also hosted a popular radio talk show.

For many opponents of the Fords, Doug's loss on election day may have seemed inevitable, given his brother's legacy and the quality of the other candidates running for mayor. However, Ford remained Tory's biggest challenger in the final months of the race, and he came in second in the election, winning nearly 34 per cent of the vote. However, Tory's victory and Chow's distant third place result were hardly foregone conclusions as the campaign progressed. In fact, Chow had been the clear favourite during the first half of the race, only to fall to, and stay in, third place during the second half.

This book analyses the outcome of the 2014 Toronto mayoral election. It considers the many twists and turns that occurred throughout the eleven-month campaign by taking an in-depth look at the attitudes and behaviour of Torontonians toward the election. Toronto is of huge importance to Canada's economy, culture, and political landscape, so developing an understanding of how voters function in this context is invaluable to the literatures on Canadian politics, local politics, and political behaviour. This book also offers many lessons about municipal elections in Toronto – and elsewhere. The 2014 Toronto election is an extreme case in terms of profile, media coverage, voter turnout, public interest, and the strong provincial and federal partisan links of the front-runner candidates for mayor. The 2014 mayoral race in Toronto was perhaps the highest-profile municipal election in Canadian history, and our analysis of it allows inferences to be made about how electors view local politics elsewhere. If, for example, Torontonians were not interested in *this* election, then they are unlikely to be more engaged in elections with less media coverage and a much less polarizing incumbent mayor. The same could be said of local electors in other municipalities, where media coverage and the availability of relevant information is less extensive.

Local elections have received only a fraction of the attention from scholars that contests at other levels of government have. We believe that much more research is needed to understand how the public views municipal politics and elections and how their attitudes and actions translate into and shape municipal policy. Municipalities are responsible for providing most of the goods and services the public relies on daily, so the common perception of them as third-rate cousins of more senior levels of government is at best misguided, at worst damaging. We hope this book, and the Toronto Election Study research project on which it is based, will foster greater discussion about municipal elections in Canada and the world.

This introductory chapter has many goals. First, it provides an account of the very limited history of the study of municipal elections, in Canada and elsewhere. Second, it makes the case for the study of local elections, noting that such contests represent a vast, untapped research site for scholars of political behaviour. Third, it introduces the reader to some early empirical findings by outlining the sources of data employed in this book and providing some background information on how Torontonians view municipal politics. We conclude with a brief summary of what to expect in the pages that follow.

What We Don't Know about Municipal Elections Could Fill a Book

Voting is one of the most thoroughly studied phenomena in the field of political science. A huge amount of research has been published aimed at explaining how voters reason and why they act the way they do come election time. However, the overwhelming majority of research in this field has focused on national or federal elections. This work is often facilitated by national election studies, in which a large number of citizens are interviewed about their political attitudes and behaviour. Commencing in the United States in the mid-twentieth century (e.g., Campbell et al., 1960; Lazarsfeld et al., 1948), election studies are now conducted regularly in dozens of countries around the world. In Canada, the Canadian Election Study has been gathering federal election survey data since 1965. For as long as they have been conducted, these large-scale election surveys have been the main drivers of our collective understanding of voting behaviour.

Canadian elections other than those at the federal level, however, have received relatively little attention, though this is an emerging area of research. As survey data become increasingly easy to collect (given the cost savings resulting from technological advances), new venues for research have opened up. In recent years, studies of provincial elections have become more and more common (Bastien et al., 2013; Cross et al., 2015; Wesley, 2015). There is a burgeoning interest, therefore, in the study of elections below the federal level.

Despite this trend, very little research has been done on municipal elections in Canada, particularly using individual-level survey data. Except for studies of Vancouver (Cutler & Matthews, 2005) and Toronto (McGregor et al., 2016, using Toronto Election Study data), municipal elections have not been subjected to comprehensive individual-level analysis of the sort that has characterized federal and provincial election studies. It is no wonder that Cutler and Matthews (2005) call municipal elections "the poor cousins in the study of elections and voting behaviour" (p. 359). This oversight is problematic for several reasons. First, the overwhelming majority of elections in this country are fought at the municipal level. Municipalities account for 99.6 per cent of all governments and 95.8 per cent of all politicians in Canada (even excluding school boards and other special-purpose bodies).[1] In focusing predominantly on federal elections, scholars of voting behaviour have largely ignored the majority of electoral contests in Canada.

This trend would be less concerning if vast differences did not exist between local and other elections. However, municipal elections are, in important ways, different from federal elections. Perhaps the most obvious difference is that most local elections in Canada, Toronto included, are non-partisan in nature – the few exceptions are all in British Columbia and Quebec. Municipal candidates anywhere in Canada are permitted to run under a party banner, but in most provinces they cannot raise party funds, and this leaves them to fend for themselves, financially; moreover, party labels typically are not allowed on municipal ballots. Thus, while candidates may share a banner and an election platform, they benefit far less from doing so, particularly in jurisdictions where the electorate may be hostile to the notion of municipal political parties. This has real implications for the transferability of existing knowledge about voting behaviour, given that it is well-established that parties have a significant impact on elections and electors. According to Dalton (2002), political parties "define the choices available to voters" (p. 125) and "shape the content of election campaigns" (p. 126). Moreover, how voters relate to parties is a central component of research on voting behaviour. Partisanship – that is, a long-standing psychological attachment to one party (Campbell et al., 1960) – has been shown to influence how voters receive and process information (Zaller, 1992), how they evaluate past government performance (Duch et al., 2000), and how engaged, interested, and attentive they are (Buchanan, 1977). It also has a significant impact on how they vote (Gidengil et al., 2012). The vast majority of research explaining voter behaviour in partisan contexts attempts to account for how predispositions toward parties affect attitudes and decisions.

Another major difference between federal and local elections is the informational context. With few exceptions, municipal elections in Canada are low-information contests. Simply put, electors tend to know less about local politics than they do about other levels of government. This trend may be less pronounced when a mayoral election is high-profile, as in Toronto. But even when it *is* high-profile, there is no doubt that little is known about down-ballot contests, such as those for council and school board. Cutler and Matthews (2005) refer to the situation facing voters in local races as "challenges of both informational quantity and quality" (p. 360). Because local elections by their nature are non-partisan and low-information, we cannot assume that the results of research into federal or provincial elections will hold in municipal contexts.

Context also matters at the municipal level because we need to recognize that voters are embedded in other levels of government as well.

Multi-level governance can entail a complex and detailed distribution of power and responsibility. It also brings with it the potential for confusion about who is responsible for specific policies and who has the power to change things. How does this affect voters, their preferences, and their reasoning? To what extent do their attitudes toward government and politicians at other levels play out in their local vote choices? This is an important question because it raises concerns about the nature of democratic governance and choice. Only by studying municipal elections can we fully understand the political lives of voters.

Additionally, though the current study is not a comparative one, municipalities offer an excellent opportunity to study the effects of institutional variations between cities in the same country. For example, some Canadian cities are divided into wards, with individual representatives for each ward. Some are "at-large," that is, councillors are chosen to govern without specific geographic assignments. Also, the local level is the only one in Canada where concurrent elections are regularly held, and there is variation in this respect, with most cities holding elections for mayor and council at the same time, while others also vote for school boards (including cities in Ontario), regional governments (in regions like Waterloo and Durham), or borough councils (in some cities in Quebec). The office of the mayor can vary substantially as well. Some mayors are institutionally powerful. While no mayor in Canada has the sweeping powers of some of the United States' "strong mayors," some, like the Mayor of Montreal, wield significant authority. Montreal's municipal party system, which is highly leader-focused, ensures that the mayor controls much of City Council. Furthermore, Montreal's mayor chairs an upper-tier local body that oversees the entire Island of Montreal. With half the members of this body coming from the City of Montreal's council, the city's mayor has significant influence over areas beyond the boundaries of the city proper. In other cities, by contrast, the mayor has little authority beyond that of a city councillor (this is the case in cities as large as Edmonton and Ottawa), and it is conceivable that this variation may have an impact on electors.

The study of municipal elections therefore holds great promise for scholars of voting behaviour to increase our knowledge of how institutions affect vote choice. This complexity is both an opportunity and a challenge. When we ignore municipal contests, we risk overlooking the ways in which citizens respond to the unique and varied features of the local level. Given the woefully inadequate literature on local political behaviour in this country, we concur with Marschall et al.'s (2011) assessment that the potential for research in local political behaviour is "practically limitless" (p. 97).

A final reason to study municipal elections is that these contests have important consequences. Local governments in Canada lack formal constitutional standing, yet they are responsible for a wide range of policies and services that directly affect voters' daily lives. Municipal politicians make decisions about services and infrastructure that Canadians often take for granted, including water and sewage, garbage removal, roads, fire and police services, land use, social services, and public transit. These governments make policy decisions that have immediate, visible, and consequential effects on the lives of citizens – from how often garbage gets picked up to how many fire stations exist to how quickly roads are ploughed after a snowstorm to which roads get resurfaced. This importance is not lost on voters. Data from the Toronto Election Study show that most Torontonians believe their municipal government has more impact on their lives than the national or provincial government, or both (the corollary of this, of course, is that nearly 50 per cent of electors view local government as the least impactful of the three orders) (McGregor et al., 2016). Being "closest" to the voter, municipal politicians are also often seen as the most responsive to the public's demands (Fischel, 2001; Olson, 1969; Ostrom et al., 1961). So it is important for researchers to develop an understanding of orientations and behaviour toward elections at this important level of government.

This is not to imply that there has been no research into local elections, simply that this type of research suffers in terms of quantity and range. We know relatively little about how voters choose who will govern their cities. In both Canada and the United States, research on local elections has focused largely on identifying the determinants of candidate success (Adams & Schreiber, 2011; Gierzynski et al., 1998; Krebs, 1998; Kushner, 2001; Kushner et al., 1997; Lieske, 1989). The underrepresentation of women has also received a noteworthy level of attention (Adams & Schreiber, 2011; Gidengil & Vengroff, 1997; Schmidt & Saunders, 2004; Selokela, 2014; Tolley, 2011; Tremblay & Mévellec, 2013). Finally, given the low turnouts for local elections, it is unsurprising that the literature on cities attempts to explain participation rates among the electorate (Kushner et al., 1997; Lassen, 2005; Niven, 2004; Walks, 2013) or among particular groups (Sheffield & Hadley, 1984; Siemiatycki & Marshall, 2014), though most of this work has been conducted at the aggregate level, which makes causal claims less certain (see McGregor & Spicer, 2016, and McGregor, 2018, for exceptions).

Until recently, research on municipal vote choice has focused largely on explaining aggregate-level outcomes, with the aim of understanding the success rates of incumbents and challengers (Berry & Howell 2007; Krebs, 1998; Oliver & Ha, 2007) or minority and non-minority candidates

(Barreto, 2007; Barreto et al., 2005; Brockington et al., 1998). Only with individual-level data have scholars been able to conduct more thorough examinations of the determinants of vote choice. Cutler and Matthews (2005) identified several correlates of vote choice in the 2002 Vancouver election, and several pieces have been written on the 2014 Toronto election (due to the availability of Toronto Election Study data), covering topics such as economic voting (Anderson et al., 2017), gender and ethnic affinity voting (Bird et al., 2016), strategic voting (Caruana et al., 2018), partisanship (McGregor et al., 2016), and incumbency (Moore et al., 2017). The vast majority of this work has emerged in the last few years, and researchers are just beginning to scratch the surface of what will no doubt prove to be an exceptionally bountiful research area.

Also conspicuously absent in the literature on local political behaviour is a book-length academic treatment of a single case. Stephen Clarkson's (1972) *City Lib*, published more than four decades before the 2014 Toronto election, remains the only book-length study of a Canadian municipal election that we know of, and even then, it is largely a personal record of the author's unsuccessful campaign in the 1969 mayoral race; thus it lacks any detailed individual-level analysis of voter opinion to definitively qualify it as a study of political behaviour. Such studies have, however, long been a feature in the study of federal elections (see, for example, Blais et al., 2002; Dornan & Pammett, 2016; Johnston et al., 1992), and they are becoming increasingly common provincially (Bastien et al., 2013; Cross et al., 2015). This current study represents the first such treatment of a local election in Canada.

The Unique Nature of Municipal Elections

This book provides the first comprehensive, survey-based examination of a Canadian mayoral election. Our focus is on what was perhaps the highest-profile mayoral contest in the country's history – the 2014 contest in Toronto between Doug Ford, John Tory, Olivia Chow, and more than sixty other candidates. Ultimately, we are interested in understanding the outcome of the election as well as what it can tell us about politics in Toronto and elections in Canada's other cities. In the chapters that follow, we provide the reader with an understanding of the politics surrounding the city at the time of the election, present relevant background on the major candidates, consider the importance voters attached to policy concerns (as opposed to the personalities of the contestants), and consider the bases of support for the outgoing, scandal-ridden mayor, Rob Ford, and his brother Doug. In the penultimate chapter, we examine how Torontonians viewed their elected officials, and the city's performance, two years after the election. Finally, we reflect on what our analysis of Toronto 2014 says about voters in large cities in general, and provide a short epilogue addressing the 2018 election results. When considering the wider applicability of our findings, we ask two broad questions pertaining to the study of municipal elections in political science. First, how do Canadian voters make decisions in a non-partisan environment? Setting aside two of Canada's territories (NWT and Nunavut), this is the only order of government in Canada where parties do not dominate and structure elections.[2] Second, do municipal politics and elections matter to voters? Are electors engaged with politics at this unique and important level of government? We now briefly discuss why these are important questions to consider.

The Absence of Parties at the Municipal Level

The local level is the only one in Canada where non-partisan contests are the norm rather than the exception.[3] Schattschneider's (1942) famous claim that "modern democracy is unthinkable save in terms of political parties" (p. 1) has simply not been borne out at the local level in this country (or in much of the United States). The absence of parties at the municipal level is enough justification alone to study such elections in Canada.

Canadians are accustomed to partisan elections at the federal and provincial levels. In electoral contests where parties are present, they structure competition, provide institutional and financial resources for candidates, and centrally control and dominate the campaign narrative. For voters, the presence of parties provides an important information shortcut – in the absence of the time (or willingness) to educate oneself regarding candidates and issues at each election, one can fall back upon what is already known about a party. Over consecutive elections, voters can develop a sense of a party's ideology and positions on a range of issues, making it unnecessary to collect this information at every election. For those individuals who develop a strong partisan attachment to a party, vote decisions become easy and are made largely insulated from changes in leaders or salient issues. In studies of partisan elections, partisanship is a constant and fundamental consideration – so fundamental that much of what we know about partisan contests cannot simply be assumed to apply to non-partisan local elections.

In most municipalities in Canada, including Toronto, candidates do not campaign as members of specific parties. As a result, each candidate must first establish name recognition, raise their own campaign funds, do their best to make the electorate aware of their policies and platform, and prove to the electorate that they are the best candidate to govern the city. We already know that this burden on individual candidates largely favours incumbents, who, by way of their incumbency, are already widely known (Moore et al., 2017). However, aside from this reliance on name recognition, we know little about how or on what basis municipal voters decide how to vote. The fact that a number of high-profile candidates ran for mayor in the 2014 Toronto municipal election, and the extent of the media coverage, makes this a good case for delving into the mind of the municipal voter – to understand how individuals arrive at voting decisions when no formal partisan cues are available to them. We do recognize (and discuss in more detail later) that strong partisan cues were available in the Toronto 2014 election – Tory was a former leader of the provincial PCs, and Chow was a former NDP MP. Yet voters did not universally identify these cues (McGregor et al., 2016), and in any case, the structure and resources that parties bring to election campaigns at the provincial and federal levels are absent at the municipal level in Ontario. The election was, therefore, formally non-partisan, even if it was somewhat quasi-partisan in practice. We therefore ask: in the absence of formal party cues and party campaigns, how important are policy considerations and the personal characteristics of the candidates? Analysing a non-partisan Toronto election can teach us a great deal about how politics works in other Canadian cities.

Are Municipal Elections Important to Voters?

In addition to the absence of political parties, municipal elections differ from those at the federal level in that many political scientists see them as "second order" contests. The theory of second-order elections was developed by Reif & Schmitt (1980) to apply to European Parliament contests, and the term has since been widely applied to elections other than those held at the national level, including provincial and municipal elections (see Golder et al., 2017, for a discussion of this literature). The label "second order" derives from the belief or perception that little is at stake in these races, as compared to national elections. As a consequence, voters will perceive these elections as relatively unimportant.

Literature on the subject suggests that such elections generate low public interest and voter turnout and result in relatively greater success for parties that are not usually successful at the national level. Also, in circumstances where party systems at the second-order and national levels match, the party in power nationally tends to perform relatively poorly (Marsh, 1998; Schmitt, 2005). All of this makes it debatable, however, whether the term "second-order election" can be applied to Toronto in

2014, which saw relatively high turnout and was technically non-partisan in nature. Still, it is quite likely that electors view their local elections differently than those at other orders of government.

National elections tend to be of high importance to citizens, for national governments are the most visible and tend to oversee broader policies that can shape the entire country. However, governments at other levels do important work as well, and these elections can be hard-fought and highly visible. Not surprisingly, some academics have questioned whether all subnational elections in Canada should be labelled as "second order," particularly at the provincial level (Cutler, 2008). In a highly decentralized federation such as Canada, all levels of government have important responsibilities and all levels of elections have the potential to attract significant public interest.

What does this mean for a study of the 2014 Toronto mayoral election and for municipal elections in general? Had that election been truly "second order," Torontonians would surely have shown relatively little interest in it. If voter turnout is any indication, however, this does not appear to have been the case. Turnout was 54.7 per cent – more than 11 percentage points higher than the average (43.1 per cent) for municipal elections held in the province that day (AMO, 2014), and higher than for the provincial election held that same year (51.3 per cent), though lower than for the 2015 federal election (68.3 per cent). In this sense, and given the formally non-partisan nature of the Toronto contest, the "second order" label does not appear to apply neatly.

However, voter turnout does not equal engaged and informed voters. While significant media coverage and the antics of Toronto's incumbent mayor may have driven more voters to the polls, whether these voters were interested in the election beyond deciding whether a Ford should continue to be mayor remains to be seen. If the council races in the 2014 Toronto election are any indication, the high turnout may have masked an otherwise uninformed and blasé electorate. After all, 97 per cent (36 of 37) of incumbent councillors won re-election, with 70 per cent (26 of 37) winning a majority of the vote in their ward. Such results do not point to an engaged and informed electorate.

The Data

To understand better the 2014 Toronto mayoral election, and uncover what it can tell us about municipal elections in Canadians cities more broadly, we use the 2014 Toronto Election Study (TES),[4] a two-wave survey of Torontonians conducted before and after the election. The pre-election survey wave includes the responses of 3,000 eligible Toronto voters, collected after the candidate nomination deadline (12 September) and before election day (from 19 September to 27 October). In the post-election survey wave, conducted in the week after the election (28 October to 3 November), almost three quarters of respondents who completed the pre-election wave answered another questionnaire (n = 2,232).[5] Surveys were conducted online and administered by Nielsen Consumer Insights. Respondents were recruited from pre-existing panels and provided with incentives in accordance with the survey provider's standards. The surveys included a variety of questions probing attitudes toward government, the candidates, and the election, as well as political behaviour. Many of the questions were modelled after comparable national and provincial election studies, though a number were designed to account for the unique nature of local elections and of the 2014 contest in particular (for more information on the questions used in analyses throughout, refer to Appendix I).

The above-noted dearth of research into municipal political behaviour stems in part from a lack of available individual-level survey data, a problem that is remedied by the TES data. A significant share of existing work on explaining municipal election outcomes has been based on qualitative approaches (Breux & Bherer, 2011; Chiasson & Mevellec, 2013; Chiasson et al., 2014; Sussmann, 2006). Quantitative work on municipal elections has largely been at the aggregate level (Kushner et al., 1997; Walks, 2013; see Siemiatycki & Marshal, 2014; Stanwick, 2000; Taylor, 2011), but it is difficult to draw conclusions from aggregate data about the decisions of individual electors. The large sample size and individual-level nature of the TES dataset enable us to move beyond aggregate-level analyses and impressions and data gathered by pollsters and politicians.

The second data source we use is a follow-up survey conducted with Torontonians in the fall of 2016. A limitation of political behaviour research is that it typically draws upon data collected around the time of an election. However, citizen engagement with their government does not begin or end with each election. Little is known about how voters reason about politics between elections, the extent to which electors "tune out" from politics after election day, and the implications of post-election shifts in attitudes for representation and accountability. The 2016 survey results provide another data point we can use to evaluate the attitudes of Torontonians, in particular how attitudes may have changed after the election. The survey was conducted two years after the 2014 Toronto election, two and a half years after the 2014 Ontario election, and more than a year after the 2015 Canadian election. We gathered responses from just under 1,500 Torontonians (n = 1,487) between 8 November and 21 December. This online survey was conducted using Qualtrics software, and the sample was provided by Research Now. Respondents were recruited from an existing panel and provided with incentives in accordance with provider norms.

Finally, we augment these two datasets as appropriate with polling information and a variety of news accounts. In so doing, we aim to provide a comprehensive, data-driven examination of the attitudes of Torontonians toward the 2014 election.

How Do Torontonians View Municipal Government?

As lamented repeatedly above, there is a sizable gap between what academics know about local elections and voters and what they know about the federal and provincial levels. Before "jumping in" to focus on the specifics of the Toronto 2014 race, it makes sense to provide some background as to how electors view local politics and politics in a more general sense, and to compare attitudes toward the different orders of government. Until now, the lack of individual-level data has made such an examination difficult if not impossible.

Given that so little is known about municipal elections and voters, we begin by considering basic orientations toward this level of government, to evaluate how these views compare with those held about federal and provincial politics. We focus on how citizens view local government in general, setting aside the specific individuals who represent them on City Council (or hope to). More specifically, do they view local politics as important and local government as influential? Is local politics interesting, and do voters feel a duty to participate in local elections? Does the municipal government have a greater impact than the provincial and federal governments or a lesser one? We compare orientations toward local politics with those toward the provincial and federal levels, about which we know a great deal more. We ask these questions in a largely exploratory manner, with the goal of providing the reader with some context about Toronto politics in general, before proceeding to discuss the 2014 election in particular.

Local politicians preside over a government that provides a variety of important services. In investigating views on the importance of local government, we are asking (albeit indirectly) whether voters view elections in Toronto as "second order." In terms of what is perhaps the most significant indicator of importance – turnout – municipal elections tend to lag behind federal elections, though (as noted above) participation in Toronto in 2014 was higher than in the 2014 provincial election. We consider here several additional measures that can reasonably be viewed as proxies for the level of importance electors assign to the three orders of Canadian government, including levels of interest in politics and whether or not the decision to vote in elections is one's democratic duty. We also consider in detail the relative impact of municipal government on one's quality of life, as compared to the provincial and federal governments.

Toronto 2014 was hardly typical of municipal elections in Canada (given the size of the city and the profiles of the candidates). Indeed, it represents an extreme case that allows us to draw inferences about how electors in other cities view their local governments. If the local government of the largest city in the country, with the largest budget and state apparatus, is viewed as unimportant, then it seems very unlikely that the governments of other cities will be seen differently. We suggest that the timing of data collection allows us to comment about how important local governments are generally perceived to be. The results that follow are based on responses to surveys conducted in the fall of 2014, either during the election campaign or immediately thereafter. Given the strong focus on municipal politics during this period, one would expect evaluations of the importance and impact of local politics to be at their maximum during this period. If voters do not care about municipal politics at the zenith of the election cycle, they likely never will.

TES data suggest that despite the timing of data collection, and the size and scope of the government of the City of Toronto, Torontonians are relatively less interested in local politics. Perhaps not surprisingly, data suggest that Torontonians view the national government as the most interesting order of politics. On a scale from 0 to 10, the average level of interest in the federal level was 6.37. The corresponding values for the provincial and municipal levels were 6.19 and 6.07, respectively (both these figures differ from the federal estimate at a 99 per cent confidence level).[6] Though the levels of interest in municipal and provincial politics are statistically indistinguishable, the finding that local politics are of less interest to electors than federal politics fits well with the second-order theory of elections.

Also in line with the finding that voters see municipal politics as relatively uninteresting is evidence that Torontonians are less likely to view voting in a municipal election as one's democratic duty than they are to hold this opinion toward provincial and federal elections. Fewer than 65 per cent (64.6 per cent) of respondents viewed voting in local elections as a duty, compared to 67.7 per cent and 69.4 per cent for the provincial and federal elections, respectively (the municipal value differs from the others at p < 0.01).[7] The belief that voting is a duty (as opposed to simply a choice) is widely viewed as one of the best predictors of voter turnout, if not *the* best (Blais, 2000). As such, our data suggest that even over

Figure 1.1. Relative government impact on quality of life

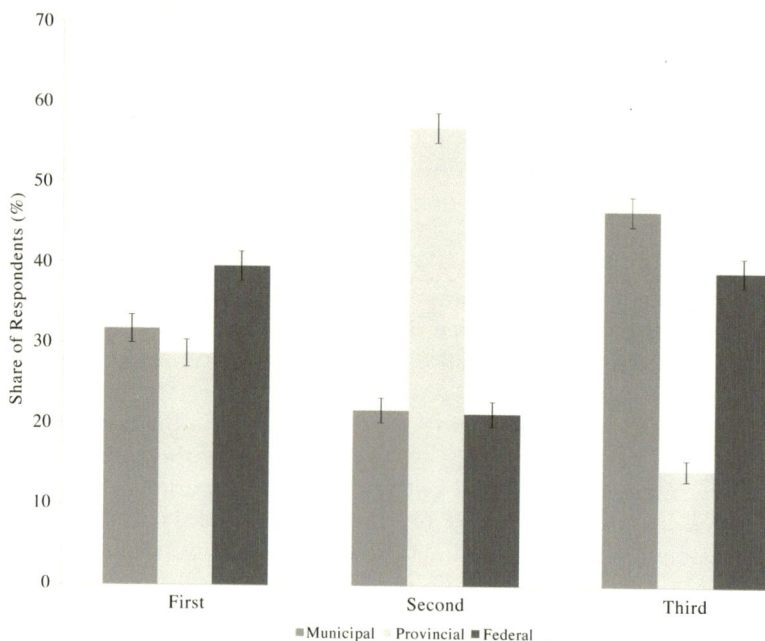

the course of the highest-profile mayoral election in Canadian history, Torontonians were less interested in the local election than in those for other levels of government and felt less of a duty to participate.

Why this lack of interest and sense of duty? One possibility is that electors simply believe that municipal government has less impact on their lives. If this were the case, we would expect interest in local politics in general to be weak, regardless of how many sensational headlines were written about municipal politicians and politics.

To test this assertion, we measured government impact as the respondents perceived it. They were asked to rank the three orders of government with regard to how much impact each had on their quality of life. Each order of government was assigned a rank from first to third. The results of this question are seen in Figure 1.1, which shows the share of respondents who ranked each level of government in each position. Note that the "whiskers" on each bar indicate the lower and higher bounds of the 95 per cent confidence intervals.[8]

Though the results shown in Figure 1.1 are not completely straightforward, on balance they seem to indicate that most Torontonians view their local government as having relatively little impact on their lives. Perhaps surprisingly, nearly one third of respondents (31.7 per cent) were of the opinion that the municipal government has more of an impact on their lives than other levels of government. Though this value is slightly higher than for those who selected the province (28.7 per cent), it is substantially lower than the analogous value for the national government (39.6 per cent).

It is at the other end of the figure, however, that opinions on the impact of the municipal government become clear. Nearly half of respondents (46.5 per cent) believe that the local government is the least impactful order of government – a figure substantially higher than for the federal (39.0 per cent) and provincial (14.4 per cent) governments. Far more respondents view local government as having the least impact than as having the most – a gap of 14.8 percentage points.

Together, these data suggest that on the whole, Torontonians view local politics as relatively unimportant and as having comparatively little impact on their lives. These views were present even when attitudes were measured during the height of one of the highest-profile municipal elections in Canada's history, in the country's largest city (which has the largest municipal government). If electors in an extreme case such as Toronto have such opinions, it is very unlikely that those in other cities will believe that local politics are either interesting or more important. These findings may not be encouraging to those who champion the importance of municipal politics or even to municipal politicians themselves. On the academic front, however, such trends simply reinforce that municipal elections are unique within the Canadian federation and thus worthy of their own scholarly attention.

Understanding the Torontonian Voter

Municipal elections have consequences; they are also different from provincial and federal contests in important ways. At the same time, however, they have been largely overlooked by scholars of political behaviour. This study, which represents the first book-length academic work on a Canadian municipal election, contributes toward closing the gap between the study of municipal and other elections. Its purpose is to develop an understanding of the outcome of the 2014 Toronto mayoral race and to consider what these lessons tell us about how Torontonians, and Canadians more generally, reason and behave toward municipal politics.

To understand the Toronto voter, and the outcome of the 2014 Toronto election, a few steps are crucial. First, we must establish the context in which the voters came to the polls. In this chapter we have demonstrated that Torontonians view local politics as less important than politics at other levels of government. In chapter 2, we turn to the 2014 mayoral contest in particular, and begin by focusing on the contenders for the position of mayor. How did Torontonians view the candidates, which issues were important to supporters of the major candidates, and what kind of character traits did voters prioritize? In chapter 3, we focus on the campaign, tracking attitudes toward the candidates over time.

The book then turns to explaining the election result. Chapter 4 examines the outcome of the election from the perspective of what mattered to voters. Here we consider, in detail, the role played by candidate personality as compared to the policy preferences of voters. Given the high profiles of the mayoral candidates, coupled with the election's formally non-partisan nature, it is conceivable that evaluations of the candidates' personal characteristics were of particular importance in this election. In chapter 5, we examine "Ford Nation," the loosely defined group of voters said to make up the core of Rob's, and later Doug's, electoral support. After all, the elephant in the room regarding this election was Rob Ford's legacy. So we look closely at the geographic make-up of Doug Ford's support, comparing it to that of the 2010 election Rob Ford won. We also consider whether the election's outcome would have been different had Rob remained on the ballot instead of being replaced by his brother. In chapter 6 we discuss the future, and municipal elections more generally, drawing on data from the 2016 survey of Torontonians. Our goal in this chapter is to determine how electors viewed the performance of the city and those who governed it two years after the election.

We close the book with a chapter that considers how findings from the 2014 Toronto mayoral election apply to other Canadian cities. In particular, we ask how the non-partisan nature of local elections affects voters, and, more simply, whether local elections matter to Canadians. As an extreme case in terms of the size of the city, the nature of the candidates, and the intense media coverage, the 2014 Toronto election can tell us a lot about municipal elections and electors in the rest of Canada. In a short epilogue, we discuss the 2018 election.

Though this book is by no means an exhaustive account of every noteworthy feature of the 2014 Toronto mayoral contest, together its chapters provide a comprehensive overview of municipal electoral politics in Toronto. By the conclusion, readers will have gained an understanding of why, on 27 October 2014, John Tory became the fourth mayor of the amalgamated City of Toronto. They will also have gained new insight into how municipal politics and politicians are viewed in Toronto. And finally, we believe the 2014 Toronto mayoral election offers a number of important insights into the nature of municipal elections in Canadian cities more broadly.

Chapter 2

The Contenders

Given that Toronto is Canada's largest constituency and draws much of the attention of Canada's news media, running for mayor of the city is no task for the meek. Because there are no municipal political parties and the barrier for registering as a candidate is low, it is also an easy race to enter, which is probably why some eighty individuals signed up to run for mayor in 2014. In the end, though, only a handful of candidates generated any traction with the electorate and news media. For those few legitimate contenders, the decision to run was no small thing. The election would, after all, be expensive, and a failed bid could have a strong impact on a candidate's political future. Even absent major gaffes, the campaign for mayor in Canada's largest fishbowl can be very unforgiving.

Karen Stintz, a Toronto city councillor considered to be a serious threat to incumbent Rob Ford a few months before the campaign began (Toronto Star, 2014, 2 January), found this out the hard way. Having announced her candidacy before the race began, Stintz waited until late February to officially enter, hoping to generate a buzz as the first "high-profile challenger" to Mayor Rob Ford (Church, 2014, 22 February). Unfortunately, she chose the same day to enter the race as eventual winner John Tory, who, conveniently, showed up at City Hall to register a few hours before her. So Tory "scooped" her on the day of her entry into the race; to make things worse, she suffered the indignity of being turned away initially because she did not have photo identification with her (James, 2014, 22 February).

For Stintz, the 2014 election may simply have been a case of bad timing. Before the 2010 campaign, during which former Ontario provincial cabinet minister George Smitherman ran against Rob Ford, candidates for mayor were almost always current or former city councillors (or former mayors of the former constituent municipalities of Metro Toronto). For instance, both Rob Ford and his predecessor David Miller were sitting city councillors when they chose to run. Very early on, before Olivia Chow and John Tory entered the race, it seemed that Rob Ford's main competition would be Karen Stintz and former city councillor David Soknacki. But by election day, Rob Ford, Stintz, and Soknacki had dropped out of the race, leaving Doug Ford, Olivia Chow, and John Tory as the three front-runners. Therefore the ballot for mayor of Toronto in 2014 was an unusual one, due to the number of high-profile candidates and the route some of them took to enter the campaign.

This chapter introduces readers to those three and to a few of the high-profile "also-rans" who dropped out of the race before it ended. It also examines how voters perceived each of the three front-runners as election day approached. Candidates are always central to elections, and how voters perceive them is particularly important in non-partisan municipal contests. Absent partisan ties and party cues (which activate pre-existing perceptions of the parties and what they stand for – shortcuts often used when voting), voters are largely left to decide their vote based on the candidates' personal traits and policy positions. By examining attitudes toward the leading mayoral candidates, we hope to uncover the issues that are important to local voters, which personal traits are valued, and how these factors relate to vote choice.

As Rob Ford, Karen Stintz, and David Soknacki had all withdrawn from the race on or prior to the nomination deadline of 12 September, our analysis focuses on Olivia Chow, Doug Ford, and John Tory. That Chow and Tory were the only viable challengers to the Ford brothers was clear early on in the election. Chow ended the race in third place behind Tory and Ford, with 23 per cent of the vote. In contrast, while the fourth-place candidate, Ari Goldkind, did receive some modest news coverage in the final month of the campaign (Powell, 2014, 22 April), he finished well back with less than 0.5 per cent of the vote.

Regarding the main three contenders, we consider two questions. First, what did the electorate as a whole think of them? To answer this, we asked survey respondents to rate the candidates both in absolute terms and in order of preference. This allowed us to consider how these attitudes toward candidates would have translated into an election outcome under a ranked ballot electoral system, which is relevant given the discussions and decisions around ranked ballots at the provincial level. It also sheds light on whether the eventual outcome, based on a winner-take-all, first-past-the-post electoral system, was influenced by strategic voting. Second, what qualities did the supporters of the three different candidates prioritize? Answering this question indicates which traits each group of supporters valued in mayoral candidates, as well as which issues were important to them. Our analysis provides insight into the preferences of electors and also suggests how the public viewed the candidates themselves.

The Candidates

The "Also-Rans"

It is striking that two candidates with such strong credentials – Karen Stintz and David Soknacki – eventually found themselves relegated to "also-ran" status, but such was the nature of the 2014 Toronto mayoral election. It may also be a sign of things to come in Canada's major cities, as more and more provincial and federal politicians turn to municipal politics. Stintz was the higher-profile candidate of the two, having served as chair of the Toronto Transit Commission (TTC) while city councillor. During her time as TTC chair, she gained notoriety as well as significant support from Ford's opponents when she managed to scrap the mayor's transit plan and replace it with a new one, which City Council backed in 2012. This defiance of Rob Ford was one of the first signs that his influence in City Council was slipping. When Soknacki entered the race, he had been out of politics for eight years, having relinquished his council seat in 2006. Despite his long absence from politics, his stint as former mayor David Miller's budget chief ensured that he had a level of citywide recognition, an important factor in winning the mayoral office in a large city.

A poll conducted in November 2013, months before the start of campaign, suggested that Stintz and Soknacki were, in fact, Ford's main rivals. It suggested that Stintz was actually leading Ford by a wide margin among the electorate, with 52 per cent support compared to Ford's 33 per cent, with Soknacki in third at 14 per cent (Toronto Star, 2014, 2 January). Of course, the poll focused solely on those three candidates because, at the time, they were the only major candidates who had indicated their intention to run.

Despite the strength of Stintz and Soknacki's respective political résumés, once John Tory and Olivia Chow entered the race they were quickly relegated to fourth and fifth place, typically registering around 5 per cent support in polls conducted throughout the campaign. Eventually, running out of campaign funds and seemingly stuck with single-digit support among voters, first Stintz and then Soknacki dropped out of the race.[1]

But they were not the highest-profile candidates to withdraw from the race. That honour fell to incumbent mayor Rob Ford. Despite his admission that he had smoked crack cocaine while mayor and his entry into rehab during the campaign, by August Ford found himself sitting comfortably in second place to John Tory in most polls. His populist conservatism had strong appeal – during his tenure as an outlier on City Council, he had called for lower taxes and less spending and had ferociously attacked his fellow councillors (Wanagas, 2001, 10 March) – and it kept him buoyant during the 2014 campaign. In the end, it was neither a major political gaffe nor dwindling funds nor declining voter support that ended his campaign – it was his health. Diagnosed with a rare and deadly form of stomach cancer, he abandoned the race for mayor late in the campaign, paving the way for his brother Doug to take his place.

The Final Three: John Tory

On Monday, 24 February, John Tory, former mayoral candidate and former leader of the provincial Progressive Conservatives, announced his candidacy, making it official by registering to run (Toronto Star, 2014, 24 February). Tory brought with him experience in running in major elections (he had by then lost a mayoral campaign and a provincial election), and, more importantly, a high profile as a moderate conservative. According to some observers, these qualities immediately undermined Karen Stintz's campaign (Hepburn, 2014, 23 January). Tory quickly became Ford's strongest rival (Dale, 2014, 26 February), though he would soon lose that status (at least temporarily) following the entry of Olivia Chow. However, after months sitting in third place in the polls, it would be Tory, not Chow, who defeated the Ford brothers and became Toronto's new mayor.

Tory was born into a life of privilege as the son of John Tory Sr, of the influential law firm Torys LLP. Tory Jr would himself become a lawyer, though his interests did not lie in practising law. At an early age, his thoughts turned to politics and civic engagement (Diebel, 2014, 25 October). His early foray into the political spotlight did not go well. As Prime Minister Kim Campbell's campaign manager during the 1993 Canadian federal election, he gained infamy when he approved a TV ad that seemed to make fun of Liberal candidate Jean Chrétien's partial facial paralysis (Hepburn, 2014, 6 August). After the fallout from that commercial and Campbell's defeat, Tory moved away from politics for a time, at one point helming the Canadian media giant Rogers Communications. He would return to politics a decade later, entering, for the first time, the mayoral race in Toronto. Considered a frontrunner for much of the campaign, he would eventually lose to David Miller, a Toronto city councillor, by 43 to 38 per cent.

But his mayoral campaign had undoubtedly raised his profile within the city. This may have acted as a launching pad for his successful bid to become leader of the Ontario Progressive Conservative Party. As PC leader, Tory went into the 2007 provincial election with polls showing his party in the lead against Dalton McGuinty's struggling Liberals. One major miscalculation – his reluctance to back away from an unpopular promise to publicly fund faith-based schools – played a large role in his eventual defeat by the Liberals (Hepburn, 2014, 6 August).

After his successive political losses, Tory again took a break from politics. However, he remained publicly engaged. At various times, he served as chair of the United Way of Greater Toronto and the Greater Toronto Civic Action Alliance (now CivicAction). Perhaps more importantly, he also launched his own political radio talk show, one that proved popular with many listeners, particularly women. On the radio, Tory was able to portray himself as fiscally conservative but socially progressive (Preville, 2011, 6 June). His ideological position likely helped him win converts from the Ford camp in the 2014 election, for the Fords, while fiscal conservatives, at times demonstrated prejudicial tendencies (for example, when he was mayor Rob Ford repeatedly refused to walk in Toronto's Pride Parade). It is also likely that Tory's profile and political leanings undermined the campaigns of Soknacki and Stintz, both of whom, like Tory, positioned themselves as centre-right on fiscal issues while progressive on social issues.[2]

The Final Three: Olivia Chow

At the start of the campaign for mayor, Olivia Chow was the sitting federal MP for Trinity-Spadina, a federal riding in downtown Toronto. She was also a former city councillor. Supporters and the news media had expected her to enter the race long before her campaign actually began (Doolittle, 2014, 15 March), but she waited until mid-March to step down from her seat in Parliament and do so (Morrow & Hui, 2014, 11 March). As soon as she announced her candidacy, she took a commanding lead in the polls; however, her campaign faltered in the second half of the summer, in part due to circumstances beyond her control. In the end, she would finish third in the race behind Tory and Doug Ford.

Chow represented something quite different from the other major candidates running for mayor. Toronto is a very diverse city – half the population was born abroad. Yet all of the leading candidates for mayor were Caucasian and Canadian-born, except for Chow. She was also the only major candidate hailing from the left of the political spectrum, as well as the only downtowner. In many ways, she was the antithesis to the suburban conservatism of her fellow front-runners (Morrow & Hui, 2014, 11 March).

Chow was born in Hong Kong and moved with her parents to Toronto in her teens. In sharp contrast to Tory and the Ford brothers, she began life in Canada relatively poor. Both her parents were well educated, yet they struggled to find work in Canada. She would grow up in the towers of St James Town, a neighbourhood known at the time for its poverty, crime, and high density. In spite of that rough start, Chow would go on to graduate from university and at times teach at the college and university level (Doolittle, 2014, 15 March).

Like Tory, Chow had a long history in politics. She won the first election she entered, for the Toronto Board of Education, in 1985. After six years as a board trustee, she ran for and won a seat on Metro Toronto Council in 1991. After Metro Toronto was amalgamated with its six constituent lower-tier municipalities in 1997, Chow served on the new City Council for another nine years. After more than two decades serving Toronto at the municipal level, she made the leap to federal politics, representing the riding of Trinity-Spadina from 2006 until 2014, when she stepped down to run for mayor.

During her time on City Council, Chow served as chair of the Community Services Committee and vice-chair of the TTC. While an MP, she served as the NDP's critic for transportation, infrastructure, and communities. Of all the major candidates, Chow had the strongest political pedigree, having served in elected office for more than a quarter century. She was also one half of a political power couple. Her late husband, Jack Layton, had served on City Council with her before also making the jump to federal politics. As leader of the federal NDP, he had led the party to its best ever electoral result, in 2011. Chow played a major role in that campaign and in the NDP's shadow government after the party became the Official Opposition in Parliament for the first time in its history. Given her background and formidable profile, it is clear why she was considered the front-runner in the race even before she entered.

The Final Three: Doug Ford

Doug Ford began the 2014 Toronto municipal election by choosing not to run for re-election in his Etobicoke ward, leaving his nephew Michael Ford to run in his place. Instead, he chose to focus on his brother's campaign for re-election as mayor. During the early part of Rob's campaign, Doug was often seen at his brother's side. As Rob's health began to fail, however, the Ford campaign team prepared a backup plan: running Doug in place of Rob. After Rob was hospitalized and diagnosed with an abdominal tumour in early September, that plan was triggered. Doug joined the race for mayor, replacing his brother, on the last day of registration (Church & Hui, 2014, 12 September).

Rob had served on City Council for ten years before running for mayor; Doug had much less experience in public office. He had won the first election he ever entered, in 2010, replacing his brother in the Etobicoke North ward. Prior to that, he had never held public office. However, his lack of experience in office masked a longer history in politics.

According to an article in *Toronto Life* magazine, it was Doug Ford Jr, the second of three boys and one daughter, who started his family down the path to politics. Prior to entering politics, Doug spent much of his time working in his father's – Doug Ford Sr's – label-making business, DECO Labels and Tags, eventually replacing his father as company president and later expanding the business to the United States (Canadian Press, 2014, 12 September; Rider, 2014, 26 October). It was through DECO that the middle Ford brother entered politics. In 1994, Ford was approached by then Etobicoke city councillor Doug Holyday, who was looking to recycle his campaign signs for City Council for use in his run for mayor of Etobicoke, a former constituent municipality of Metro Toronto. Ford obliged, and then joined the Holyday steering committee. Doug Ford was also the impetus for his father's successful run for provincial politics in 1995 (McDonald, 2012, 15 May).

Though he was interested in politics, Doug Ford focused on running his family's company while his younger brother, Rob, pursued a career in public office. Doug would largely remain in the political shadows until he ran for City Council in 2010. Though he was a neophyte on the council, his close relationship with the mayor ensured that he attracted significant attention from the news media. The brothers' decision to ply the city's airways in 2012 with their own weekly radio show only expanded their audience (McDonald, 2012, 15 May). More importantly, Doug Ford's close association with his brother, and their mutual branding as "Ford Nation," ensured that the two were closely linked in the minds of the electorate. This made the transition from Rob to Doug in the mayoral race much easier, despite the many differences between the two (White, 2014, 12 September).

Attitudes toward the Candidates

Candidate Ratings

We begin our analysis of the public's perception of the candidates by focusing on summary indicators of attitudes toward the three main contenders. TES respondents were asked to rate each candidate on a scale from 0 (very negative) to 100 (very positive), with a score of 50 being the neutral point (such 101-point "feeling thermometers" are common in election studies). These summary measures do not speak to *why* electors feel the way they do toward candidates, but they are closely linked to vote choice. Indeed, TES data reveal that 82.5 per cent of respondents who gave one of the candidates a higher rating than the other two voted for the candidate they ranked most highly (n = 1,596).[3]

A descriptive analysis of these feeling thermometer data provides important insight into how the typical Torontonian viewed the candidates. Ford received the lowest average feeling thermometer score among the three major contenders, 41.0, with a standard deviation (indicating how consistent views toward the candidate were) of 36.0. Despite receiving fewer votes than Ford on election day, Chow had a somewhat higher average feeling thermometer rating, 46.0 (standard deviation = 31.1). Tory came out on top, with a mean value of 55.3 (standard deviation = 28.5).[4] Tory was the most popular, and had the most consistent ratings, while the opposite can be said of Ford.[5] On the basis of these values, it is easy to see why Tory was able to win the mayoralty by a fairly comfortable margin.

Feeling thermometer data can also be used to evaluate the distribution of attitudes among electors. Are attitudes toward candidates normally distributed? That is, do electors more or less view politicians in a similar manner, with ratings clustering around the mean? Or are some candidates more polarizing than others, causing voters to either "love them or loathe them"? To consider this, we present Figure 2.1, which shows histograms of the feeling thermometer results for each candidate.[6] The x-axis in the histograms shows the range of candidate ratings, while the height of the bars shows the share of respondents who assigned the candidates each value.

Figure 2.1 reveals several noteworthy patterns. Perhaps most strikingly, feeling thermometer results suggest strongly that Doug Ford was indeed a highly polarizing candidate. Nearly 13 per cent of TES respondents gave Ford a score of 0, and more than one third (33.6 per cent) gave him a score of less than 10. In comparison, Chow and Tory received the lowest possible feeling thermometer score from only 5 per cent and 2.7 per cent of respondents, respectively. Less than one fifth of respondents (19.1 per cent) rated Chow lower than 10, while fewer than one in ten (9.6 per cent) Torontonians gave Tory such a score. At the same time, Ford was also the most likely to receive a "perfect" score from Torontonians; 7.4 per cent of respondents gave him a rating of 100 (10.8 per cent gave him a score higher than 90). Both of his competitors received a score of 100 from fewer than 5 per cent of respondents (though Chow and Tory

Figure 2.1. Candidate ratings – histograms

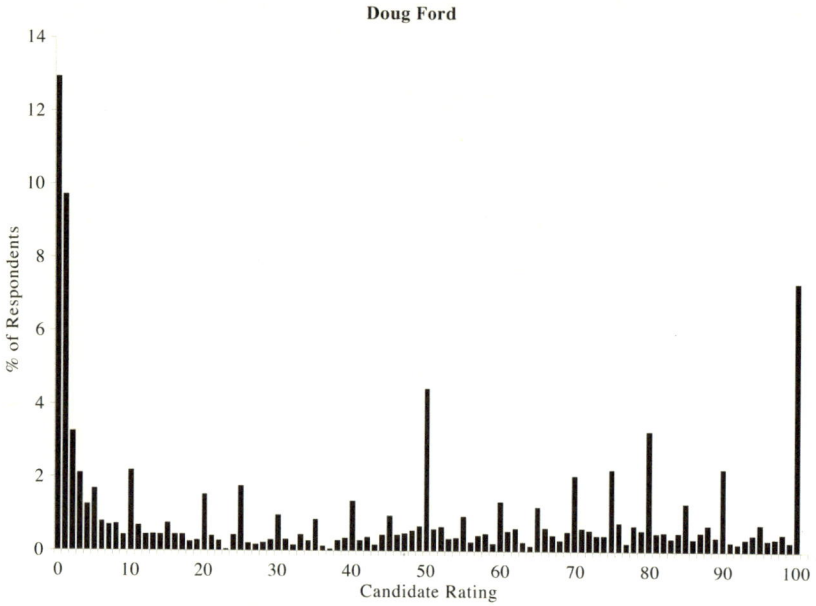

Doug Ford

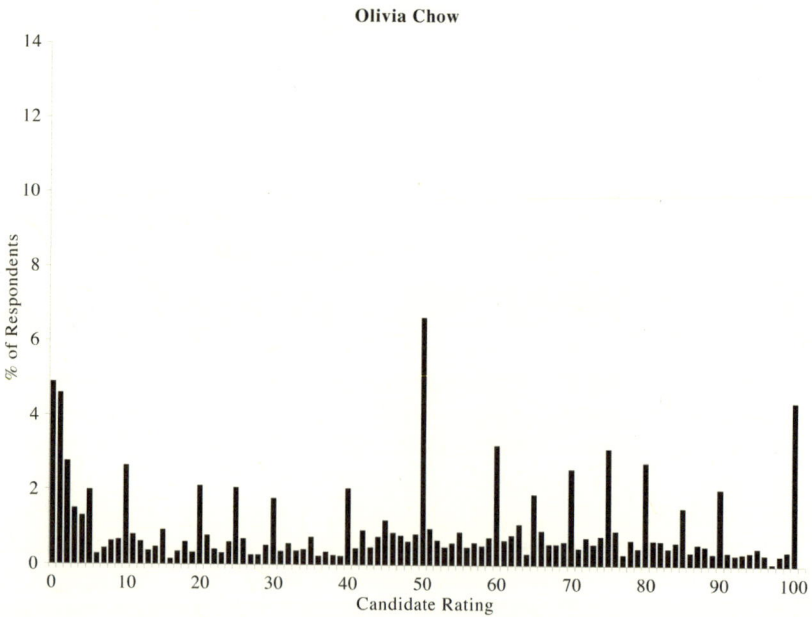

Olivia Chow

Figure 2.1. (Continued)

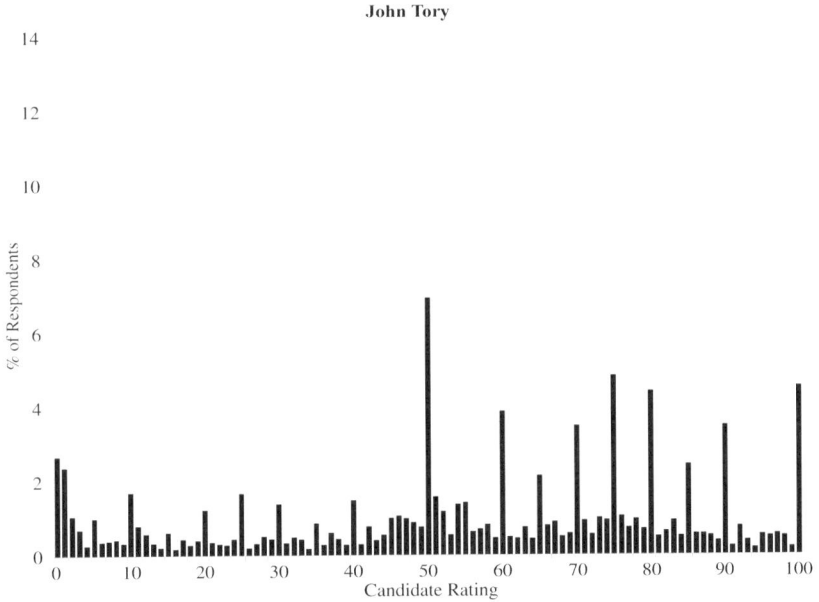

did receive scores greater than 90 from 7.2 per cent and 8.5 per cent of electors, respectively). Ford, then, was both loved and loathed by more electors than either of the other main contenders.

It is also worth evaluating the *skew* of the feeling thermometer data. The skew of a variable speaks to how symmetrical a distribution is, and, more importantly, whether respondents tended to assign positive or negative ratings to candidates. The histogram of John Tory's ratings shows that many more Torontonians rated him positively than negatively (the height of the bars on his histogram tends to be greater on the right than on the left).[7] Views toward the eventual mayor were thus generally quite positive – 56.9 per cent of respondents assigned him a score greater than 50, while only 34.5 per cent assigned him a negative value (less than 50).

The opposite is true for Ford, whose histogram shows that respondents were more likely to dislike than like him: 55.1 per cent of respondents gave Doug a negative score, compared to 39.9 per cent who assessed him positively. Thus, besides being the most polarizing candidate, Ford was also the most disliked by the electorate as a whole. Finally, Chow's histogram displays relative balance – nearly the same number of respondents assigned her negative (48.5 per cent) as positive (44.8 per cent) values. Chow was thus liked by nearly as many people as disliked her.

So there is clearly much more to candidate ratings than average values. Though she finished third in the election, Chow received the second-highest average rating from electors. At the same time, she was the least polarizing contestant in the race, as her nearly symmetrical histogram shows. While perhaps not a recipe for victory, these findings hardly point strongly to a third-place finish. By contrast, in addition to having a low average rating, Ford was extremely polarizing. More Torontonians gave perfect 0s or 100s to him than they did to either of the other candidates. Those voters who liked Ford, however, tended to *really* like him, and this may have propelled him to second place on election day. The key to Tory's success seems to have been consistency. He did not polarize the electorate, and far fewer electors viewed him negatively than positively. That such factors could lead to victory should be a shock to no one.

2014 and Ranked Balloting

Though of significant interest, the ratings of individual candidates provide only limited insight into the preferences of electors, and thus their voting behaviour. If individuals assign high ratings to multiple politicians, for example, being viewed positively can be of little use to a candidate if a rival is viewed even just slightly more positively. Similarly, some voters may have a generally negative view of politicians, potentially assigning all candidates low feeling thermometer scores. When forced to choose a candidate while in the voting booth, such voters will inevitably support a candidate of whom they are not fond. Absolute ratings, therefore, are less important for vote choice than *relative* ratings.

In the first-past-the-post electoral system employed in elections in Toronto, voters must eventually choose a single candidate to support. What matters for vote choice, therefore, is how candidates are rated *in comparison* to one another (though other factors, such as strategic calculations, may also play a role in determining which single candidate one will support on the ballot). Other electoral systems prioritize different decision-making criteria. In a ranked ballot electoral system (alternatively referred to as "instant runoff preferential voting"), voters rank candidates in order of preference. Ballots are then counted on the basis of each voter's first choice. If any candidate secures a majority of votes after the initial tally, that candidate wins. If not, the candidate with the fewest first-choice votes is eliminated from consideration, and the second choice votes from those ballots are counted. This process continues until a single candidate receives more than 50 per cent of the votes.

In June 2016, the Province of Ontario granted municipalities the authority to use ranked ballots in future elections, permitting voters to select as many as their top three options on a single ballot (Ontario, 2016). The province was responding to a grassroots movement to reform voting at the local level (which was accompanied by a high-profile national debate on the issue of electoral reform). Ranked ballots are used in municipal elections in a growing number of American cities, including San Francisco, California, Minneapolis, Minnesota, and Portland, Maine. The decision to adopt the system at the municipal level in Ontario is thus not without precedent (Moore, 2017). This is the same system widely believed to have been favoured by Prime Minister Justin Trudeau and the federal Liberal Party prior to the abandonment of their promise to reform the electoral system in 2017 (Grenier, 2015, 26 November). Interestingly, this is also the electoral system used by all of Canada's major federal parties when selecting leaders. Organizations such as the Ranked Ballot Initiative of Toronto (RaBIT) have argued that ranked ballots would prevent mayoral and council candidates from winning elections with less than a majority of the vote, eliminate vote-splitting, and reduce strategic voting at the municipal level (RaBIT, n.d.). The putative motivation for this movement is the sense that current electoral systems in municipalities are unable to translate residents' sentiments and preferences into an elected body that accurately represents their interests.

All Ontario municipalities were given the option to adopt ranked ballots for the 2018 election cycle, but only one, London, did so in advance of the provincial deadline of 1 May 2017.[8] The City of Toronto at first supported the adoption of ranked ballots; in 2013, City Council was at the forefront of the battle for ranked balloting, having petitioned the province to allow for it at the local level (provincial permission is required for such a change). However, council reversed its decision in 2016, in a 25–18 vote led by rookie city councillor Justin Di Ciano, who argued that a ranked ballot voting system would be too costly and overly complex and that there was limited public support for it (Di Ciano, 2017, 27 March). In 2020, the (now Conservative) provincial government abruptly stripped cities of the option to use ranked ballots. As a result, ranked ballots do not seem to have a future in Toronto, especially given the province's 2020 reversal on this issue.

A debate over the merits of various electoral systems falls outside of the purview of this book. Still, knowledge of how electors ranked the candidates can provide insight into how the competitors were viewed in relative rather than absolute terms. This enables us to conduct a counterfactual exercise, in which we use information about the attitudes of

Table 2.1. Ranking of mayoral candidates (%)

		Candidate			
		Ford	Chow	Tory	Others
Ranking	First	31.4	20.6	45.1	2.9
	Second	14.5	35.9	34.0	15.6
	Third	17.1	23.8	14.8	44.3
	Fourth	37.0	19.7	6.1	37.3

n = 1,385

Torontonians toward the 2014 mayoral candidates to speculate about what the election outcome would have been had the contest been run under a ranked ballot system. Admittedly, the candidates might have campaigned differently, and the electors might have responded and reasoned differently, had a different electoral system been used in 2014. Even so, this exercise is still informative for understanding electoral system–induced strategic behaviour.

In the campaign-period TES questionnaire, respondents were informed that the province had passed legislation that would allow the city to use ranked ballots in future elections, and ranked balloting was described to them. They were then asked to rank the candidates as if ranked balloting were currently in place. Table 2.1 shows the results of this question, indicating how many first, second, and third place votes each candidate would have received. We consider the three major candidates, as well as an "other" category to capture all minor candidates simultaneously, and limit our analysis to voters, as we are interested in speculating on the outcome of the hypothetical election.[9] Entries in the table report column percentages.[10]

Not surprisingly, the first-place rankings in Table 2.1 fairly closely mirror the actual election outcome. Tory, who received 40.3 per cent of the vote on election day, was ranked highest by 45.1 per cent of TES respondents. Ford was ranked first by 31.4 per cent of respondents, which closely matches the 33.7 per cent of votes he actually received. Chow was the most preferred candidate of 20.6 per cent of Torontonians and received 23.2 per cent of the actual vote. Such a pattern suggests that little strategic voting occurred in the election, a contention that is compatible with the work of Caruana et al. (2018), who estimate that a mere 1.3 per cent of ballots cast in the election were "strategic" (i.e., voters supported a candidate who was not their most preferred, in order to prevent a disliked candidate from winning).

Table 2.2. First- and second-choice preferences (%)

		First choice			
		Ford (n = 434)	Chow (n = 286)	Tory (n = 625)	Other (n = 40)
Second choice	Ford	–	10.9	26.7	7.5
	Chow	26.9	–	57.1	58.5
	Tory	57.0	73.5	–	34.0
	Other	16.1	15.6	16.2	–

Another striking observation from Table 2.1 is that, among those who did not rank him first, Doug Ford performed very poorly. In fact, the brother of the outgoing mayor was ranked last (fourth) by many more respondents than were Chow and Tory combined. He was also the recipient of relatively few "second place" rankings. Fewer than one in six voters who preferred a candidate other than Ford listed him as their second choice. In contrast, both Chow and Tory were the recipients of greater than one third of second place votes. These patterns suggest strongly that Ford would not have fared well had the 2014 election been fought under a ranked ballot system.

This supposition raises the question of which candidates were the "second choice" among the supporters of various contenders. In a traditional first-past-the-post election, this question is of little importance, for only first preferences are considered. In a ranked ballot election, however, second choices become important if no candidate receives the majority of first choice votes necessary to be declared the victor. In such a scenario, second place preferences would also need to be considered. For insight into such preferences, Table 2.2 shows the cross-tabulation of first and second place rankings. As with Table 2.1, entries report column percentages.

Though the official election results align closely with the first-choice preferences of Torontonians revealed in Table 2.1, such results provide no insight into who voters might have supported had their preferred candidate not been an option. So the second-choice preferences in Table 2.2 are vital for understanding potential outcomes in a ranked ballot election. Important for the outcome of a hypothetical election is the fact that, among those who favoured one of the three major candidates, there were clear patterns of second preferences.

More specifically, the finding in Table 2.2 most relevant to the matter of ranked balloting is that Tory was the second preference of a large majority of those who ranked either Ford or Chow first. Such a pattern may reflect the fact that the electorate viewed Tory as conservative but a more moderate one than Ford (Chow was viewed as on the left of the ideological spectrum (McGregor et al., 2016)).[11] On that basis, Downs (1957) would suggest that it would have been logical for supporters of Ford (on the right) and Chow (on the left) to rank Tory second, given that he was more ideologically proximate to their first choice. This may help explain Tory's support for ranked balloting in future elections.

An ideological explanation does not necessarily hold, however, when we attempt to explain why Ford was so infrequently the recipient of second-place rankings. As one would expect on the basis of the results in Table 2.1, Ford was the second choice of very few of those who ranked Chow, Tory, or any other candidate first. That he was not even the second choice of most Tory supporters is surprising given that, again, both candidates were viewed as ideologically conservative (McGregor et al., 2016). One might at the very least expect Ford to win more second-place support than Chow from those who ranked Tory first. This is, in fact, the opposite of what happened – Chow received more than twice as many second-place votes from this group.[12]

In some elections fought under a ranked ballot electoral system, however, it is not just first and second place preferences that matter. As noted above, votes must continue to be counted until one candidate receives the support of a majority of voters, and more than two rounds of counting would have been necessary to settle the 2014 Toronto election. After the first round of counting, those in the "other" category would have been dropped sequentially, and the second-place preferences of those voters considered. Given that few people supported such candidates in this election, however, further rounds of counting would have been needed.[13] Olivia Chow would likely have eventually been dropped from the candidate pool, leaving an "instant runoff" between Ford and Tory. Table 2.3 shows the hypothetical round by round results, based on the same TES question used to create Tables 2.1 and 2.2.

Based on TES data, we can conclude that John Tory would have won the 2014 Toronto mayoral election had the contest been fought under a ranked ballot electoral system. All three major candidates would have received a modest boost in support from the second-place votes of those who supported "other" candidates. No candidate would have reached the 50 per cent threshold, however. With Chow eliminated, Tory would have leapt past the 50 per cent mark, receiving the support of 65.3 per cent of electors, compared to 34.7 per cent for Ford.[14] In this case, therefore, the outcome of the election did not depend upon the electoral system in place.

Table 2.3. Ranked balloting results by round (%)

	Ford	Chow	Tory	Others
Round 1	31.4	20.6	45.1	2.9
Round 2	31.6	22.3	46.1	–
Round 3	34.7	–	65.3	–

n = 1,385

Still, one can imagine instances where ranking might affect an election outcome. John Tory was the recipient here of a large number of second-place votes, quite possibly because he was ideologically moderate. In an election where the front-runner was less moderate, however, he or she might well receive relatively fewer second place votes, potentially allowing a more centrist candidate to surpass them in later voting rounds. This may very well be the logic that led Tory to support ranked balloting in the first place, and to oppose City Council's 2017 decision to back away from ranked balloting.

Regardless, based on both feeling thermometers and rankings, it is not difficult to see why John Tory was victorious on election day. Attitudes toward him were more consistent and more positive than toward any other candidate, and he was the most popular second choice of supporters of both other major candidates. In other words, it is hard to imagine an electoral system in which John Tory would not have become mayor of the City of Toronto in 2014.

What Did Torontonians Look for in a Candidate?

Candidate ratings and rankings are useful summary measures: they provide an overall "score" for candidates. They do not, however, tell us *why* candidates received the scores (or votes) that they did. Voters' opinions may be shaped by any number of factors, including (but not limited to) both personal and policy considerations. However, ratings and rankings do not tell us how voters view the personal qualities or policy stances of candidates. One way the TES provides insight into these matters is through questions about the importance of various policy areas and the personal traits of candidates.

On the first matter, TES respondents were asked how important a series of five policy fields were to them: public transit, property taxes, traffic and congestion, housing affordability, and managing the city's finances. If supporters of the three candidates held different policy priorities, it would strongly indicate that the candidates were viewed differently in those policy areas. If, for instance, Ford voters placed a low value on public transit, and Chow supporters a high value, it would say something about the supporters of the two candidates (i.e., that they held different issue priorities). It would also suggest, however, that the candidates themselves were viewed differently on the matter, not simply that Chow had a "better" position on transit. Rather, for whatever reason, it could suggest that she attracted people who valued public transit. It could also imply that she was seen as "owning" the issue (meaning that she was viewed as having a better capacity to handle the matter). (See Bélanger, 2003, and Bélanger & Meguid, 2008, for a discussion of issue ownership at the federal level in Canada.)

Besides examining differences with regard to various policy fields, we compared supporters of the three major candidates with respect to the importance they placed on six candidate traits: intelligence, honesty and trustworthiness, effectiveness (the ability to "get things done"), caring about people, sharing political beliefs with the candidate, and approachability. If one group of voters valued different traits than another, it would indirectly suggest that the candidates themselves were seen as possessing those traits (or not).

We make no claims of causality here. That is, we are not suggesting that voters necessarily supported the candidate they did because that candidate was seen as best able to handle a policy area or possessed a valued trait. We recognize that a candidate who is perceived as having a trait such as intelligence may well attract voters who value that trait. In other cases, though, a voter's decision to support a candidate may lead that voter to state that he or she values a trait that candidate possesses, *after the fact*. Such attitudinal shifts may be easily explained by cognitive dissonance theory, which suggests that incongruence between attitudes and behaviour can lead to a shift in attitudes (Festinger, 1957). Vote choice is one such behaviour, and supporting a particular candidate has been shown to affect attitudes toward that candidate (Beasley & Joslyn, 2001; McGregor, 2013a; Mullainathan & Washington, 2009).[15]

We have two responses to this endogeneity concern. First, all questions about policy importance and candidate traits were measured prior to election day, while vote choice was measured after. As many voters were still undecided at the time of the pre-election interview (which in some instances was conducted more than a month before the election), this order of questioning had the effect of minimizing the impact of vote choice on opinions about the importance of policy areas and candidate traits. Second, and more importantly, as the purpose here is to gain some insight into how voters viewed the candidates, it does not matter whether they selected candidates because of their opinions on policy and candidate traits, or altered their opinions in response to their decision to support a particular candidate. Perhaps voters supported a particular candidate due to that person's policy stances or personal characteristics, or perhaps that person's policy stances or personal characteristics changed because they had decided to vote for that person. In either case, the analysis that follows still tells us how the candidates were viewed by their supporters.

Issue Importance

TES respondents were asked how important they believed a series of five policy issues to be, on a scale from 0 to 10. We chose the five policy issues – public transit, property taxes, traffic and congestion, housing affordability, and managing city finances – based on their prevalence in media coverage of the election campaign. Cases have been broken down on the basis of vote choice to determine whether the individuals who supported the three major candidates had different priorities in the 2014 election. Figure 2.2 show the results of this analysis, with the mean "importance" score for each issue shown for each group of voters, as represented by the height of each bar in the figure (whiskers show the limits of the 95 per cent confidence intervals).[16]

Figure 2.2 reveals several noteworthy differences between the three groups of voters. First, supporters of the incumbent mayor's brother prioritized management of the city's finances over all other issues. The average value for this issue was 8.5/10, the highest of any in the figure. This issue was more important than any other for Ford supporters, and more important than it was for both Tory and Chow voters ($p < 0.05$ in all comparisons). Public transit, by contrast, was particularly unimportant for Ford voters. With a value of 7.1, only one value in the entire figure is lower (the "property taxes" issue among Chow supporters). Rob Ford's long-time emphasis on "stopping the gravy train" at City Hall and fighting against the "war on the car" may help explain why his brother attracted those who prioritized city finances and cared relatively little about public transit.

The results for Chow supporters stand in stark contrast to those for Ford. On three of five policies, Chow and Ford voters had statistically significant differences in opinion regarding issue importance. Chow supporters placed relatively less emphasis on managing the city's finances (though in absolute terms, this issue remained relatively important, at 7.9). More striking are the differences regarding public transit and property taxes. Transit was more important for Chow voters than for any other

Figure 2.2. Issue importance by vote choice

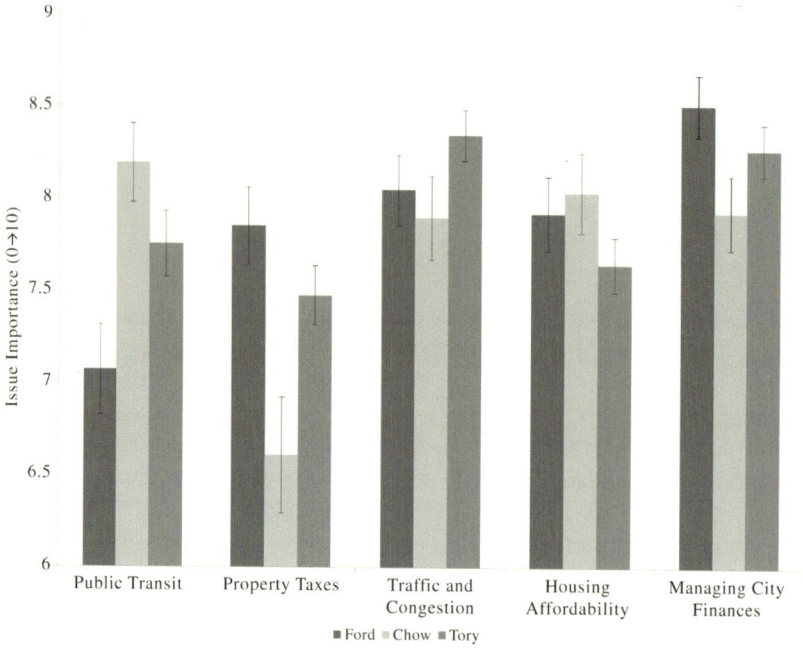

group (which is perhaps not surprising given her strong support in the downtown core, where parking space is at a premium). By contrast, property taxes were of very little importance for this group – the average value of 6.6 is the lowest score for any issue for any candidate. Ford and Chow thus attracted very different policy constituencies.

Finally, there are no overwhelmingly strong outliers regarding issue importance for Tory supporters. Those who backed him cared more about traffic and congestion, and less about housing affordability, than both Chow and Ford supporters, but the differences on both fronts are hardly drastic. On the issues where Ford and Chow supporters differed most (public transit and property taxes), Tory supporters were in between in both respects. With respect to policy, therefore, Tory's constituents were moderate on all fronts. The largest contrasts in Figure 2.2, and thus the most important patterns, are between supporters of Chow and Ford.

Candidate Traits

We now know that supporters of the three major mayoral candidates had differences of opinion regarding issue importance, but what about opinions of the traits they valued in the candidates themselves? In non-partisan races (meaning that parties are absent), candidates' characteristics stand to play a larger role in voter decisions. In such races, image management on the part of the contenders becomes increasingly important, and displaying specific personal characteristics may attract or repel voters. So it is worth considering which characteristics were deemed important by electors and whether vote choice was associated with different priorities.

We thus turn to consider whether supporters of the three major candidates valued different personal characteristics in municipal politicians. TES respondents were provided with a series of characteristics and asked which ones they believed to be most important for politicians. As above, the sample has been divided on the basis of vote choice, allowing us to compare the responses on the basis of candidate support.[17] Figure 2.3 shows the results of this analysis. Note that the height of each bar represents the share of supporters of the major candidates that selected each trait as most important. As above, whiskers indicate 95 per cent confidence intervals.

There are some similarities between supporters of the candidates, but there are also some noteworthy differences with respect to how character traits are valued. The modal choice for supporters of all three candidates is "honest and trustworthy." More than four in ten of those who voted for each candidate identified this as the most important trait. There is a difference between Tory and Ford voters, with the former group being more likely to select this trait than the latter, but for the most part there is agreement that this is the most important trait a candidate can have.

There is less agreement with respect to some of the other traits, however. First, Ford voters were less likely to select intelligence as the most important trait than were either Tory or Chow voters (who did not differ from each other in this regard). The reverse pattern is observed, however, with respect to the ability to "get things done." More than one third of Ford voters selected this as the most desirable candidate trait, while the same can be said of fewer than one fifth of either Chow or Tory voters (again, these two groups did not differ from each other in any statistically significant sense). Ford voters thus prioritized candidate efficacy over intelligence, or action over "smarts," while this was not true of Chow and Tory supporters.

Finally, we see that few voters from any camp chose the final three traits (caring about people, sharing political beliefs, being approachable). Approachability was particularly unimportant, while sharing one's political beliefs was selected by fewer than one in ten voters for all three

Figure 2.3. Most important candidate trait by vote choice

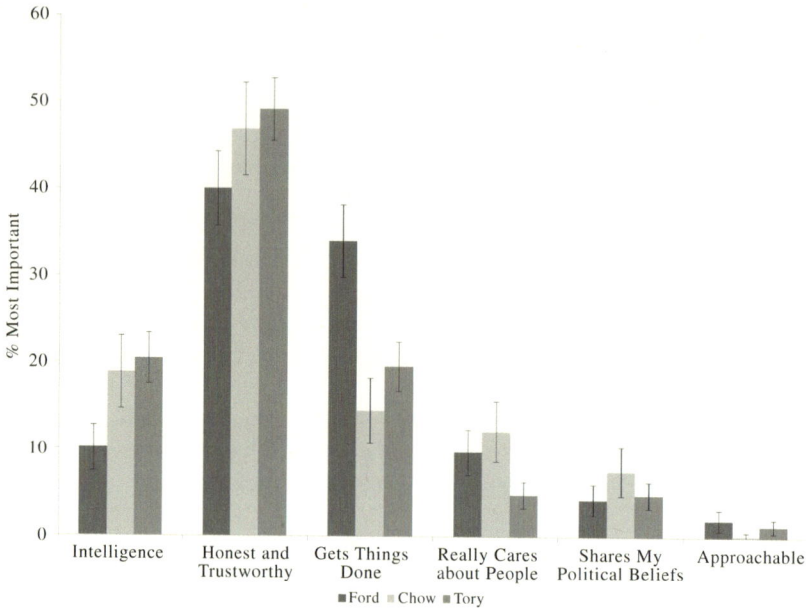

candidates (which suggests that policy was less important for many voters than were the candidates' personal characteristics – a contention we return to later in this book). Finally, though few voters placed great value on candidates "really caring about people," Tory supporters were less likely to value this than were Chow or Ford voters – an interesting finding, though potentially a difficult one to explain.

As was the case when examining the relationship between vote choice and issue importance, the results of this analysis point to important differences between supporters of the various candidates. Ford supporters clearly prioritized effectiveness over intelligence, whereas supporters of the other two candidates perceived these traits as equally important. Interestingly, Chow and Tory supporters varied very little from each other with respect to candidate trait preferences. Tory supporters were slightly less likely to prioritize "really caring about people" and just a bit more likely to prioritize "getting things done," but on neither front were these differences anywhere near the magnitude of those observed when comparing Ford and his rivals with respect to the first three traits in Figure 2.3. It was Doug Ford supporters who were the outliers with respect to the importance of various candidate traits.

Conclusion

In chapter 1 we focused on how Torontonians think about municipal politics in general. In this chapter, we changed our focus to consider the major candidates in the 2014 mayoral race. Any election for a "top job" necessarily puts the spotlight on candidates, and that is even more true when there are no parties or partisan loyalties to consider. Therefore, understanding who the candidates were and what voters thought about them is crucial to understanding the election outcome.

When considering the ratings of the candidates themselves, in terms of both absolute values and relative measures, John Tory received the highest rating of the three candidates, and he was also the most preferred in a relative analysis. In contrast, Ford was the most polarizing, and disliked by a majority of voters. This polarization seemed to transpose onto the voters themselves: Ford supporters differed significantly in the traits they looked for in a mayor, placing an ability "to get things done" second only to honesty and trustworthiness.

Overall, the findings in this chapter suggest that John Tory was a good compromise candidate for Torontonians. Supporters of both Ford and Chow were more likely to prefer him to the other candidate, and his backers were not sharply motivated by any particular policy or personality trait. Chow's middling rating among voters was insufficient to defeat Tory at the ballot box, despite her appeal to voters who prioritized public transit rather than property taxes. Ford's perceived ability to "get things done" and his focus on managing city finances was not a powerful enough combination to win his brother's old job. Tory, with his consistently high ratings among the electorate, seemed destined to win the 2014 Toronto election, regardless of the electoral system under which it was fought.

Chapter 3

In the Thick of Things: The 2014 Campaign

Apart from the victory of John Tory, the 2014 mayoral campaign in Toronto will be remembered largely for the antics of the Ford brothers. From the day Rob Ford announced his intention to seek re-election on 2 January until election day on 27 October, the Fords' campaign was a tumultuous one. While the brothers were ever present in the media, however, the narrative of the first half of the election campaign was very much about the inevitability of an Olivia Chow victory. Well before she entered the race, the *Toronto Star* touted the election as "Chow's to lose" (James, 2014, 22 February). On officially entering the race on 13 March (Church & Hui, 2014, 13 March), she catapulted to first place in the polls (Toronto Star, 2014, 15 March). Supposedly, a splintered right would allow the sole left-wing candidate to win (James, 2014, 13 March). This narrative persisted for months. Chow was perceived as the strongest candidate in early debates (Gee, 2014, 27 March) and was still leading by a healthy margin in June. Yet on election day, she finished a distant third behind John Tory and Doug Ford. Chow's fall from favour is indicative of the long, gruelling nature of the 2014 campaign. The 2014 mayoral election in Toronto was like no other before.

In the Thick of Things

This chapter considers the effects of the 2014 municipal campaign on voters and on the final results. To that end, we map, and attempt to explain, changes in candidate support over the nearly ten-month campaign. We begin by presenting a detailed narrative account of the campaign; we then combine polling and TES data to determine the extent to which voter attitudes changed during the campaign, briefly comparing attitudinal change during the Toronto campaign to that found during recent federal elections. Polling data are employed to track voter attitudes for the first eight months of the municipal campaign, and TES data are used to consider attitude changes in the period after the nomination deadline. These data help explain the election outcome; they also suggest whether electors were influenced during the campaign, and if so, how. Did voter attitudes toward the candidates change over the months? Did ratings of candidates, vote preferences, or attitudes about a candidate that one would "never vote for" change? Relatedly, did expectations regarding the election outcome change over time? Changes to any or all of these attitudes across time would provide strong evidence that voters were being influenced by the campaign.

The Campaign Narrative

And They're Off …

The 2nd of January, 2014, marked the beginning of the nomination period for mayoral, council, and school board candidates and the start of the 2014 Toronto election campaign.[1] With almost ten months to go before election day, the only notable element at this fairly early stage was Rob Ford's decision to run for re-election despite having been stripped of most of his authority as mayor by City Council a month and a half earlier (Toronto Star, 2014, 2 January). The first two and a half months of the campaign for mayor were spent waiting to see which heavyweights would decide to enter the race. By the end of February, polls showed a close race between Ford and Tory, with Tory having the edge. However, these early polls proved a distraction; the news media and political pundits were waiting to see whether Chow, then a sitting federal MP, would enter the race (Toronto Star, 2014, 26 February). The *Toronto Star*, in particular, waited with bated breath for Chow, the presumed front-runner, to declare her much-anticipated candidacy. The *Star's* focus on Chow was based on more than the dreams of some left-wingers. In polls conducted at the end of 2012 (Rider, 2012, 18 December) and in May 2013 (Flavelle, 2013, 13 May), she was the only potential candidate who performed better than Mayor Ford among voters. That meant the campaign would not truly begin until she made her decision, which she did by entering the race on 13 March 2014. A poll conducted two days later showed her already in the lead (Toronto Star, 2014, 14 March).

With Chow's entry into the race, the field of candidates appeared to be set. Tory, Chow, and Ford were the three front-runners, followed by Stintz and Soknacki, the only other candidates to register noteworthy support among the electorate (albeit in single digits). The first of many debates was held at the end of March. By most accounts, Chow performed strongly in that event, cementing herself as the front-runner, while Tory came out flat. Ford, despite the increasing spectacle of his time as mayor, proved to still be a formidable opponent, leading one observer to suggest that voters not overlook him as a legitimate threat (Gee, 2014, 27 March). This first debate would turn out to be the most civilized of the mayoral debates, and the least controversial.

Provincial Politics and Shifting Tides

For a time in spring 2014, the campaign for mayor was overshadowed by a much shorter one – on 2 May, a provincial election was called for 12 June. The result was a surprising majority government for the ruling Liberal Party under Kathleen Wynne (Diebel, 2014, 14 June). While the provincial election dominated headlines during this period, the contest for mayor continued apace, and at times the two elections converged, particularly around the issue of transit. For instance, John Tory's Smart-Track, his new transit proposal for Toronto, called for the expanded use of the tracks utilized by the province's regional transit system (Moore, 2014, 28 March). This led to inevitable questions for provincial leaders about their support for transit, and for specific transit projects in the city. After the provincial election, the importance of the transit issue in Toronto was made abundantly clear when Kathleen Wynne inserted herself into the mayoral campaign, warning the leading candidates against cancelling existing plans for transit in the city (Benzie, 2014, 28 June).

The dropping of the writ for the provincial election coincided with another important event in the mayoral campaign. On the same day, Mayor Rob Ford announced that he would be taking leave from the campaign, and his curtailed role as mayor, to seek treatment for substance abuse (Church & Hui, 2014, 2 May). He would not return to the campaign until 30 June (Dale, 2014b).

The immediate effect of Ford's entry into rehab was a plunge in voter support for his campaign, leaving him trailing Chow and Tory in third place (Alamenciak, 2014, 3 May). In Ford's absence, the two leading candidates switched to attacking each other (Toronto Star, 2014, 17 June), with Tory taking advantage of Chow's high negativity ratings to present himself as the best option among the centre-right candidates (Hepburn, 2014, 8 May). A poll conducted just before Ford's return to the race showed the incumbent mayor in second place, ahead of Tory and behind Chow (Toronto Star, 2014, 25 June). Although pundits and Tory campaign organizers would later identify Ford's entry into rehab as the turning point in Tory's campaign (Warnica, 2014, 27 October), it appears not to have registered with voters.

In the first debate in which Ford took part following his leave of absence (16 July), Tory demonstrated new vigour. He went on the offensive, attacking the mayor's record. Chow, in contrast, seemed to have lost some of the edge with which she had begun the campaign (Dale, 2014, 16 July). By 9 August, a day after Rob Ford unveiled his plans to bury the proposed Eglinton Crosstown line through Scarborough (Peat, 2014, 8 August), a new poll placed Tory firmly in the lead, with Chow, the former front-runner, dropping to third place (Visser, 2014, 9 August). Tory would remain in the lead for the rest of the campaign.

Things Get Nasty

The remaining weeks of the nomination period saw Karen Stintz and David Soknacki drop out of the election. Having run out of money, and apparently hitting a ceiling in her support, Stintz left the race on 20 August (Rider & Dale, 2014, 21 August). This proved to be a boon for Tory, as many of her advisers moved to Tory's campaign (Rider, 2014, 22 August). David Soknacki would last another three weeks before also ending his ill-fated bid for the mayoralty (Boesveld, 2014, 9 September).

The weeks leading up to the last day for nominations coincided with a growing intensity and nastiness in the campaign (Gee, 2014, 21 August). In August, Warren Kinsella, a high-profile operative for the Chow campaign, took to Twitter to accuse John Tory of being a segregationist, for his SmartTrack proposal did not serve the predominantly lower-income black neighbourhoods of Jane/Finch and Rexdale. Kinsella went so far as to say that if one did not come "from his [Tory's] demographic, he doesn't give a s— if you lose transit service" (quoted in Dale, 2014, 20 August, p. A1). Tory attacked Chow for not immediately firing Kinsella (Dale, 2014, 20 August), who would eventually leave her campaign of his own accord (Powell, 2014, 28 August). Two weeks later, before ending his campaign for mayor, Soknacki accused Rob Ford and his brother Doug of using city resources to fund their campaigns, suggesting he had proof (D'Souza, 2014, 3 October). This change in tone toward greater negativity would continue for the duration of the campaign.

A Quick Change

The 12th of September was the last day for candidates to enter the election. In most campaigns, nomination day goes by with little fanfare, as most candidates have already entered the race and any also-rans have already left it. In 2014, however, this day was hugely consequential: Rob Ford had been admitted to hospital with a tumour two days earlier. This had turned the race topsy-turvy, making nomination day 2014 one to remember (Boesveld, 2014, 10 September).

On this day, a representative of Rob and Doug Ford withdrew Rob's candidacy and immediately submitted Doug's candidacy for mayor (CBC News, 2014, 12 September). On learning of Rob's exit and Doug's entrance into the campaign, Olivia Chow responded with restraint. One of her spokespersons remarked that Rob Ford had been a formidable foe. In contrast, Tory immediately began to attack Doug Ford, demonstrating a level of ire he had not directed at Rob. Asked his opinion of Doug Ford entering the race, he stated: "Doug Ford, who is now a candidate for mayor, has repeatedly put down the members of city council who were his colleagues, and he has publicly disparaged the premier of this province and members of her cabinet ... I don't think Doug Ford offers four more years of the same. In fact, he may offer Toronto something that is worse" (from Hui et al., 2014, 8 May).

Not surprisingly, the final month of the campaign was at least as rancorous as what had come before. The low point was the vitriol directed at Chow for her ethnicity; at times, she had to endure heckling and questions about her ancestry (Strashin, 2014, 2 October). Doug Ford, for his part, did little to help his own cause when he tried to defend his brother against charges of anti-Semitism (Kenez, 2014, 5 October); later in the campaign, a number of people claimed to have heard him refer to a prominent reporter as a "little bitch" (Peat, 2014, 23 October). Tory did not relinquish his lead in the polls during this period, but his support took some hits as a result of Doug Ford's pointed attacks (Rath, 2014, 10 October). Some polls put the brother of the former mayor within striking distance of Tory (James, 2014, 11 October), who was busy defending himself from both Ford and Chow (Pagliaro, 2014, 24 September).

Notwithstanding the odd scare for the front-runner, John Tory would triumph on election day with a large plurality of the vote. The lengthy campaign had involved many twists and turns, including the replacement of Rob with Doug Ford, Olivia Chow's fall in support, and the rise of John Tory. Which events, if any, help account for these changes? In what ways were voter attitudes changed over the course of the election? At what point, if any, was the outcome a foregone conclusion? We turn now to these questions.

Campaign Effects

We will consider *why* voters voted for Tory (or another candidate) in later chapters. This chapter considers whether the 2014 mayoral campaign influenced voters' attitudes and decisions, and if so, how. The scholarly consensus on campaign effects has evolved significantly in recent decades. Early studies of voting behaviour (Campbell et al., 1960; Lazarsfeld et al., 1948) reported that campaigns had "minimal effects" on voters. That is, scholars generally believed that campaigns were rarely able to overcome the knowledge and prejudices that voters already held. More recently, this view has been challenged, and it is now widely accepted that campaigns, and new information that voters are exposed to during those campaigns, can significantly affect voter attitudes and behaviour (Blais et al., 2003; Fournier et al., 2004; Jacobson, 1983; Johnston et al., 1992).

Federal and provincial campaigns tend to be much shorter than Toronto's ten-month electoral odyssey was in 2014 (federally, the average length of a campaign period since 2000 has been just over forty-six days, and provincial elections in Ontario have been even shorter, lasting on average less than thirty-three days). If significant campaign effects have been observed in these relatively short campaigns, it stands to reason that we should see similar shifts during Toronto's ten-month contest. Additionally, if present, we might expect campaign effects to be much more noticeable in Toronto than in other municipalities. Municipal politics in Canada tends to receive much less attention than federal and provincial politics; that said, the 2014 Toronto election was one of the most high-profile municipal contests in Canadian history. Given the exceptional publicity the race attracted, if campaign effects are to be observed in a municipal setting, *ceteris paribus*, we would expect to see them in Toronto's 2014 election.

Alternatively, an argument can be made that we should expect to find relatively little in the way of attitudinal change over the course of the Toronto contest, at least in the weeks leading up to election day. The fact that the official campaign attracted so much attention could mean that attitudes toward the candidates may have been quite well-anchored long before voters went to the ballot box. Zaller's (1992) receive–accept–sample (RAS) model of decision-making suggests that attitudes are formed as a result of the summation of considerations, or beliefs or pieces of knowledge, relevant to some decision (such as vote choice). During a campaign, new considerations are combined with existing ones. All else being equal, the more considerations that are present, the more strongly anchored a belief may be and the less likely it is that new considerations will change one's opinion. In the context of a long, high-profile campaign such as the 2014 Toronto mayoral race, it stands to reason that many voters will already have a great number of existing considerations by the nomination deadline. In such a scenario, attitude change may be particularly unlikely in the later stages of a campaign. In short, the substantial length of the Toronto campaign may very well mean that voter attitudes and preferences were set well in advance of election day. Campaign effects in the final weeks before election day may, therefore, have been muted in Toronto, when compared to federal and provincial contests.

It is between these two possibilities that we adjudicate. After using publicly available polling data to chart public preferences during the first eight months of the election (prior to the candidate nomination deadline), we employ TES data to map several attitudinal measures over the remainder of the campaign (a period comparable to the length of federal and provincial campaigns). The fact that TES data are restricted to the thirty-eight days immediately before election day means that we needed to look elsewhere to analyse campaign dynamics for the first eight months of the campaign. In the remainder of this chapter we ask: Did the campaign affect voter attitudes and preferences in the final weeks of the 2014 Toronto municipal election, as has been found to be the case at other levels of elections in Canada, or were opinions and knowledge levels relatively stable over this time?

Measuring Attitudes over Time

Fortunately for this study, the significant scrutiny devoted to the mayoral contest in Toronto meant that an abundance of polls were conducted over the course of the campaign. For our analysis of the first eight months of the election period, we rely on the polls carried out by Forum Research. While other firms conducted polls, Forum collected the most data by far. Focusing on polls from a single firm allows us to use consistent measures as well as questions that were collected the same way, ensuring comparability across time.[2] We were able to obtain Forum data on voter intentions for the entirety of the campaign (beginning in January). From April onwards, Forum also asked questions about "candidate approval" for the major contenders (basically, respondents were asked to rate candidates on a feeling thermometer scale from 0 to 100). These polling data complement TES data and indeed are an important part of explaining the election outcome, as a number of important events occurred before the nomination deadline and the roll-out of our own survey.

Despite their abundance, however, Forum's data are far less detailed than those included in the TES. Forum-type polls usually ask only a handful of questions, while the TES contains dozens of measures of attitudes and behaviour. Forum polls are thus valuable but limited. For the first months of the campaign, then, our analysis is more rudimentary than for the later weeks.

For the pre–nomination deadline component of our analysis, we use two measures consistently included in Forum polls: vote preference and candidate approval/disapproval. The first asked, "If a mayoral election were held today, who would you vote for if the candidates were Rob Ford, Karen Stintz, John Tory, Olivia Chow, and David Soknacki?" The second asked, "Do you approve or disapprove of [candidate's name]?"

For the period after the nomination deadline of 12 September, TES data are available. We conducted the pre-election wave of the TES using a modified type of rolling cross-section design (Johnston and Brady 2002), meaning we staggered data collection throughout the weeks leading up to the election, collecting a portion of the sample each week.[3] This meant that new respondents were interviewed each week. In essence, this is what pollsters (like Forum) do when they collect new samples every few days to measure and track public opinion. For our purposes, such a design allowed us to monitor potential opinion changes during the final weeks of the campaign. Major academic surveys such as the Canadian Election Study employ a version of this sampling method for the same purpose (see Fournier et al. 2013 for an analysis comparable to one found below).

The collection of TES data began one week after the nomination deadline (on 19 September) and continued for the remaining five and a half weeks before the 27 October election. For our analysis, we have grouped respondents according to interview date, dividing them into five categories. The first group includes those interviewed between 19 and 28 September (ten days); each of the other four groups covers a period of seven days.[4] This approach has allowed us to mimic the repeated cross-section design of Forum's polls.

We examine the effects of the campaign on voters' perceptions and preferences by considering four measures: perceptions of how competitive the three major candidates were, ratings of the candidates, anti-candidate sentiment (i.e., whether there is a candidate that one would not consider supporting), and vote intention. Though related, these measures provide different types of information regarding perceptions and attitudes across time.

We begin by considering how competitive the candidates were perceived to be by the electorate, using survey questions that asked respondents to rate each candidate's chance of victory. Such perceptions are important for they have been known to shape voter preferences (Blais et al., 2006; Fey, 1997; Nadeau et al., 1993). Changes in these evaluations would suggest that voters were influenced by election period stimuli of some sort, thus providing support for the possibility of campaign effects.

With respect to affinity for candidates (i.e., how much survey respondents liked or disliked each candidate), we consider three distinct though related indicators. The first is based on a series of feeling thermometer questions. As with the Forum polls, TES respondents were asked to rate their feelings toward candidates on a scale from 0 (negative) to 100 (positive). With their range of 0–100, feeling thermometers are relatively sensitive indicators of attitudes toward candidates; they allow us to identify changes in attitudes toward candidates, even if vote preferences remain unchanged.

The second measure of candidate affinity is based on responses to a question that asked TES respondents whether there was a candidate for whom they would "absolutely not vote." It is well-established that people process negative information and attitudes differently than positive information and that negative information often has a stronger effect than positive (Baumeister et al., 2001; Kahneman & Tversky, 1979). This measure, which is the opposite of vote choice, provides insight into whether there is a specific candidate who evokes a particularly strong negative sentiment among the public. Third, and finally, we consider vote intention, the "classic" measure of voter attitudes and the one that is most similar to the question voters are presented with on election day. The question "Which mayoral candidate do you think you will vote for?" forces respondents to choose a single candidate (or none).

By comparing attitudes across time we can identify changes in, and draw inferences about, the electorate as a whole. Any observed difference across time, in either the pre- or post-nomination period, would suggest that voters had changed their attitudes, presumably due to events that occurred over the course of the campaign; widespread changes in attitudes must have been the result of some stimulus. Conversely, the absence of differences would suggest the absence of campaign effects and that the campaign had little if any effect on voters.

Findings

Pre-Nomination Deadline

To begin our analysis, we first look at vote intentions (whom respondents intend to vote for) for the period between the beginning of the campaign and the nomination deadline. Figure 3.1 shows the support for the five leading candidates (Ford, Chow, Tory, Stintz, and Soknacki) over the first eight months of the campaign.

The lines represent the percentage of respondents intending to vote for each candidate. In the first poll (conducted in January), Rob

Figure 3.1. Vote intentions for 6 January through 8 September

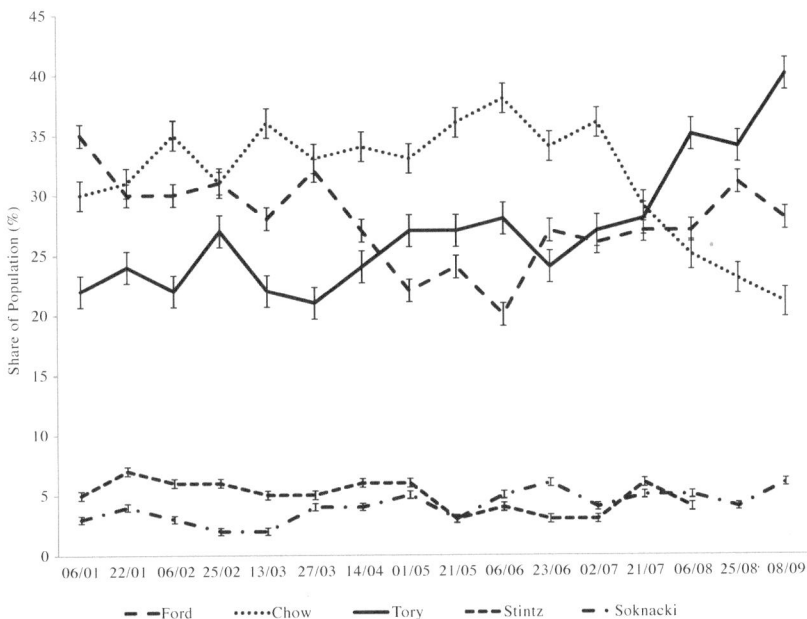

Note: These data were compiled using Forum Research's "TO Horserace" news releases from 15 April 2014 through 26 October 2014, inclusive. The news releases are available online at http://poll.forumresearch.com/category/3/toronto.

Ford led, though he and Karen Stintz were the only candidates to have announced their candidacy at this point. This would be the only time Rob Ford had the support of a plurality of respondents. Even though she would not officially declare her candidacy until 13 March, Olivia Chow led or was tied for the lead after the first poll. Following her entry into the race, she slowly developed a substantial lead. Up until the poll held on 1 May, the race seemed to be a contest between Chow and Ford, with Tory hovering around 20 to 25 per cent. After that, however, Ford's support dropped significantly, with Tory moving into second place and Chow taking a commanding lead. This period of the campaign coincides with Ford's entry into rehab, suggesting that his admission of substance abuse and his absence from the campaign significantly influenced voters' support, at least for a time (his support recovered slightly toward the end of his stint in rehab and upon his return to the race).

Aside from the easily explained dip in support for Ford during this period, the most important findings in Figure 3.1 are Chow's precipitous decline and Tory's massive surge in the late summer. After leading for nearly six months, from 22 January through 2 July, Chow's support plummeted, leaving her in third, well behind Ford and Tory. At the same time, from 21 July, Tory's support grew to over 40 per cent. Clearly, there was a dramatic swing in voter sentiment during this period, suggesting that some event in the campaign either negatively influenced Chow support or positively influenced Tory support.

This change is perplexing because the narrative of the campaign in the news media does not suggest any single event that could have triggered this swing in public support for the two candidates. Tory's campaign team posited that their candidate found renewed vigour following Ford's entry into rehab (Warnica, 2014, 27 October); however, this event took place over two months before Chow and Tory switched places in the polls. Moreover, Tory had introduced SmartTrack, his new transit proposal, a month and a half before the 21 July poll that showed him neck and neck with the two other candidates for the first time.

Some observers of the first debate following Ford's return criticized Chow's performance (Lee, 2014, 15 July), but one untelevised debate out of dozens is an unlikely cause for such a shift. Except for promising to rid the city of handguns, Chow made few campaign announcements during this period, and she committed few gaffes. Furthermore, she did not unveil her entire transit plan until late August (Hennessy, 2014, 20 August), though she had promised before then to improve bus service (Dale, 2014, 29 July). It is also possible that the provincial election had an impact on the two candidates, though the election had taken place on 12 June, at which point Chow was still firmly in the lead.

To unravel this mystery, we first examine poll respondents' approval for each of the candidates from April to the beginning of September. Forum asked respondents to rate their approval of each candidate on a scale of 0 to 100. Much like the feeling thermometer we employ when analysing our own data below, this measure is relatively sensitive, so changes in attitudes should be relatively easy to observe. Figure 3.2 reports the results of these questions. Note that for the sake of simplicity, the rest of this chapter focuses solely on the three major candidates.

Tory's rise seems to have been due to changes in attitudes toward the other candidates rather than himself. Figure 3.2 shows clearly that, though he enjoyed a meteoric rise in the polls beginning in July, his approval rating remained quite flat (though he consistently had the highest approval rating among the candidates). In contrast, Ford's approval rating declined greatly after his entry into rehab at the beginning of May, and Chow's saw a slow decline beginning in July – after hovering around sixty points, it dropped to fifty by the end of the campaign.

Figure 3.2. Voters' approval of candidates

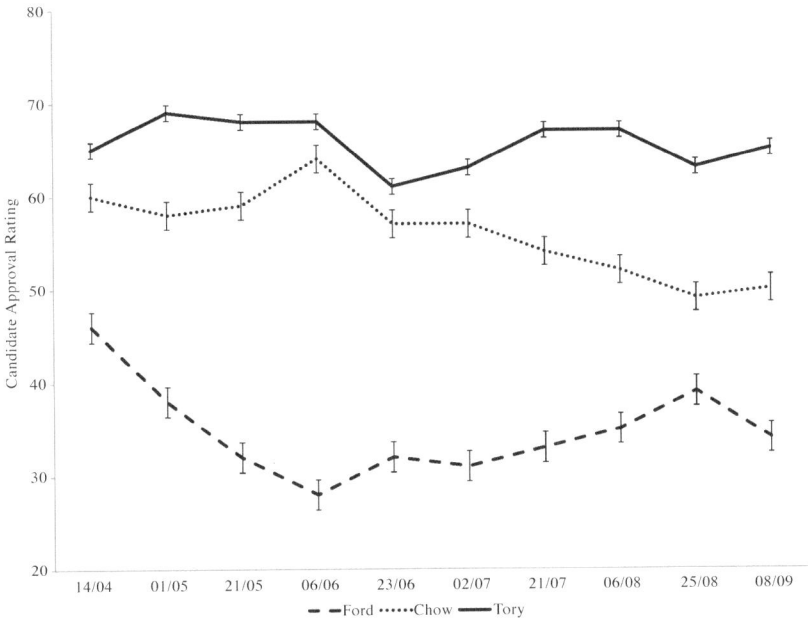

Note: These data were compiled using Forum Research's "TO Horserace" news releases from 15 April 2014 through 26 October 2014, inclusive. The news releases are available online at http://poll.forumresearch.com/category/3/toronto.

Chow's approval drop corresponds to the decline in her voter support, suggesting that the shift in momentum from Chow to Tory resulted less from Tory's campaign than from something affecting Chow's.

Clearly, the decline in Ford's support, and ratings, was precipitated by his entry into rehab. He never regained pre-rehab levels with respect to vote choice or approval. Explaining Chow's decline, however, is more difficult. While the format of polling data makes it impossible to be certain why attitudes toward Chow began to slip in June, we wish to briefly speculate as to why this may be.

A strong case can be made that Chow fell victim to her NDP roots.[5] As noted above, the Ontario provincial election was held right in the middle of the Toronto municipal campaign, on 12 June. The result of that election was clearly a disaster for the NDP. Though the party had lost only a little support since the previous election (roughly one percentage point in the popular vote) and actually increased its representation at Queen's

Park by four seats, the Liberal majority victory meant that the NDP was no longer a "kingmaker" in a hung Parliament; it was now merely the second opposition party in a majority legislature. Adding more salt to this wound, the 2014 provincial election had been precipitated by the NDP's decision to vote against a Liberal budget.

Among voters who associated Chow with the NDP, that stinging result might conceivably have affected attitudes toward her candidacy for mayor. Indeed, the work of McGregor et al. (2016) shows that most voters (68.5 per cent of TES respondents) associated Chow with the NDP and that NDP partisanship was positively associated with support for Chow, even after controlling for various socio-demographic and attitudinal characteristics. Though the 2014 Toronto mayoral election was formally nonpartisan, Chow's fortunes appear to have been tied to those of the NDP.

That relationship was problematic for Chow, given that the provincial NDP had fared quite poorly in Toronto ridings in 2014 (reduced to two seats, from five in 2011). Moreover, NDP leader Andrea Horwath saw her voter approval decline across the province over the course of the provincial election campaign, with her approval rating in Toronto, typically a stronghold of NDP support, taking a particularly steep dive. Forum data show that between 3 May to 4 July (the dates of the first releases of polling data during and after the election), Horwath's provincial approval rating as NDP leader dropped from 36 per cent (versus 41 per cent disapproval) to 28 per cent (with 47 per cent disapproval). And this drop was significantly higher in the 416 region (Toronto), where it fell from 42 per cent approval (and 40 per cent disapproval) to a staggering 17 per cent approval (and 63 per cent disapproval).[6] This precipitous decline no doubt helps account for the NDP's poor result in Toronto (the NDP lost three long-held ridings), and it may have had spillover effects into municipal politics.

So it is perhaps no coincidence that Chow's voter support fell after the provincial election. Chow was a federal MP, but the federal and provincial wings of the party are highly integrated so it is quite possible that voters' disaffection with the provincial leader, and the party, after the provincial election negatively impacted her support. This may well have cost her the mayor's seat.

Tory's renewed vigour as well as his policies may well have played some role in his rise in popularity in the months leading up to the nomination deadline, but it is equally likely that the decline in attitudes toward Chow and Ford in the summer of 2016 were the more proximate cause. Ford's entry into rehab and the decline of the provincial NDP in Toronto (two events that are quite distinct from municipal policy debates) seem to have had a significant positive effect on Tory's electoral prospects.

Post-Nomination Deadline

The weeks that followed the nomination deadline saw an increasingly nasty campaign but little change in the polls, even after Doug Ford replaced his brother as mayoral candidate. Tory maintained his lead for the most part, with Ford in second place and Chow in third (Stintz and Soknacki had dropped out by then). Does the consistency in voter preferences during this period mean that the campaign had largely been decided in the summer, months before the election, or does it mask change with respect to other attitudes? We now turn to our own survey data to answer this question. We consider several attitudinal measures besides vote intention to see whether any of these other attitudes changed during this period.

The first indicator of campaign effects that we consider is the perceived competitiveness of the candidates. Survey respondents were asked what the chances of each candidate winning the mayoral race were, from 0 to 100 per cent. Ideally, voters would realize that the sum of responses for the three candidates should equal no more than 100 (i.e., the three candidates cannot each have a 50 per cent chance of winning), and adjust their responses accordingly. However, as with other surveys that use similar questions (including the Canadian Election Study), they did not. Nevertheless, these questions can provide insight into how competitive the candidates were seen to be and to identify changes in competitive expectations across time.

Given the outcome of the election, Figure 3.3 suggests that as a group, voters had a good understanding of the candidates' chances. Throughout the period considered here, Tory was seen as the most likely victor, consistently hovering around 66 per cent. Between 19 and 28 September, Chow and Ford were seen as equally competitive, though after that point Chow's perceived chances declined, and from then on she was seen as the least likely to be the next mayor of Toronto. At no point did Ford and Chow's perceived competitiveness ratings rise above 50 per cent and 40 per cent, respectively.

On the whole, these perceptions remained fairly constant from mid-September until election day. Aside from the divergence of Chow and Ford after 28 September, there is very little observable change to report. Tory's perceived chances of victory remained statistically constant for the entire period under study. Ford saw a slight "bump" during the second-last week before the election, only to dip (as did Chow) immediately before the election.

Besides competitive expectations, many other indicators can be affected during a campaign. We will consider three, the first being

Figure 3.3. Candidate chances of victory

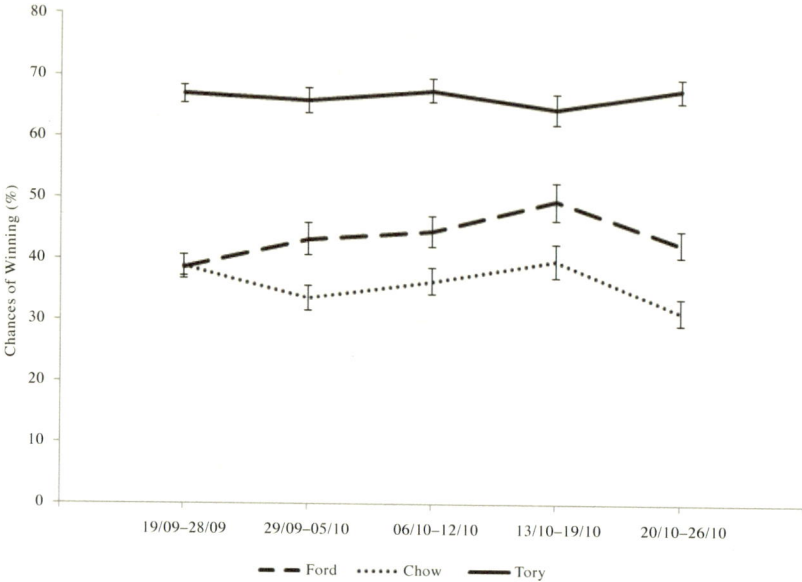

candidate feeling thermometers. Figure 3.4 shows the mean feeling thermometer value for the three major candidates over time, in the final weeks of the campaign.

Figure 3.4 reveals at least two striking findings. The first is that, though Chow came a distant third in the election, she consistently received the second-highest feeling thermometer score, averaging roughly ten points higher than Ford, the runner-up in the election. Although her approval did drop over the course of the summer, it appears to have largely stabilized by the end of the campaign, remaining above Doug Ford's throughout.

This finding no doubt reflects the polarizing nature of the Ford brothers. Unsurprisingly, Doug was highly rated among those who voted for him while receiving very low ratings from those who did not. Individuals who voted for Doug assigned him an average feeling thermometer score of 77.8 (n = 419); for individuals who voted for another candidate, this value was only 21.8 (n = 1,171). A difference of this nature is to be expected, given that voters are bound to rate the candidate they vote for more highly than other candidates. However, the magnitude of this gap – 56 points – is higher than the corresponding values for Tory and Chow. Indeed, the gaps for the other candidates were only 31.3 points for Tory

Figure 3.4. Candidate feeling thermometers

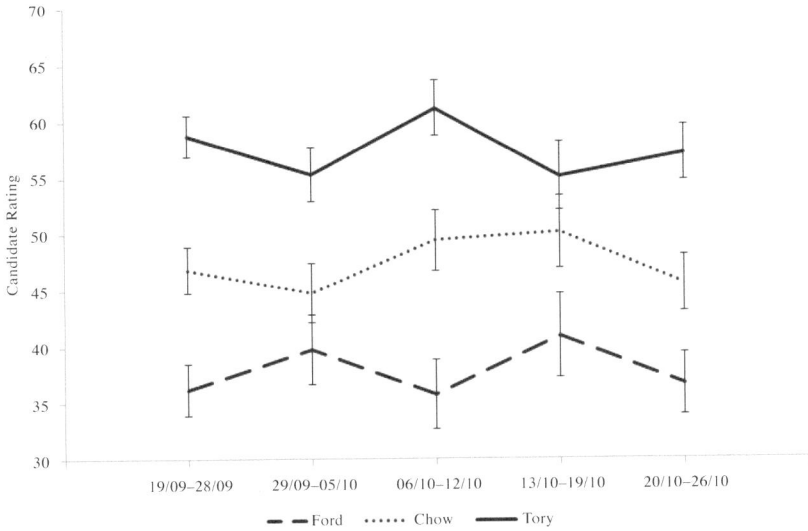

and 36.2 points for Chow. Such a difference helps explain why Ford had such a low average feeling thermometer score among the population as a whole, despite being the runner-up in the election.

The second noteworthy feature of Figure 3.4 has to do with consistency. Throughout the campaign – according to data from both Forum and the TES – respondents rated Tory the highest among the three candidates, followed by Chow, then Ford. At no point did the candidates change positions with one another. In the final weeks of the campaign, the candidate ratings remained consistent, a fact that is perhaps striking given the intensity of media coverage during this period. The ratings for Ford and Chow reveal no statistically significant change across the five time periods considered here. Tory was the only one who saw his ratings shift at all. Even then, it was only a temporary spike in his rating during the period from 6 to 12 October, before he fell back to his "normal" value of about 56 the following week. On the whole, we see little evidence of changes in attitudes toward the three major candidates during the final weeks of the campaign.

One might expect to observe campaign effects when evaluating feeling thermometer questions. Since we saw little of that during the later stages of the campaign, it would be no surprise to see little if any variation in other attitudes, including in terms of vote choice or anti-candidate sentiment. It is to the latter that we now turn.

Figure 3.5. Candidate would never vote for

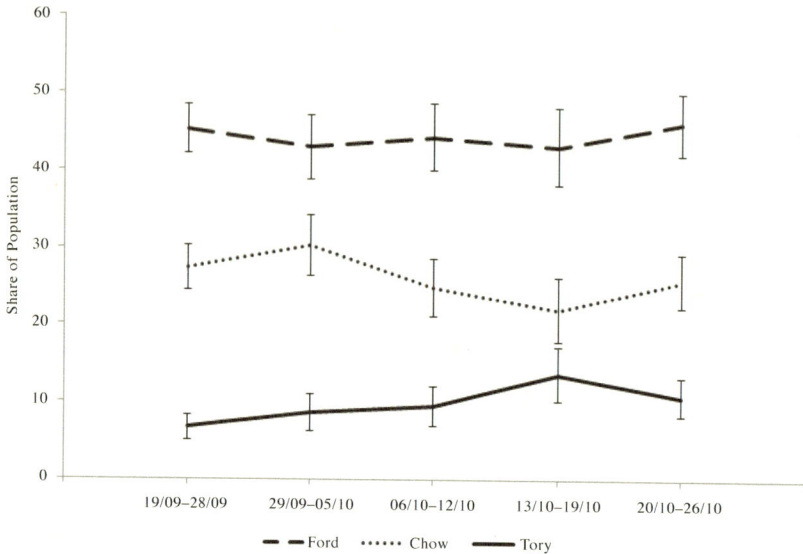

TES respondents were asked if there was a candidate for whom they absolutely would not vote. In partisan contests, "negative partisanship," or revulsion for a particular party, has been shown to influence many types of behaviour, including vote choice and turnout (Abramowitz & Webster, 2016; Caruana et al., 2015), and anti-candidate sentiment at the municipal level is known to influence rates of strategic voting (Caruana et al., 2018). Accordingly, Figure 3.5 shows the share of respondents who stated that they "absolutely" would not vote for one of the major candidates (note that respondents also had the option to not rule any candidate out).

Given that he received the lowest average feeling thermometer score, it is no surprise that more TES respondents stated they absolutely would not vote for Doug Ford. In fact, Ford was ruled out by more respondents than were Chow and Tory combined. Given that roughly 45 per cent of electors would have never even considered voting for Ford, it is clear that he was fighting an uphill battle in his bid to win the mayoralty. Chow, who came in third in the race but received the second-highest average rating, was the recipient of the second-highest number of "would not vote for" responses, which perhaps helps explain her poor performance on election day. Finally, and not surprisingly given the election outcome, Tory had the lowest rate of anti-candidate sentiment – only about 10 per cent of the population stated they would not consider voting for him.

As was the case with competitiveness measures and candidate feeling thermometers, Figure 3.5 tells a story of consistency. Candidate ordering remained constant in the weeks leading up to election day, and there was little change over time in the share of the population holding negative sentiments toward each contender. Anti-Ford sentiment was constant throughout this period (i.e., no statistically significant change). Anti-Chow and anti-Tory attitudes saw a modest decrease and increase, respectively, between 13 to 19 October, but both scores returned to previous levels in the week before the election. On the whole, then, Figure 3.5 indicates general consistency in anti-candidate attitudes.

The flipside of anti-candidate views, and indeed the most important variable in the field of voting behaviour, is vote choice. While anti-candidate sentiment might push voters away from certain choices, it is their choice of whom to eventually support that matters most for an election outcome. In addition to questions on candidate ratings and anti-candidate sentiment, TES respondents were asked which candidate they planned to vote for. As above, Figure 3.6 tracks vote preference over the weeks leading up to the election, focusing on decided voters.

For the most part, the vote intentions in Figure 3.6 consistently mirror candidate ratings and anti-candidate sentiment. Except for the period from 13 to 19 October, there is no statistically significant difference in pledged support for Tory, Ford, or Chow. Tory is consistently ahead of the other two candidates, while Chow has the lowest level of support (though she is tied statistically with Ford in three of the five periods). The most important takeaway from this figure is that vote preferences at the end of the campaign were virtually the same as they were after the nomination deadline, with Tory receiving the support of the highest number of voters, followed by Ford, then Chow. Moreover, the level of support pledged for each candidate is statistically indistinguishable between the first and last time weeks considered in the figure.

The one break from this consistency relates to the period from 13 to 19 October, when we see a sudden decline in support for Tory, accompanied by an increase in support for Chow (and a suggestive, though statistically insignificant, increase in support for Ford). There was no obvious reason for this change. A Forum poll conducted on 6 October 2014 registered the same Ford surge.[7] Most media outlets considered the results an outlier, given that no recent events during the campaign could account for Ford's rise and Tory's decline (CBC News, 2014, 7 October; Gillis, 2014, 7 October; James, 2014, 11 October). Whatever the reason for this "blip," vote preferences had returned to more common levels by

Figure 3.6. Vote intentions

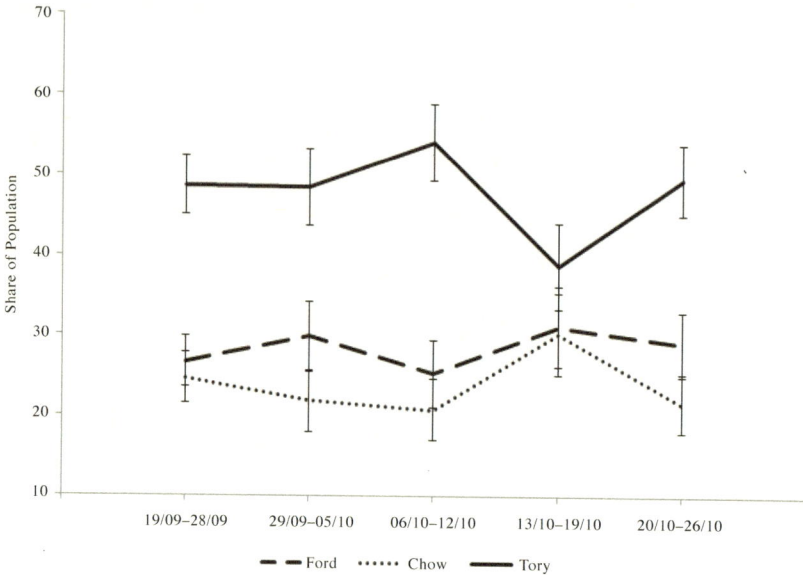

the week before the election.[8] As with the measures considered above, therefore, our indicator of vote preference shows little evidence that the period after the nomination deadline influenced the attitudes of voters, or the election outcome, in any meaningful way.

Consistent, but Compared to What?

Before completely ruling out the presence of substantial campaign effects during the period after the nomination deadline, it is important to recognize that "consistent" in the sense that we are using it is a relative term. Is the paucity of statistically significant effects observed in Figures 3.3 to 3.6 "standard" for elections in Canada, or was the post nomination-period of the Toronto campaign relatively inconsequential?

To answer such a question, some comparison must be made. The TES is the only major study of a municipal election in Canada that allows a thorough examination of the stability of voter attitudes. The closest comparable dataset is the Canadian Election Study (CES). Like the TES, the CES is based on data from multiple interviews; also like the TES, the pre-election wave of the CES consists of a rolling cross-section design. Furthermore, pre-election CES data were collected during a timeframe comparable to that of the TES (in the five or six weeks preceding the election). All of this means that data from federal elections can be compared to TES results to determine whether the post-nomination period of the Toronto campaign really was the non-event that the above results seem to suggest it was.

Were voter preferences affected less in the final weeks of the Toronto 2014 campaign than during the corresponding period in federal elections? To make this comparison, we draw upon data from pre- and post-election TES and CES questionnaires (from several recent federal elections). These datasets all ask respondents, prior to the election, whom they intend to support or whether they are undecided. Pre-election responses can thus be compared to actual vote choice, reported in the post-election survey.

Using data from multiple survey waves in this manner allows us to examine attitudinal consistency at the individual level. Repeated cross-sectional data of the type reflected in Figures 3.3 to 3.6 suggest that vote intentions remained quite consistent over time at the aggregate level; however, to rule out the possibility that attitudinal change is being masked at the individual level, it is necessary to take repeated measurements from the same individuals at multiple points in time. For example, Doug Ford may receive 35 per cent of support in two consecutive weeks, but it may be that different people are supporting him each week. If, for instance, some of his supporters go to Tory between these two periods, but an equal number of Tory's supporters shift to Ford, the repeated cross-sectional analysis will miss that shift. When we examine responses from the same individuals at multiple points in time, we can be more confident in the conclusions regarding attitudinal stability.

To compare the stability of voter attitudes, therefore, we focus on two different albeit related measures, which are directly comparable between the TES and CES datasets. First, we consider the share of voters who claim to be undecided at the time of the pre-election survey and who do not pledge support for any candidate (TES) or party (CES); by definition, such individuals must have made their decisions during the campaign period, meaning that campaign events likely influenced them. The second measure indicates the stability of vote preferences among those individuals who expressed a preference in the pre-election survey, compared to vote choice measured post-election. Relative stability on this measure would indicate relatively weak campaign effects. Table 3.1 shows the results of these analyses, comparing the 2014 Toronto election to the 2008, 2011, and 2015 Canadian federal elections.[9] Note that both sets of analyses are limited to voters.[10]

Table 3.1. Stability across time, Toronto and Canadian election studies

	Toronto 2014	Canada 2008	Canada 2011	Canada 2015
Share of respondents undecided at pre-election interview (%)	16.7	25.1	25.0	17.8
n	1,719	1,937	2,696	3,329
Share of respondents that changed preference between survey waves (%)	13.5	13.8	14.7	21.2
n	1,388	1,376	1,968	2,704

By both of the measures considered in Table 3.1, the final thirty-eight days of the 2014 Toronto election appear to have had relatively little impact on voters. Relative to all three of the federal elections, fewer Torontonians (16.7 per cent) were undecided at the time of the pre-election interview, which suggests that fewer voters were actively contemplating their vote choice by this point in the campaign. Furthermore, the number of voters who changed preferences was lower in Toronto than in any of the federal elections. Only 13.5 per cent of respondents who expressed a preference at the time of the pre-election interview had changed their minds by election day. Such a finding is particularly striking in light of the fact that the outgoing mayor was replaced on the ballot by his brother just weeks before the election.

These findings go a long way toward explaining the consistency of attitudes toward candidates observed in Figures 3.3 to 3.6. Fewer voters were undecided in the weeks leading up to the Toronto election than tends to be the case at the federal level, and those individuals who did have a preference were relatively unlikely to change their minds. These results thus support the findings above that the last thirty-eight days of the 2014 Toronto campaign had relatively little impact on voters or the election outcome.

Conclusion

The story of the last weeks of the 2014 Toronto mayoral campaign is that this part of the campaign had little if any effect on either voter attitudes or the outcome of the election. In the period after the nomination deadline there were no noteworthy changes in competitive expectations, the order in which the candidates were ranked, anti-candidate sentiment, or vote preferences. Moreover, as compared to their counterparts in federal elections, voters in Toronto made their decisions relatively early and maintained stable preferences throughout the campaign. All indications are that the outcome would have been the same had the election been held on any of the dates covered by TES data.

This is not to suggest that the 2014 Toronto campaign did not "matter." Instead, it was only the late weeks and months of the campaign that had no discernible effect upon voters. All indications are that the major shifts in public opinion occurred months in advance of election day, far in advance of the nomination deadline. Rob Ford's support plummeted upon news of his entry into drug rehab in May, and neither he nor his brother was able to regain enough support to win the election. Olivia Chow, who for so long held a dominant position in the polls, saw her lead slip away in the wake of the 2014 provincial election, in June. By mid-summer, the positions of the candidates had been set. In the last several months, therefore, the campaign had no discernible effect on the electorate, or on the election outcome.

The absence of post-nomination campaign effects is noteworthy and bears some examination. Indeed, this period was of a similar length to federal and provincial contests, during which there are often major swings in public support. We suggest that the most likely source for this relative inactivity during the late stages of the campaign was the length of the official campaign period. At nearly ten months, the official campaign length dwarfed that of other levels of government. In the eight months preceding the nomination deadline, electors had ample opportunity to learn about the candidates and their policies, and they likely had fairly well-formed attitudes of the candidates by the time the nomination deadline rolled around. In terms of Zaller's (1992) RAS model (discussed above), voters had two thirds of a year to collect and store considerations. Any new information obtained during the final weeks of the campaign that might be inconsistent with existing beliefs (and thus which might affect attitudes) thus had a tremendous number of considerations to overcome.

That said, it is doubtful that the length of the campaign was solely responsible for the absence of late-campaign effects. In municipalities with lower-profile elections, voters may receive relatively little information on municipal politics. In Toronto, however, the attention paid by the media to the 2014 campaign was nothing short of unprecedented; the highly publicized antics of the outgoing mayor put the politics of Toronto in the spotlight like never before. Though data are unavailable to test this contention, it stands to reason that Torontonians were quite enlightened with respect to municipal politics, relative to their counterparts in many other cities. In sum, we suspect that this high level of existing knowledge, combined with the sheer length of the mayoral campaign, contributed to the absence of late-campaign effects in Toronto in 2014.

Chapter 4

Policy versus Personality: Correct Voting and the Outcome of the 2014 Toronto Mayoral Election

Without question, the exceptionally high-profile nature of the 2014 Toronto mayoral election stemmed from the larger-than-life personalities of the Ford brothers. Rob, in particular, was infamous in Canada, but also well-known around the world for his various struggles and scandals. *The Globe and Mail* referred to the Rob Ford "saga" as the "biggest Canadian story in [the] U.S. this century" (Pannetta, 2013, 4 December), citing data showing that the story received more media coverage in that country than did any other Canadian news item since the year 2000. Outside of North America, outlets such as *The Guardian* (2014, 1 May), *The Irish Times* (2014, 1 May), *Le Monde* (Chabas, 2014, 2 May), and *Al Jazeera* (2014, 1 May) introduced the former mayor of Toronto, and his many foibles, to the world.

Importantly, the news coverage beyond Toronto made little or no mention of either Rob's policy stances or his past performance governing the city. Instead, the media focused almost exclusively on Ford's personal characteristics, including his battles with substance abuse, his propensity to use offensive language, his weight, and his generally bombastic nature.

While such stories may help sell newspapers, the coverage of the personal characteristics of politicians, as opposed to policy, is of questionable value to Toronto's democracy. In fact, the extent to which electors vote in accordance with their own principles and priorities has been proposed as an important metric of a democracy's health (Lau & Redlawsk, 1997). If the purpose of a democracy is to see the wishes of the electorate translated into policy, then voters should arguably be making their vote decisions on the basis of policy considerations rather than the personal characteristics of candidates. According to this line of reasoning, if voters are unable to identify the candidate who best reflects their policy preferences or are unwilling to vote for that person because other considerations weigh more heavily on their vote decisions, then the quality of democracy is weakened.

Did Torontonians focus primarily on policy considerations in the 2014 mayoral election, or did their evaluations of the personal characteristics of candidates lead them to stray from the candidate they would otherwise have supported? The answer to this question has implications for the quality of Toronto's democracy and government as well as for the legitimacy of the city's rulers.

Policy versus Personality

In this chapter we consider two questions. First, to what extent did Torontonians vote in accordance with their policy preferences in the 2014 mayoral election? Second, how important were the personal characteristics of candidates, as opposed to policy stances, in the decision-making calculus of voters? In short, we want to know whether the outcome was based on voters making "good" decisions, and whether they made those decisions on the basis of policy or personality.

In answering these questions, we draw upon the concept of a "correct vote," first introduced by Lau and Redlawsk (1997). A correct vote is one that is cast for the candidate who best reflects the policy positions and priorities of an individual voter. This simple, attractive concept has drawn considerable attention from scholars (see for example, Blais & Kilibarda, 2016; Ha & Lau, 2015; Lau & Redlawsk, 1997, 2001; McGregor, 2013b; Milic, 2012; Ryan, 2011).

We focus on the idea of "correct" issue voting in this chapter as a way to gauge the extent of policy-based decision-making. However, we recognize that the potential for voting on the basis of something other than policy is significant. Scandals, partisan biases, or even a simple desire for "change" might motivate voters to cast their ballot for a particular candidate. In the Toronto election, it is easy to see how these types of factors might have been important: the Ford scandal exhausted many who desired clear change for the city, and Tory and Chow had clear partisan ties. Nonetheless, there is a strong argument to be made that voting based on policy considerations is desirable because it directly corresponds to the main purpose of government: creating policies that reflect the interests of, and impact the quality of life of, citizens. In contrast, the personal characteristics of decision-makers have no such discernible impact on Torontonians (aside from potential embarrassment if a mayor becomes a global laughing stock).

The analysis that follows proceeds in two stages: first, we calculate the rate of correct voting (on the basis of issue considerations) in the mayoral election and determine the extent to which the three major candidates suffered or benefited as a result of *incorrect* voting. Our analysis reveals that Doug Ford was harmed significantly and that John Tory benefited greatly. Second, we examine the sources of incorrect voting to see whether personality concerns trumped policy considerations. Specifically, we consider the level of importance that Torontonians attached to policy when choosing between mayoral candidates and when evaluating those candidates. Toronto Election Study data suggest that most Torontonians claimed that policy was more important than personality when formulating attitudes toward candidates. Finally, given the high profile and divisive nature of some of the individuals associated with the election, we consider whether enough voters made their decisions on the basis of candidate personality to sway the outcome of the election.

The Logic of Correct Voting

Elections give citizens not only the opportunity to determine who will control government, but also (and perhaps more importantly) the chance to have input into the types of policies adopted by decision-makers. Elections are often seen as providing mandates, or permission from the public, for politicians to pursue specific policy goals. This view of elections is central to the case for democracy; liberal theory suggests that government decisions should be made on the basis of the preferences of the citizenry, rather than for the benefit of dictators or monarchs (Locke, 2003). The best way for citizens to ensure that their wishes are translated into policy is to elect representatives who most closely reflect those preferences.

It follows that the quality of a democracy can be indicated by the extent to which individuals vote in accordance with their personal principles and priorities. "Good" democracy, in which government policies reflect the will of the people (Dahl, 1967), is therefore heavily dependent on the quality of inputs (votes). Even the earliest voting studies conceded, however, that many voters did not meet the standards expected of them by democratic theorists. As early as the 1950s, when voter turnout was higher, scholars demonstrated that large portions of the electorate were disengaged, inattentive, and unknowledgeable (see for instance, Berelson et al., 1954; Campbell et al., 1960). These same classic studies also recognized that uninformed or inattentive citizens might not make good vote decisions; yet it was not until the late 1990s that scholars began to measure the quality of individual vote decisions. In this vein, Lau and Redlawsk (1997) introduced the concept of "correct" voting, referring to the extent to which electors vote in accordance with their personal values and priorities. The authors suggest that a correct vote is the choice that voters would make if they had perfect information as well as the cognitive capacity to process this information. Put another way, a correct vote choice is represented by the candidate who has policy stances most similar to those of the individual voter. The concept of correct voting assumes a normative position that is supported by democratic theory: some vote decisions are simply democratically *better* than others.

There are several plausible reasons, however, to expect many citizens to vote incorrectly. Electors do not have perfect information about campaigns, candidates, and policy promises. Research has demonstrated clearly that voters are not the fully informed citizens who are expected to inhabit an ideal democracy (Delli Carpini & Keeter, 1996; Fournier, 2002). Even if voters did have a perfect understanding of the electoral options before them, the average citizen would not have the capacity or the time to sort through and interpret all of this information. Moreover, decisions may be made on the basis of factors other than policy preferences. Evaluations of the personal characteristics of candidates, for example, could cause voters to support the candidate who seems the most likely to support positions and interests similar to their own. But without full information, how likely is it that their subjective judgments will match objective reality?

This is not to say that the prospects for democracy are necessarily bleak. Much of the literature suggests that voters are very good at using shortcuts, or heuristics, to gather enough information to vote on the basis of policy (Popkin, 1994; Sniderman et al., 1991). In essence, voters can use readily available information to make inferences about the unknown. Knowledge of candidate characteristics or partial information on policy stances might allow voters to speculate regarding unknown policy positions. This phenomenon is often referred to as "low information rationality" (Popkin, 1994); such an approach to decision-making can be sensible, as the effort required to collect complete information can be daunting for many. Fortunately, research has shown that heuristics, or cues, can be very helpful when it comes to political decision-making (see, for example, Lau & Redlawsk, 2001; Lupia, 1994) and that the inferences made by voters on the basis of such cues are often correct. That voters can use cues to make the same choices they would have made had they been fully informed gives us reason not to be completely pessimistic about the quality of democracies.

The most powerful, frequently used, and pervasive cue employed by voters is partisanship. Knowing which party a candidate is affiliated with is a powerful shortcut for estimating likely policy positions with minimal effort, particularly among experienced and knowledgeable voters (see Downs, 1957). Party cues improve rates of correct voting in partisan contests (Lau, 2013; Lau et al., 2008), based on the logic of low-information rationality as we have just described it. Other research, however, has demonstrated that reliance on such cues can lead to *worse* decisions (Arceneaux, 2008; Dancey & Sheagley, 2013; Lau & Redlawsk, 2001; Merolla et al., 2016; Rahn, 1993), particularly if voters ignore information suggesting that a party toward which they are biased has stances inconsistent with their own personal preferences (or if a party they have a bias against has stances that are compatible with their own).

The democratic implications of a lack of party cues are thus worth examining. If shortcuts enable voters to make accurate inferences, then the presence of parties may improve rates of correct voting. If party labels can lead voters astray, however, then the fact that so many elections are contested by parties may bode poorly for the legitimacy of a democracy.

Regardless of the outcome of this debate, the widespread tendency toward relying on party labels leads to questions about which factors voters use to structure their choices in non-partisan elections, including the 2014 Toronto mayoral race. Research has shown that many voters attempt to draw on party cues even in officially non-partisan situations, by attempting to associate candidates with parties (Bonneau & Cann, 2015; McGregor et al., 2016; Schaffner & Streb, 2002; Squire & Smith, 1988). For other voters, however, it is also conceivable that candidate policy positions will take on a larger role in non-partisan contests, as voters look to make their decisions on the basis of other information. This latter approach would have positive democratic implications; when citizens focus more heavily on policy then, *ceteris paribus*, it stands to reason that rates of correct voting could be high.

Yet it is also plausible that factors other than policy may take on increased importance in non-partisan elections. In particular, we suggest that the personal characteristics of candidates may become more important to the decision-making calculus of voters. For instance, research has shown that the socio-demographic characteristics of candidates – or, more specifically, how similar their characteristics are to those of individual voters – are important factors in vote choice in both partisan (Cutler, 2002) and non-partisan (Bird et al., 2016) elections.

Beyond socio-demographics, what other factors might matter when the characteristics of individual candidates take on increased importance? One possibility is that voters may consider the personality (defined broadly) of the candidate over and above what that person is expected to do in office. If a candidate has a particularly undesirable characteristic or trait, it may decrease the possibility that voters will support him or her, regardless of the policy stances of that individual. Opinions about candidate personalities may overwhelm opinions about policy stances.

Certainly this is more likely to be the case in non-partisan elections than in analogous partisan contests, where party cues remain a central influence.

Again, we see reasons to expect the absence of parties to have both positive and negative effects on rates of correct voting. It stands to reason that if voters focus on the policy promises of candidates, as opposed to party labels, then rates of correct voting will increase. If, however, the personal characteristics of candidates – which are completely independent of policy – take on increased importance in the absence of parties, then the chances of voting against one's policy interests may increase.

The Toronto 2014 mayoral election is an excellent case for evaluating the extent to which candidate evaluations may overwhelm issue preferences and affect vote choices and rates of correct voting. The race involved larger-than-life personalities who were extremely well-known to the population. As already noted, the incumbent, Rob Ford, was known widely among Torontonians as a boor due to his many inappropriate and off-colour remarks. It was the release of a video that showed him smoking crack (Dale, 2013, 5 November), however, that led to him being relieved of his power at City Hall and becoming infamous outside of the city. For many voters, this was deeply embarrassing. If there was ever a candidate for whom personal characteristics could be more important than policy positions in the formation of voter attitudes, it would be Rob Ford. Of course, he did not end up being on the mayoral ballot, but the three major candidates (Doug Ford, Tory, and Chow) were also well-known, high-profile individuals with partisan ties. Did the conspicuous personalities of the major candidates influence correct voting rates in Toronto in 2014, and, in turn, the election outcome? Before addressing this question, we explain how we assessed correct voting in the election.

Measuring Correct Voting

Following McGregor (2013b), our measure of correct voting is based on a series of policy questions and involves comparing the preferences of individual voters to the policy stances of the candidates themselves.[1] This type of analysis is based on the "spatial theory" of party competition (Downs, 1957), which supposes that voting behaviour can and should be understood on the basis of the "distance" between the preferences of voters and the positions of candidates. In short, a voter should support the candidate who is most similar to him/her on important issues.

We consider five policy areas: public transit, property taxes, traffic and congestion, affordability of living, and managing the municipality's finances. These issues were chosen for the TES based on a review of news coverage and polls that circulated in the media. TES data confirm that respondents believed these issues to be the primary foci of the election, for when asked which issue was most important to them, 93.9 per cent of respondents chose one of these five policy areas. We were able to gather the policy positions of candidates from official campaign websites and policy debates held during the campaign.[2] More than twenty debates were held leading up to the election. Not all candidates took part in every debate, but together these events provided ample opportunity for voters to learn about the candidates' stances.

In the TES survey, we asked respondents for their policy preferences on each issue and provided them with the official candidate positions as options to choose from. For example, the options provided to survey respondents when asked about their preferred policy on public transit were: build subways instead of planned light rail transit on Sheppard and Finch (Ford's policy); build planned light rail transit routes on Sheppard and Finch (Chow's position); and electrify GO transit lines, add more stops along them, and increase frequency of service (Tory's policy).[3] Some respondents might have preferred policies not represented by these options; but for our purposes, they were forced to either choose from among the three official policy stances of the candidates or indicate they did not know their preference.

For four issues (public transit, property taxes, traffic and congestion, and affordability of living), the official candidate policy positions were provided without the candidate names, to avoid providing any sort of cue that might lead respondents to select the policy associated with their favoured candidate. For the fifth and final issue, "managing the city's finances," an exception was made, and survey respondents were asked which of the candidates would be best suited to manage the municipality's budget.[4]

Policy preferences aside, individuals have different priorities and place varying degrees of emphasis on each. Public transit may be the only issue that matters for one voter; another might prioritize affordability and taxes. Our analysis of correct voting took policy preferences into consideration while allowing for heterogeneity in terms of issue salience, drawing on responses to questions about the importance of each of the five policy areas. Mean issue salience scores ranged from 7.3 for property taxes to 8.3 for managing the city's finances.[5]

To identify the correct vote choice, we calculated a "compatibility" score for each survey respondent for each candidate. We considered how many policy positions individual voters shared with each candidate, and how important each issue was, to determine which candidate was most compatible with the voter (the "correct" vote choice). If a policy position was shared, but unimportant, the compatibility score for that candidate increased very little. If a position was not shared, but important, the compatibility score decreased a lot.

On each dimension, for each candidate, respondents were assigned a value of 1 if they supported the policy of the candidate, –1 if they supported a different candidate, and 0 if they replied "don't know." These values were multiplied by the relevant policy salience scores, which ranged from 0 to 10. After summing the values for each policy, the compatibility scores ranged from –50 to 50. Higher values indicated higher compatibility with a candidate; a low value indicated lower compatibility. For example, if a respondent shared all policy positions with a candidate, and assigned all five issues a salience score of 10, the compatibility score would be 50. For each individual respondent, the candidate with the highest value was considered to be the "correct" vote choice.

After calculating the rate of correct voting in the 2014 mayoral election, we considered whether personality factors had led individuals to vote incorrectly according to their issue preferences. We considered two indicators of attitudes related to policy and personality to determine the relative importance of each type of consideration in shaping the "correctness" of the vote choices of Torontonians. First, we considered whether voters reported voting for a candidate on the basis of policy or personality. Then we considered anti-candidate attitudes, using questions that asked whether they were unwilling to vote for a specific candidate based on policy or personality considerations. These measures help us determine whether the decisions of voters in the 2014 Toronto mayoral election were driven by policy or personality.

Results

To begin, we consider the average values for the compatibility variables among the voting population as a whole. The average "distance" values for the candidates are as follows: 3.4 for Ford (std. dev. = 23.2), –15.6 for Chow (std. dev. = 22.0) and –22.2 for Tory (std. dev. = 15.6).[6] As higher values indicate similarity, the average Torontonian was closer to Ford's policy stances than to those of either of the other major candidates. Meanwhile, Tory's stances were the least compatible with those of the average voter. These findings are striking, given that Tory, not Ford, won the election.

Looking more closely at specific policies also suggests that Ford was favoured by the typical Torontonian. Table 4.1 presents the share of respondents who preferred each candidate, on each policy area.

Ford placed second in the election even though he scored extremely well on all issue dimensions: all five of his policy positions were favoured

Table 4.1. Share of respondents who preferred each candidate on each policy dimension (%)

	Ford	Chow	Tory	Don't know
Public transit	51.5	26.1	13.7	8.7
Property taxes	47.6	31.5	9.1	11.9
Traffic and congestion	57.5	25.2	57.5	17.2
Affordability	35.7	27.0	22.2	15.2
Managing city's finances	39.8	15.3	33.0	12.0

n = 1,454

by at least a plurality of voters. The eventual mayor, John Tory, scored lower than both of his competitors on three dimensions. On the basis of overall distance values, as well as individual policy areas, one might therefore reasonably expect Ford and Tory to have performed well and poorly, respectively. Given the apparent incompatibility between policy preferences and the election results, however, it stands to reason that the rate of correct voting was relatively low.

According to the method outlined above, the overall rate of correct voting in the 2014 Toronto mayoral election was 57.3 per cent (n = 1,454). Whether this rate is high or low is a matter of debate. Compared to voting at random (where we would expect a correct voting rate of 33.3 per cent, assuming a three-way race between the major candidates), this value might be considered high. Random voting is not, however, a very high bar to set for voters if one is an advocate of the idea that the quality of democracy depends on voters' ability to identify the candidate who best reflects their personal policy preferences.

The figure of 57.3 per cent is middling compared to examinations of correct voting in other settings. In their study of decades of presidential elections, Lau and Redlawsk (1997) estimated that 75 per cent of Americans vote correctly in contests for the White House. Rates of correct voting in the 2008 presidential primary elections were decidedly lower, however, being estimated at 50 per cent for Republicans and 56 per cent for Democrats (Lau, 2013). Studies of correct voting in Canadian federal elections produced estimates of 71.0 per cent and 77.1 per cent for the 1997 and 2004 elections, respectively (Lau et al., 2014), and 47.4 per cent (again for 2004) with a method very similar to the one we use here (McGregor, 2013b). The rate of correct voting in Toronto therefore appears to be neither particularly high nor especially low. There is limited value, however, in comparing our results to other studies and settings. The methodological differences used to operationalize correct voting, the number and types of policies important in an election, and

Table 4.2. Correct voting statistics

	Ford	Chow	Tory
Vote share (%)	34.7	23.8	41.5
% who should vote	62.8	22.2	15.0
% of those who should that do	57.0	51.5	66.8
% of those who do that should	88.8	47.5	29.1

the number of serious candidates or parties in a race can all have a significant impact on estimates.

Comparisons aside, one way to assess whether incorrect voting rates were high, or potentially *too* high (from a normative standpoint regarding the quality of a democracy), is to consider the impact of incorrect voting on the outcome of the election. Would the election result have been different had all voters cast their ballots correctly? If not, then incorrect voting should be of little concern. If so, however, then incorrect voting may be considered problematic for those who believe that the policies enacted by representatives should reflect the wishes of the populace.

So, what would the result of the 2014 mayoral election have been if 100 per cent of voters had cast their ballots correctly? We consider this question in detail in Table 4.2. The table shows a number of important statistics, including the actual share of the vote received by each candidate in the TES sample, but also the share of the vote that each *would* have received had the rate of correct voting been 100 per cent.

Had all voters cast their ballots on the basis of policy considerations (and had they all possessed perfect policy knowledge), Doug Ford rather than John Tory would have won the 2014 mayoral election. Indeed, Tory would have come in third, winning a mere 15.0 per cent rather than 41.5 per cent of the vote. Ford would have won the support of a large majority of voters: 62.8 per cent. In reality, however, he received a little over half of the vote share (34.7 per cent) that he "deserved" on the basis of policy compatibility. For her part, Chow's vote share was hardly affected by incorrect voting.

Table 4.2 also provides two pieces of information that help explain why incorrect voting led to an incorrect election outcome. First, it shows the percentage of voters who *should* have voted for each candidate that actually *did*. These figures indicate how successful the candidates were at capturing those voters who should have supported them. Second, the table shows the percentage of voters who supported each candidate and *should* have, on the basis of policy compatibility. A low value for this measure

Table 4.3. Correct versus actual vote choice

		Who *should* respondents have voted for?		
		Ford	Chow	Tory
Who *did* respondents vote for? (%)	Ford	57.0	14.8	7.2
	Chow	14.2	51.5	26.1
	Tory	28.9	33.7	66.8
	n	898	328	227

Note: Values represent column percentages.

indicates that a candidate was able to attract a large number of voters who should have supported other candidates.

The last two rows of Table 4.2 go a long way toward explaining the discrepancy between the actual and "correct" election outcomes. First, Ford was less successful than Tory (though more successful than Chow) at attracting voters who should have voted for him on the basis of policy stances. Fifty-seven (57) per cent of these voters supported him, as opposed to 66.8 per cent for Tory; Tory was the most successful of the three candidates on this front. Given that such a large number of voters should have supported Ford, this difference harmed him significantly. Second, the final row in the table indicates how successful candidates were at winning the support of voters who, according to their own policy preferences, should have supported others. Among Ford supporters, nearly 90 per cent of his voters were closest to him on the basis of policy. On the other end of the spectrum, fewer than one in three of John Tory's voters shared policy preferences most closely with the eventual winner of the election. In other words, Tory was very successful at poaching the support of voters who should have supported other candidates, while Ford was not (again, Chow is in the middle in this regard).

Before moving on to try to explain why rates of correct voting were so low, we present Table 4.3, which considers the question of how the voters who *should* have supported each of the three major candidates actually cast their ballots. Table 4.2 has shown already that Ford was the least able to attract incorrect voters, while Tory was most successful in this regard. Table 4.3 shows which of their competitors the candidates won and lost votes to on the basis of incorrect voting.

Two findings of note emerge from Table 4.3. First, Tory was, by far, the most likely recipient of votes from individuals who *should* have backed someone else. More than one third of voters who should have supported Chow instead voted for Tory, while fewer than 15 per cent of these individuals backed Ford. Nearly 30 per cent of voters who should have cast their ballots for Ford did so for Tory, while just over 14 per cent voted for Chow. Tory was therefore the primary recipient of incorrect votes from both of his competitors.

The second finding worthy of discussion is that patterns of incorrect voting appear to adhere to our understanding of the ideological ordering of the mayoral competitors. Individuals for whom a correct vote would have been to back one of the candidates on the exterior of the ideological scale (Ford on the right and Chow on the left) were much more likely to instead select the relatively centrist candidate (Tory) than they were the other exterior candidate. Among those who should have voted for Ford, more than twice as many ended up voting for Tory as Chow. A similar pattern holds for those individuals who should have (but did not) support Chow: here, Tory outperformed Ford by an even greater margin. In the ideological sense, therefore, there seems to be a pattern in the observed relationship between how Torontonians should have voted and how they actually did. In terms of policy, Tory seems to have been somewhat of a compromise candidate. We turn now to a discussion of why this might have been, examining the possibility that personal characteristics played a particularly great role in shaping the vote choices of Torontonians.

Policy versus Personality

As we have seen, Doug Ford lost a great many voters who should have supported him, while John Tory attracted many who should have cast their ballots for other candidates. So, what accounts for rates of incorrect voting being high enough to affect the outcome of the election? Given the peculiarities of the Toronto 2014 election, we suggest that one possible explanation is that voters focused on factors other than policy when formulating their decisions. As explained earlier, *who* became mayor, possibly even more than *what* the new mayor promised to do, was of great salience for voters. The extra-governmental activities of Rob Ford embarrassed many Torontonians. That Doug Ford held many of the same policy views as his brother, and was known for being equally bombastic, may have factored into vote calculations for many members of the electorate. John Tory, while clearly not the policy choice for most voters, would have represented a considerably less risky choice. Might it be the case that policy took a back seat to other considerations, such as those related to the candidates' personal characteristics? Did how voters felt about the candidates personally lead them to vote against their own policy interests?

TES data provide compelling support for the contention that for most voters, policy was a more important consideration than personality. There are two sets of TES questions that indicate convincingly that Toronto-nians prioritized policy congruence over the personal characteristics of candidates. First, after reporting vote choice, survey respondents were asked why they voted for the candidate they did, with the options being because they liked the candidate personally or because they liked the candidate's policy ideas. Second, prior to the election, respondents were also asked if there was a candidate for whom they *would not* consider vot-ing. Those who responded that such a candidate existed were similarly asked if they disliked the candidate personally or if they disliked the can-didate's policies.

Responses to these two sets of questions indicate that policy was a more important consideration for voters than were personal characteristics. Among all voters, 73.0 per cent of respondents reported supporting the candidate they did because they liked the individual's policies, mean-ing that a mere 27.0 per cent made their selection because they liked the candidate personally. When it comes to negative evaluations, TES data similarly suggest that policy was the more important consideration, though by a lesser margin: 48.7 per cent of respondents stated that there was a candidate they could never support due to policy, while 34.9 per cent stated as much because they disliked a candidate personally (the remaining 16.4 per cent of respondents did not have a candidate for whom they would never vote).[7] On both positive and negative fronts, therefore, policy was more commonly cited by respondents as driving attitudes and decisions.

While the population as a whole seemed to privilege policy over per-sonality considerations, it is conceivable that supporters or opponents of various candidates differed. Such a difference might go some way toward explaining why incorrect voting had the effect it did upon the election. If, for instance, voters tended to disproportionately dislike Ford on the basis of personality, it could help explain why he lost the election despite being the most compatible with the average Torontonian in policy terms. Similarly, if policy was relatively unimportant among those individuals who supported Tory, it would help explain why he performed better than he "should" have.

Table 4.4 indicates the relative importance of policy and personality among those individuals who liked and disliked the three major candi-dates. The first two columns of results indicate the share of voters who supported each candidate on the basis of policy and personality. The final two columns focus on those individuals who stated that there was a candidate whom they would not support (note that 41.6 per cent of respondents claimed that they could never support Ford, as compared to 30.6 per cent and 10.7 per cent who would not consider voting for Chow

Table 4.4. Policy and personality by candidate (%)

	Share of supporters who like on the basis of policy	Share of supporters who like on the basis of personality	Share of respondents who dislike, and who do so on the basis of policy	Share of respondents who dislike, and who do so on the basis of personality
Ford	78.6	21.4	37.1	62.9
Chow	77.4	22.6	83.8	16.2
Tory	65.8	34.2	65.8	34.2
	Total n = 1,664		Total n = 1,415	

or Tory, respectively). Entries indicate the share of respondents who disliked a candidate on the basis of policy or personal considerations, among those who would not consider voting for each individual.

Table 4.4 reveals two patterns that help explain Tory's victory despite his apparent incompatibility with the electorate in policy terms. First, relatively few Tory voters supported him on the basis of policy, as compared to both Ford and Chow supporters. More than one third of Tory voters chose him on the basis of personality, while the comparable share was just over one fifth for both other candidates. Such a difference might help account for Tory's ability to attract a great many voters who should not have supported him based on policy alone.

With respect to negative attitudes, we see a second important pattern of differentiation between the contestants. Among Torontonians who claimed that they would never support Ford, nearly 63 per cent held such attitudes on the basis of personality. The comparable values for those who would not support Chow and Tory were only 16.2 per cent and 34.2 per cent, respectively. Thus, Ford was much more likely to be ruled out by voters, and he tended to be ruled out on the basis of personal rather than policy considerations.

Returning to the question of the relative importance of policy and personality, Table 4.4 tells a largely consistent story of the primacy of policy. Though fewer Tory voters supported him on the basis of policy than did Ford or Chow supporters, policy considerations were nevertheless chosen by nearly twice as many respondents as was personality. Attraction to candidates was overwhelmingly driven by policy. In terms of being repulsed by a candidate, only among those individuals who disliked Ford was personality a more important consideration than policy. While Table 4.4 helps explain why Tory and Ford performed better and worse than they should have on the basis of policy, it nevertheless suggests that, on the whole, policy considerations played a greater role in this election than did personality. We turn now to consider the effect of the decision to focus on policy or personality on correct voting.

Explaining (In)correct Voting

Thus far, we have calculated the rate of correct voting in the 2014 Toronto election and determined that, had voters cast their ballots purely on the basis of policy, the outcome of the election would have been different – "Ford Nation" would have ruled the day. TES data have revealed that despite the high-profile nature of the election's primary contestants, policy considerations were more important than personality in the decisions of most Torontonians, but that supporters and opponents of the various candidates differed with respect to what they focused on when forming positive and negative assessments. We seek now to quantify the impact of focusing upon either policy or personality on the likelihood of voting correctly.

To that end, we conducted a series of logistic regression models, where a correct vote was the outcome variable (0/1). Our explanatory variables of interest were based on answers to the questions asking survey respondents to explain their vote choice and why they would never consider voting for a candidate. Those individuals who claimed that their vote choice had been made on the basis of policy were compared to those who had focused primarily on the personal characteristics of their chosen candidate. We also compared respondents who ruled out a candidate for policy reasons to those who did so based on personality, as well as to those who did not rule out a candidate (the base category in the models below).

We also included several important control variables, two of which were related to policy.[8] The first was a measure of whether respondents trusted politicians to keep their promises (most of the time, some of the time, or hardly ever). One of the generally unstated assumptions in research on correct voting is that politicians will actually follow through with the policy promises they make.[9] Our assumption was that voters who did not trust politicians were more likely to discount policy similarities when making their vote choices. The second policy-related control was an indicator of knowledge of campaign promises. This variable (an index created from a series of questions asking respondents to associate specific policy promises with candidates) should be positively associated with correct voting, for all else being equal, those individuals who know more about the policy positions of the candidates should be more likely to find the candidate most compatible with their own policy positions.

The final three controls were unrelated to policy specifically but were nevertheless expected to be associated with voting correctly. The first

Table 4.5. Explaining correct voting – policy versus personality

	Model 4A	Model 4B
Voted for candidate on the basis of policy	1.94 (0.33)***	1.86 (0.33)***
Dislike candidate on the basis of policy	2.22 (0.53)***	1.94 (0.48)***
Dislike candidate on the basis of personality	1.16 (0.28)	1.07 (0.27)
Policy knowledge	–	1.57 (0.46)*
Trust politicians	–	2.57 (0.71)***
Voted for most preferred candidate	–	2.62 (0.58)***
Municipal government has greatest impact	–	1.09 (0.18)
Partisan	–	1.13 (0.18)
n	1125	
Pseudo R^2	0.041	0.077

Entries report odds ratios and robust standard errors (in parentheses).

* $p < 0.10$
** $p < 0.05$
*** $p < 0.01$

was a measure of voter sincerity. For myriad reasons, including the desire to cast a strategic or protest vote, electors may not vote for their most preferred candidate, and such individuals cannot be expected to vote correctly. TES respondents were asked to rank the candidates, and we included a dummy variable to identify those individuals who did not vote for their preferred candidate on the basis of these rankings. Next, in their examination of correct voting in the United States, Lau and Redlawsk (1997) have identified two other important control variables. To begin with, those individuals who believe that the outcome of an election is important should be more motivated to vote correctly. The TES asked respondents how much of an impact the three levels of government (federal, provincial, municipal) had on their lives. We compared those individuals who believed that the municipal government had the greatest impact to those who did not. Lau and Redlawsk also note that political heuristics, such as partisanship, are positively associated with voting correctly. Given that several of the mayoral candidates had fairly obvious partisan links, we suspected that partisans would rely upon their identities (and knowledge of politics associated with these identities) to aid them in voting correctly. We thus included a dummy variable for federal-level partisanship, where we compared partisans (regardless of the party) to non-partisans.[10]

Table 4.5 includes the results of two models. The first (Model 4A) includes the policy/personality variables only, while the second (4B) includes the aforementioned control variables. All explanatory and out-come variables in the models are coded from 0 to 1, and entries report odds ratios. Results can be interpreted as the likelihood that those indi-viduals having the maximum value of a variable voted correctly, as com-pared to those with the minimum value.[11] For instance, a ratio of 2 would indicate that having a characteristic would make one twice as likely to vote correctly, while a value of 0.5 would suggest that one is only half as likely to do so.

The most striking and important finding in Table 4.5 is that those indi-viduals who prioritized policy, whether they evaluated candidates posi-tively or negatively, were more likely to vote correctly than those who did not. Both the uncontrolled (4A) and controlled (4B) models reveal that respondents who supported a candidate on the basis of policy were much more likely to vote correctly than those who chose a candidate for per-sonality reasons. In terms of the negativity variables, those who ruled out voting for a candidate on the basis of policy were more likely to vote cor-rectly than both those who did not rule out a candidate and those who ruled out a candidate on the basis of personality (the latter two groups had a statistically indistinguishable rate of correct voting). Whether the respondents were forming positive or negative assessments, therefore, focusing on policy was positively associated with voting correctly.[12]

These results validate our measure of correct voting, for there are strong theoretical reasons to expect correct voting and attitudes toward policy importance to be positively correlated. More importantly, how-ever, our results paint a fairly optimistic picture of the decision-making ability of Torontonians. While not all voters prioritized policy, most did when deciding which candidate to vote for and which candidate they would never vote for. Those voters who did focus on policy were also more likely than those who did not to identify the candidate who best reflected their policy preferences. In short, policy mattered for most, and when it did matter, correct voting rates were relatively high.

The impact of these variables on correct voting rates is substantial. Post-estimation, based upon Model 4B, provides a more precise indica-tion of the size of this effect. By manipulating the values of the policy importance variables (the "vote for" and "never vote for" measures), while keeping the values of all other variables unchanged, we can esti-mate the rate of correct voting in the election had all voters priori-tized policy, as compared to a scenario in which all voters prioritized personality.

This analysis suggests that the rate of correct voting if all electors sup-ported a candidate on the basis of policy *and* disliked a candidate on the basis of policy would have been 69.6 per cent. In contrast, if vote choices *and* dislike of a candidate were based on personal considerations for all voters, the estimated rate of correct voting would have been a mere 40.2 per cent. Combined with our earlier finding that the actual rate of correct voting among the population was 57.3 per cent, this difference of 29.4 percentage points represents a significant improvement in the rate of correct voting. Focusing on policy thus has a significant effect on one's likelihood of voting correctly, and had Torontonians focused more heavily on policy in 2014, the rate of correct voting would have increased substantially.

Conclusion

The analyses in this chapter reveal that the outcome of the 2014 mayoral election would have been different had all voters cast their ballot "correctly." Though an estimated 57.5 per cent of Torontonians voted in accordance with their policy preferences in the 2014 mayoral election, Doug Ford would have won had this figure been 100 per cent. Tory won because he was able to attract many voters who should not have supported him, while Ford, whose policies were most closely aligned with the electorate, lost the support of many voters whom he should have been able to count on.

This finding is striking, especially in light of the fact that, for most voters, policy was more important for vote choice than was personality. When finalizing vote decisions (both positive and negative), a large majority of Torontonians apparently based these choices on policy considerations. From the perspective of evaluating the quality of Toronto's democracy, it is encouraging to know that those individuals who did base their decisions on policy were more likely to vote correctly than those who did not.

Despite these arguably positive findings, the 2014 Toronto election presents an interesting case: the "incorrect" candidate won the election. Is it possible that a sufficient number of voters focused on the personal characteristics of the candidates to account for this outcome? The short answer to this question is yes – enough people based their vote decision on the personal characteristics of the candidates to cost Doug Ford the election.

Had voters cast their ballots solely on the basis of policy, the election outcome would have been different. Had voters supported the candidate to whom they were closest on the basis of the five policy areas considered here, Doug Ford would have become mayor of the city, having received 39.3 per cent of the vote (as opposed to the 34.7 per cent he actually received among the TES sample). Tory would have received 34.8 per cent of votes (rather than 41.5 per cent), costing him the election. For her part, Chow would have seen a modest bump in her vote share, going from 23.8 per cent to 25.9 per cent, though she would have remained in third place. Thus, while most Torontonians did indeed focus on policy when making their vote choices, enough voters based their decisions on candidate personalities to hand John Tory the keys to City Hall.

Such a finding suggests that while policy considerations may be dominant for most voters – as democratic theorists would hope – the importance of personality cannot be overlooked. Indeed, what democratic theory expects of voters can be overwhelmed by other considerations. Our results show that rates of correct voting were higher among those who prioritized policy stances and that more people prioritized policy over personality than the reverse. However, elections are often won or lost at the margins, and our findings suggest that personality considerations were highly influential in the 2014 Toronto election. So to understand election outcomes, it is important to pay attention to how personality considerations can sway voters. It seems that Torontonians wanted Ford's subways rather than Tory's SmartTrack. The result of the election belied voter preferences: too many voters turned away from Ford on the basis of his personal characteristics. Tory's (perhaps) more palatable personality gave him an edge in the election when his policies did not.

Chapter 5

Understanding Ford Nation

By late August 2014, Rob Ford was rebounding from the precipitous drop in public support that had occurred during his stint in rehab. He once again looked like a legitimate candidate for re-election, though he still trailed front-runner John Tory. The discovery of a tumour in the incumbent mayor's abdomen and his last-minute replacement on the ballot by his brother Doug had the potential to dramatically change the tide of the election. Yet as the final months of campaigning drew to a close, voters seemed to have taken little notice of the switch in brothers. Doug Ford finished the election in second place, the same place his brother had occupied in the polls when he dropped out of the race. Casual observers might have thought that those supporting (or opposing) the Fords had been largely unaffected by the change.

That the swapping of brothers appears to have had so little effect on voter intentions – at least on the basis of aggregate level polling figures – suggests that the average voter did not perceive many differences between the two. The fact that the brothers ran their campaigns in lockstep and played to the notion of a "nation" of Ford supporters suggests that the Ford brand to a large degree transcended any individual Ford. In recent years, the label "nation" has commonly been used to describe supporters of sports teams in Toronto (including "Leafs Nation" and "Raptors Nation"), and in the period leading up to the 2010 mayoral election it was extended to apply to the rather "diehard" supporters of Rob Ford and, eventually, to those who backed Doug. One might suggest, then, that the Ford brothers constituted a political "team."

The Fords themselves wholeheartedly embraced the notion of "Ford Nation." While some maligned Rob Ford's use of the term to describe his supporters (Kidd, 2011, 6 March), it was actually the news media that coined and popularized the concept. The first reference to Ford Nation we could find was in a *National Post* article published the day Rob

Ford won the mayoral race in 2010 (Carlson, 2010, 25 October). Despite the derision levelled at the label by Kenneth Kidd, the *Toronto Star* itself began popularizing the term not long after the 2010 election (see, for instance, James, 2010, 8 November; and Hume, 2010, 18 December). In fact, by April 2017, the *Toronto Star* had used the term in more than four hundred articles (LexisNexis). Today, even after the death of the former mayor in March 2016, the term lives on. In July 2016, the spectre of Ford Nation returned when Doug and Rob's nephew, Michael Ford, easily won his uncles' former council seat in a by-election (Canadian Press, 2016, 26 July). The concept of a "Ford Nation" later emerged at the provincial level – again via the *Toronto Star* – when Doug Ford ran for the leadership of Ontario's PC Party, and won (Cohn, 2018, 29 January).

It is rare in Canada to encounter a nation, or steadfast core, of supporters devoted to a specific political family (it is more common in the United States). According to many news media accounts, Ford Nation does not have a distinct partisan identity based on a specific ideology or set of policies; rather, it reflects some part of society that has been left out of political discourse for too long and wants back in. Many commentators have linked the idea of Ford Nation to the Tea Party movement in the United States (see for instance, Hepburn, 2014, 29 October; Kay, 2013, 19 November; Siddiqui, 2013, 3 November) and to supporters of Donald Trump (*Globe and Mail*, 2016, 25 March). But who exactly are the followers of this family of politicians from Etobicoke? What makes them tick? How loyal are they? Given that Rob won the 2010 mayoral election with 47 per cent of the vote, while his brother Doug won only 34 per cent in 2014, it is clear that not every 2010 Ford voter was a diehard fan of the family. Still, the fact that Doug won more than one third of the vote after several years of scandalous behaviour on the part of his brother suggests that there may indeed be something to the notion of a "Ford Nation."

This chapter answers a number of questions. First, who exactly makes up Ford Nation? The media presented several theories about this, but TES data reveal that attempts to identify the groups and attitudes associated with Ford Nation were only accurate in some instances. We begin by considering the geographic basis of Ford Nation. We look at the ratings of the Ford brothers and the other mayoral candidates, as well as vote choice by city region, and compare the geographic distribution of votes in the 2014 Toronto election to recent provincial and federal contests. After a detailed geographic account, we move on to consider the relationship between attitudes toward the Fords and a series of other individual-level characteristics, as informed by the media's portrayal of the brothers' supporters.

Next, we ask whether Ford Nation transferred its loyalty to Doug after Rob left the 2014 race. We look at differences in the bases of support for the brothers and identify several socio-demographic and attitudinal factors related to unique attitudes toward the brothers. Not all segments of Ford Nation viewed Rob and Doug as equally deserving of support. Given that finding, we conclude by considering how the results of the 2014 Toronto mayoral election might have been different had Rob been on the ballot rather than Doug. Besides being an interesting exercise in alternative history, this analysis suggests how the infamous "switch" affected the 2014 mayoral election and whether it is accurate to use the term "Ford Nation" to describe the supporters of this political family.

Political Parties and Family Dynasties

Before addressing these research questions, it is worth contemplating the exact nature of the Rob–Doug link. More specifically, we consider how the two brothers are similar to (and different from) a political party and a family dynasty, two important concepts in politics and political science. Though Toronto politics is officially non-partisan, one might reasonably view the brothers as the municipal equivalent of a political party: they shared a platform and had a long history of working together, besides, of course, the same last name. In this light, Ford Nation could be viewed as partisan supporters of a local pseudo-party.

Early on, Ford Nation was merely a label for members of the electorate who supported Rob Ford, but over time, it seemed to acquire quasi-party status in news coverage, particularly after the two brothers switched places on the 2014 ballot. The idea that this "Nation" may be the Toronto equivalent of supporters of a political party is not so far-fetched. In 2014, Doug Ford had chosen not to run for re-election as councillor in Ward 2. Instead, his nephew, Michael, entered that race (though he eventually withdrew so that Rob could run for the seat, choosing instead to run for a school board position he eventually won). What's more, John Nunziata, a former MP and MPP, and a long-time friend of the Fords, entered the race for Ward 12 at the same time that Doug replaced his brother in the contest for mayor. Nunziata came very close to beating the long-serving incumbent, Frank Di Giorgio, losing by less than two hundred votes. With more than just the two brothers running under the Ford Nation banner, and "Ford Nation candidates" largely united under one platform, the idea that the Nation represented an emerging party with an emerging partisan base seems plausible.

However, there are a number of important differences between Ford Nation and a political party (even a quasi- or nascent one). First, while parties based on an individual or family brand exist – for instance, the party of Denis Coderre, the former mayor of Montreal, was aptly named Équipe Denis Coderre (Team Denis Coderre) – they organize as parties and tend to run full slates of candidates in elections, rather than only a small number (or even just one). Second, in Ontario, parties at the municipal level cannot raise money for candidates and are not indicated alongside candidate names on a ballot, which largely nullifies some important advantages of running as part of a party. Though he campaigned under the same brand, Doug Ford had to raise his own money to run for mayor as he did not have direct access to the funds his brother had raised during the early part of the election (though convincing contributors to switch their contributions may not have been too difficult).

If the Ford brothers and their affiliates were not precisely a party, then what linked the supporters of Rob and Doug together? Clearly, the brothers' familial ties and shared last name were important factors, and these likely also played a role in Michael Ford's election to the Board of Education (in 2014) and then City Council (in 2016). The fact that familial bonds and a name united the two brothers suggests that the family could constitute a political dynasty. The term "dynastic politicians" refers to members of the same family who hold the same elected position at different times (Asako et al., 2015). For instance, Justin and Pierre Trudeau would be considered dynastic politicians because both of them served as prime minister. Likewise, Rob, Doug, and Michael Ford are dynastic politicians as they all served as Ward 2 councillor in Toronto. Though not entirely unheard of in Canada, such politicians are rarer here than in many other countries, such as Mexico (Camp, 1995), the Philippines (Mendoza et al., 2012), India (Bohlken & Chandra, 2012), and the United States (Feinstein, 2010).

During an election, familial ties (particularly shared last names) can be very important, for they function as a brand in much the same way that party labels do (Feinstein, 2010; Smith, 2012). Simply sharing a last name with a popular politician can significantly increase a candidate's exposure and electoral success. In fact, there is evidence that in the absence of other voting cues, such as partisan ties, dynastic politics is more likely to emerge, for without parties, political contests tend to become more candidate-centred (Smith, 2012).

The success of dynastic politicians has its roots in what Thompson (2012) sees as the public's willingness to associate the character of an elected official with their offspring or siblings. In this sense, the Ford familial tie has been more dynastic than partisan: a group of people, first attracted to the charisma and policies of Rob Ford, extended their support and assessment of him to his brother (and, though we lack the data to be certain, likely to his nephew). In the case of the Ford brothers, familial ties were likely reinforced by their similar branding and close association, further heightening the effects of dynastic ties. Doug Ford even kept many of the same advisers and volunteers – for example, the same spokesperson who withdrew Rob Ford's 2014 mayoral candidacy later filed the registration papers for his brother (Hui et al., 12 September). That Doug Ford largely served as Rob's lieutenant in council during the latter's time as mayor no doubt further strengthened such ties.

Ford Nation does not constitute a party. Neither do the Fords, and given the lack of institutional support for political parties at the local level in Ontario, they likely never will. They do, however, seem to represent a potentially emergent political dynasty in the city. Delving deeper to understand the who, what, and where of Ford Nation support will provide us with an important understanding of how Canadian voters respond to dynastic politics. It will also provide important comment on an interesting period in Toronto's history.

The News Media and Defining "Ford Nation"

Rob and Doug are the two most high-profile members of the Ford dynasty, which, at least on the basis of election and polling results, seems to enjoy a great deal of loyalty among certain groups within the electorate. The question of which segments of society hold the most positive views toward the brothers, in essence making up Ford Nation, remains unanswered. Similarly, it is unclear who remained loyal (or not) to the dynasty after Doug replaced Rob on the 2014 mayoral ballot. We now investigate these matters, using TES data.

Since the notion of "Ford Nation" first emerged from the ether, various political pundits, pollsters, and even politicians have attempted to pinpoint who exactly their supporters are and what attracts them to the family's political positions. These musings range from attempts at objective analysis to vitriol levelled against the supporters of a much-hated foe. A review of these attempts to define and depict Ford Nation brings to the surface some common themes and contradictions.

When one considers Ford Nation, the first question that arises is this: should all Ford voters be considered part of the Nation, or is that Nation actually a select "tribe" of diehard supporters? The size of Ford Nation is important for election outcomes, because for it to be an actual political entity with some power, as the news media often portray it, it must account for enough of the electorate to influence elections. In the one serious attempt to determine the size and qualities of Ford Nation, John

Wright of the polling firm Ipsos Reid (now Ipsos) suggested that Ford Nation accounts for about 20 per cent of the electorate (Wright, 2013, 19 November); Royson James of the *Toronto Star* speculated that it is closer to 15 per cent (James, 2013, 21 November). Given that Rob and Doug received 47.1 per cent and 33.7 per cent of the vote in 2010 and 2014, respectively, these estimates suggest that Ford Nation makes up only a fraction of the overall population that voted for the brothers. Given the absence of Ford Nation membership rolls, we can only speculate about how many of those who have voted for a Ford are "true" members of Ford Nation and how many are merely sympathetic to the cause.

Given the difficulties associated with precisely measuring the size of Ford Nation, political commentators have turned to speculating about the identity of Ford supporters. *Toronto Star* journalist Bob Hepburn succinctly captured one of the more common portrayals of members of Ford Nation, describing them as "the odd coalition of disaffected, disenchanted, poor, ethnic, working class and fiscal conservatives" (Hepburn, 2014, October 29). Ford Nation has also been described as consisting of lower-income residents from Toronto's inner suburbs (Etobicoke, North York, and Scarborough) who feel alienated from the downtown elites that dominate city politics (James, 2013, 21 November; Kay, 2013, 19 November; Simpson, 2013, 20 November).

Former mayoral candidate Olivia Chow expressed a similar view, suggesting that residents in the most impoverished neighbourhoods in the city were stalwart supporters of Rob and his brother: "These are the people who feel they are left behind ... They feel that no one cares about them; that there's these elites downtown that control all the power; that no one feels their pain ... They don't think policy at all. It's about who is on their side ... These are the folks who are committed to Ford" (in Hepburn, 2014, 29 October).

Patrick Cain of Global News, in an attempt to bring empirical data to bear on the question, suggested much the same. Using overall voter support taken from individual polling stations from the 2010 and 2014 elections and aligning them with Canadian 2006 census tract data (a census tract is the smallest geographic area in the Canadian Census), he concluded that Ford supporters are in fact from lower-income neighbourhoods, have lower educational attainment, are immigrants, and are more likely to be single parents (Cain, 2014, 8 September).[1]

John Wright's analysis of his firm's polling data from November 2013 buttressed this view of Ford Nation, albeit with some surprises. To "isolate" Ford Nation from more transient supporters, Wright presented respondents with a series of election scenarios in which Ford was pitted against various candidates. He then determined the share of respondents who pledged to support Ford no matter who he was pitted against. Contrary to expectations, he found that voters in Etobicoke, often considered the motherlode of Ford support, were less likely to be loyal Ford Nation members than residents in the former municipalities of York, East York, North York, and Scarborough. Only 16 per cent of survey respondents in Etobicoke consistently supported Rob, regardless of who the other mayoral candidates were; the same percentage he received in the old City of Toronto, where the "downtown elite" reside. His support was decidedly higher in Scarborough (30 per cent) and North York (22 per cent). More in keeping with the usual portrayal of Ford Nation, Wright found that the Fords enjoyed higher support among those with lower incomes and those with less education (Wright, 2013, 19 November).

Who exactly, then, makes up Ford Nation? Pundits, politicians, and pollsters point to several socio-demographic and attitudinal factors. Below we consider which of these factors are associated with attitudes toward the Ford brothers. We also consider the question of geography, as well as which segments of Ford Nation transferred their loyalty to Doug in 2014.

The Geography of Ford Nation

We begin our description of Ford Nation by considering the geographic basis of support for both Rob and Doug. The brothers have conspicuously right-wing leanings, and research has demonstrated that there is a clear and persistent urban–suburban ideological divide in Toronto (Walks, 2004; 2005), with people on the periphery of the city tending to vote for right-wing politicians at higher rates than downtowners. In his work on the 2010 mayoral election, Walks (2015, p. 412) argues that Rob Ford appealed directly to the suburbs: "Conservative Rob Ford's approach centred on austerity, populism and appealing to suburban interests in preventing the shifting of resources from roads to public transit." We evaluate the geographic distribution of Ford Nation here by two means. First, we consider feeling thermometer ratings for the three major candidates by region of the city. We then consider the geographic distribution of Doug Ford's vote support. We conclude by comparing mayoral results with those from recent federal and provincial elections in order to establish that this geographic divide exists at all levels of government.

First, we consider the relationship between geography and the ratings of the various candidates. Figure 5.1 shows the feeling thermometer scores for the Fords (independently), Chow, and Tory in Etobicoke, York, Toronto, East York, North York, and Scarborough (these divisions correspond with the city's community council boundaries as they stood

Figure 5.1. Geography and candidate ratings

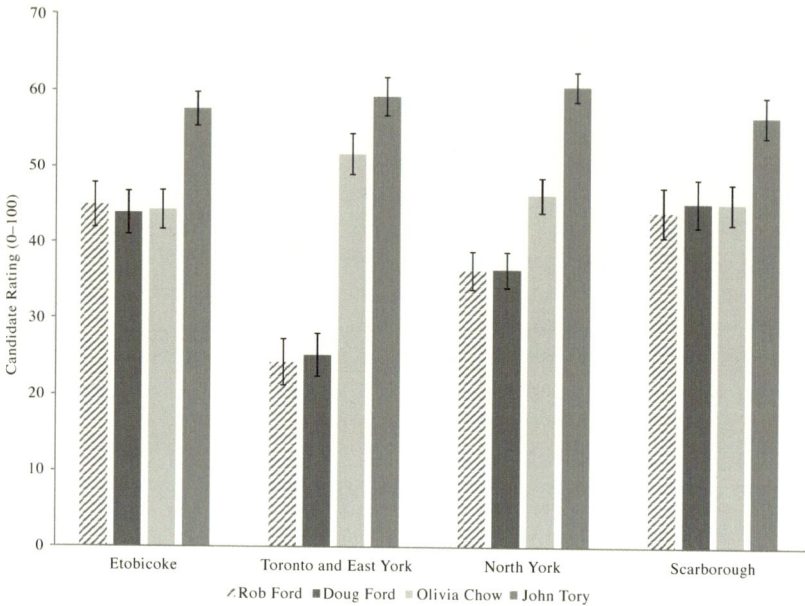

✓Rob Ford ■Doug Ford ▪ Olivia Chow ■ John Tory

in 2014). The boundaries of Toronto and East York roughly correspond to what Walks (2007) has defined as the inner city. The figure offers some interesting results. TES data suggest that the two Fords were rated essentially equally in each part of the city. In no part, however, were they significantly more popular than either Chow or Tory. In fact, Tory received the highest average candidate rating in each part of the city. The Fords did perform comparatively well in Scarborough and their home base of Etobicoke: in those places, they performed as well as Chow. Chow had her highest ratings downtown, which is perhaps unsurprising given her left-leaning ideology.

But how well did feeling thermometer scores translate into vote choices? We know from chapter 2 that average feeling thermometer scores are imperfectly correlated with aggregate-level vote choice; Doug Ford had the lowest average feeling thermometer score of the three major candidates, yet he still managed to place second in the election. As such, in Figure 5.2, we consider the geographic distribution of Ford's support on election day in map format.

Figure 5.2 shows that the relatively low ratings of the Ford brothers observed in the downtown core in Figure 5.1 indeed translated into low levels of vote support in that part of the city – the shading in Figure 5.2 is lightest in the south-central part of the city. Ford's ratings were highest in

Figure 5.2. Doug Ford vote shares by ward

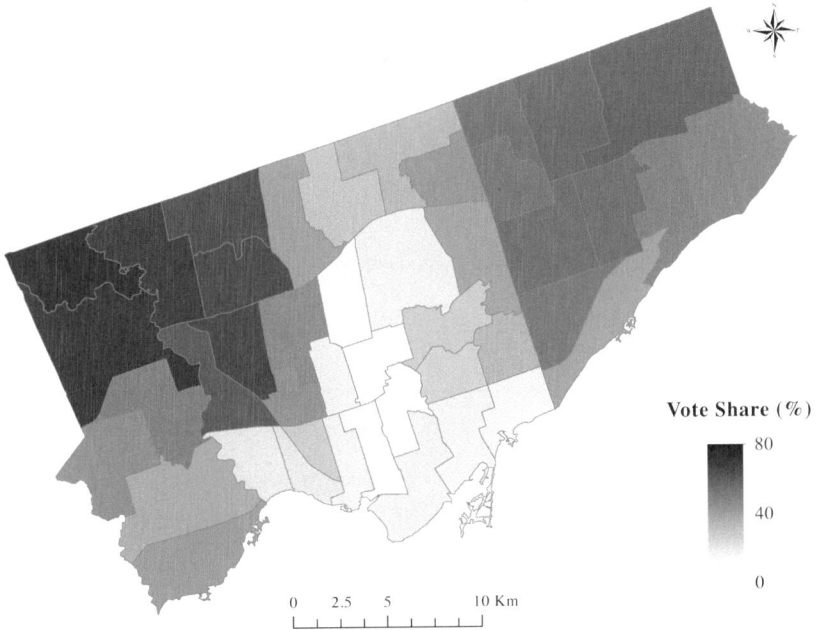

Etobicoke and Scarborough and, unsurprisingly, he received the highest vote shares in those places. The patterns in Figures 5.1 and 5.2 make it clear: Ford Nation is largely confined to the periphery of the city.

Next we consider whether the geographic distribution of support for Ford is a unique feature of Ford Nation or an artefact of a more general relationship between location and ideology. Existing research shows that Ford was widely viewed as the most conservative of the three major candidates, while Chow was seen as the most left-leaning, with Tory as the relative centrist (McGregor et al., 2016). We wish to consider whether the geographic basis of Doug Ford's support mapped closely to that of Conservative parties at other levels of government. Was he able to attract voters from parts of the city where federal and provincial Conservative parties tend to fare quite poorly? Conversely, was he perhaps more unpopular than those parties would be in other parts of the city? We consider these possibilities in Table 5.1, which shows urban and suburban support for the three major mayoral candidates in 2014, as well as the average level of support for the three major federal and provincial political parties in those same areas. We

Table 5.1. Vote shares in urban and suburban areas, municipal, provincial, and federal elections (%)

		Urban	Suburban
Toronto 2014	Chow	36.3	17.1
	Tory	44.7	35.7
	Ford	16.6	44.0
Ontario 2014	NDP	31.5	17.0
	Liberal	46.7	50.0
	Progressive Conservative	14.4	28.0
Canada 2015	NDP	31.2	12.0
	Liberal	49.5	54.0
	Conservative	15.3	31.4

categorize wards and ridings (for federal and provincial elections) as either urban or suburban, corresponding with the parts of the city used in Figure 5.1.[2]

Table 5.1 offers several noteworthy findings. For our purposes, the most important is that overall, Doug Ford's support followed a geographic pattern similar to those of the federal and provincial Conservatives. In this sense, the pattern of his support was not atypical.

What *was* atypical was the *degree* to which he performed better in suburban Toronto. In the downtown core, Ford and the two Conservative parties received similar vote shares – around 15 per cent, much lower than their vote shares on the periphery. Where Ford was unique was in his performance in the city's suburbs. While the federal and provincial Conservative parties saw increases of 13.6 and 16.1 percentage points, respectively, in suburban Toronto, Ford saw his support jump by a full 27.4 points. Indeed, he was the best-performing candidate in the city's suburbs – it was his third-place finish downtown that led to his election loss. Neither the federal nor the provincial Conservative Party won in suburban Toronto – both came in a distant second to the Liberals. Overall, the difference between urban and suburban vote choice was greater at the municipal level than it was either federally or provincially. The average difference for the three mayoral candidates was 18.5 percentage points. The comparable values for the three major parties at the provincial and federal levels were 10.4 and 13.2 points, respectively. The urban/suburban divide thus seems to matter more at the local level (for Ford, in particular) than it does at the federal and provincial levels.

Who Is Ford Nation?

The lessons from the above analysis are clear: Ford Nation is heavily based on geography. That said, we turn now to seeking other factors that may be in play. To that end, we ask which groups in society feel most positively about the Fords. Given the change in banner carrier, it is also worth considering what types of electors favoured Rob over Doug, or vice versa. Do all segments of Ford Nation feel the same way about the two brothers, or are some groups inconsistent in their support?

As noted earlier, journalists have speculated about who the Fords' core supporters are. The individual-level data in the TES allow us to test their suppositions systematically. Columnists like Bob Hepburn and Patrick Cain, and pollster John Wright, offer quite similar ideas about the composition of Ford Nation. The relevant socio-demographic factors they suggest include low incomes, visible minority status, low education levels, being an immigrant, and living outside of the city core.[3] Attitudinal factors have also been proposed, including fiscal conservatism and political disaffection. Recall that Olivia Chow herself suggested that disaffection, or feeling "left behind" by elites who don't care what they think, is more powerful in the minds of Ford supporters than policy considerations. In this section we evaluate whether the importance of these characteristics is supported with individual-level data, and also whether what was said about "Rob Ford" Nation applies to "Doug Ford" Nation – in other words, whether the composition of the group supporting the dynasty varied with the candidates.

Ideally, we would analyse individual-level data from the 2010 election to establish the nature of Ford Nation at that time; unfortunately, none are available. Nevertheless, TES data allow us to delve into attitudes toward both brothers in 2014. We consider the relationship between our explanatory factors and the evaluations of both brothers in order to identify any differences in support for the two men. If Doug is in fact the second politician in a Ford dynasty, it is crucial to find similarities between his support base and Rob's.

Our dependent variables in the analyses are the feeling thermometer scores for each Ford. During the 2014 election campaign, TES respondents were asked to rate each of the brothers on a scale from 0 to 100, where 0 meant that they really disliked him and 100 meant they really liked him (with a score of 50 representing neutrality).[4] Those factors that influenced support for both Rob and Doug could be considered the core of Ford Nation. Those that differed between the brothers would be related to each of them as unique candidates.

Table 5.2 shows the results of a series of bivariate analyses in which respondents who exhibit each demographic and attitudinal characteristic

Table 5.2. Ratings of Rob and Doug Ford – bivariate analysis

		Rob			Doug		
		Low/ No	High/ Yes	Difference	Low/ No	High/ Yes	Difference
Sociodemo-graphic character-istics	University educated	40.2	31.5	−8.7***	41.1	32.3	−8.8***
	n	502	729	–	502	729	–
	High income	36.0	34.1	−1.8	36.3	35.4	−0.9
	n	591	640	–	591	640	–
	Visible minority	31.8	43.5	11.6***	33.0	43.4	10.4***
	n	893	338	–	893	338	–
	Immigrant	30.7	43.0	12.2***	32.2	42.6	10.4***
	n	801	430	–	801	430	–
	Toronto (versus periphery)	39.2	24.3	−14.8***	39.9	25.5	−14.3***
	n	886	25.5	–	886	25.5	–
	Female	37.1	31.6	−5.5***	37.7	32.9	−4.7**
	n	761	470	–	761	470	–
	Over 50	39.0	32.4	−6.5***	39.0	33.8	−5.2**
	n	483	748	–	483	748	–
Attitudes	Disaffection – Municipal level	40.7	29.6	−11.1***	41.7	30.3	−11.8***
	n	600	631	–	600	631	–
	Disaffection – Other levels	32.6	38.5	5.9***	33.1	39.9	6.7***
	n	736	495	–	736	495	–
	Economic Conservative	29.0	39.0	10.0***	28.6	40.6	12.0***
	n	488	743	–	488	743	–
	Vote on basis of policy	30.6	36.7	6.1***	31.6	37.5	5.9***
	n	245	886	–	245	886	–

* $p < 0.10$
** $p < 0.05$
*** $p < 0.01$

are compared to those who do not, in terms of the average ratings of Rob and Doug Ford.[5] The same table shows the difference between each category of the variables, to see whether factors are indeed associated with different ratings of the Fords. All explanatory variables are coded as dummies (having two values). Some factors do not automatically lend themselves to such an operationalization, and have been converted to binary variables here for ease of interpretation, being divided at their median values (such variables include income, age, disaffection, and economic conservatism).

The socio-demographic variables considered in the table are those introduced above, including education, income, visible minority status, immigrant status, and living in the interior of the city (as opposed to its outer ring). We also include gender and age, as these are fairly standard considerations in analyses of political support. We operationalize disaffection with the following question: "How much does the ___ government care about what you think?" TES respondents were asked about all three levels of government, so we use the data to create two separate measures, one for the municipal level and one for the provincial and federal levels of government combined. As Rob was the incumbent mayor, we expect that Ford supporters would react differently to questions about disaffection at the municipal level than they would when asked about the provincial or national governments. Our measure of economic conservatism is an index based on a series of questions related to government intervention in the economy. Finally, we have a measure that taps into the relative importance of policy considerations in the decisions of voters. After reporting vote choice, survey respondents were asked whether they supported the candidate they did because they liked him or her personally, or because they liked his or her policy ideas (note that this was the same question used in the previous chapter). If Olivia Chow's comment that Ford supporters care relatively little about policy is correct, the "policy" group should give Doug Ford a lower rating than the "personality" group.

Table 5.2 reveals that a great many characteristics that were expected to form the basis of Ford Nation are indeed related to attitudes toward both Rob and Doug Ford. In fact, every single factor considered in the table displays the same relationship (or lack thereof) with attitudes toward the two brothers. All but one of the socio-demographic characteristics considered in the table is correlated with ratings of the Fords. So the pundits were correct that low levels of education, visible minority status, being an immigrant, and living in the periphery of the city are associated with relatively high ratings. Against expectations, however, income exhibits no relationship with such attitudes. Finally, women and voters over the age of fifty have relatively negative attitudes toward both brothers. The individual-level data in the TES reveal that in socio-demographic terms, Ford nation supporters are more likely to be less educated, minorities, immigrants, men, and younger, and to live in the city's suburbs.

All four of the attitudinal factors in Table 5.2 are associated with ratings of the Fords, though not all work as one might expect on the basis of the above discussion. Perhaps unsurprisingly, disaffection toward the municipal government is *negatively* associated with such attitudes. Given that the outgoing mayor so dominated the discussion on municipal politics in Toronto in the years prior to the election, it stands to reason that many electors would immediately think of Rob when asked about the municipal government, and therefore those who answered that the municipal government does not care what they think would give a low rating to both Rob and (by dynastic extension) Doug. Conversely, disaffection toward the other levels of government is positively associated with ratings of the brothers. The pundits were therefore partly correct in their assessment that disaffection is an important component of Ford Nation. It was not disaffection toward the municipal government that drove Ford support in 2014 (though it might have been relevant for supporting Rob in 2010). However, we see that negative attitudes toward the other levels of government are part of the composition of Ford support. This seems to suggest that Ford supporters are indeed disaffected by politics in general.

An attitudinal variable that works in a more straightforward fashion is economic conservatism. Respondents with economic views on the right wing of the political spectrum are much friendlier toward the Fords than are those on the left. Interestingly, the table seems to contradict Olivia Chow's assessment that Ford Nation is made up of individuals who care relatively little about policy. In fact, the opposite is true: respondents who reported voting on the basis of policy gave both brothers a higher rating than did those who voted on the basis of personality. Such a finding is congruent with the results in chapter 4, which showed that Ford's policies were generally more compatible with those of the electorate than were those of either Tory or Chow. Recall that Table 4.4 showed that nearly 80 per cent of Ford voters supported him on the basis of policy rather than personality. Policy thus appears to be of great import for Ford Nation.[6]

While bivariate comparisons of the type contained in Table 5.2 are useful for identifying the groups in society that make up Ford Nation, such uncontrolled analyses provide no insight into which factors *drive* attitudes toward the Fords. Many of the factors considered are strongly correlated with one another. For instance, age and education are related to income, and visible minority status and immigrant status are strongly associated with each other. While Table 5.2 is useful in mapping out Ford Nation, it does not identify which factors are most important and which are unique sources of support for Rob and Doug Ford.

To address this, we present Table 5.3, which shows the results of several multivariate analyses, with all of the variables in Table 5.2 considered simultaneously. In the first two results columns of this table we consider the ratings of both Ford brothers to begin to see which factors drive

Table 5.3. The correlates of attitudes toward the Ford brothers – multivariate analysis

		Rob	Doug	Rob – Doug
Sociodemographic characteristics	University educated	−10.5 (2.7)***	−10.9 (2.6)***	0.4 (1.4)
	High income	2.1 (2.7)	2.4 (2.6)	−0.4 (1.2)
	Visible minority	5.8 (3.5)*	5.6 (3.4)*	0.2 (1.9)
	Immigrant	8.9 (3.2)***	4.9 (3.1)	4.0 (1.7)**
	Toronto (versus periphery)	−13.6 (3.1)***	−14.6 (2.9)***	1.0 (1.8)
	Female	−4.6 (2.7)*	−2.1 (2.6)	−2.5 (1.4)*
	Over 50	−6.5 (2.9)**	−5.8 (2.8)**	−0.6 (1.4)
Attitudes	Disaffection – municipal level	−11.2 (2.9)***	−11.6 (2.9)***	0.4 (1.2)
	Disaffection – other levels	10.7 (2.9)***	11.7 (2.9)***	−1.0 (1.2)
	Economic conservative	5.5 (2.8)*	8.3 (2.8)***	−2.8 (1.4)**
	Vote on basis of policy	5.2 (2.9)*	5.6 (2.8)**	−0.5 (1.3)
	Constant	43.4 (4.5)***	42.0 (4.5)***	1.4 (2.3)
	R-squared	0.127	0.132	0.027
	n	1,231		

Entries report coefficients and standard errors (in parentheses).

* $p < 0.10$
** $p < 0.05$
*** $p < 0.01$

attitudes toward them. The outcome variables (the ones we are seeking to explain) are in the same format as in Table 5.2: feeling thermometer scores ranging from 0 (strong dislike) to 100 (strong like). If Ford Nation is indeed made up of distinct segments of the population that are loyal to the brand, we would expect the same factors to be associated with attitudes toward both brothers.

In addition to comparing the results of these models, Table 5.3 includes a third model, where the dependent variable reflects the difference in ratings for the two brothers. For instance, if a respondent assigned Rob a rating of 50 and Doug a score of 45, the value for this variable would be 5. Statistically significant results in this model suggest that a group or attitude is associated with assigning different ratings to Rob and Doug; positive values indicate that Rob is preferred. We use this type of "difference" variable (which has a hypothetical range from −100 to +100) to identify factors that are related to holding different attitudes toward the two brothers and to see which segments of Ford Nation were most (or least) loyal.

Table 5.3 reveals several patterns of note. First, most variables retain their statistical significance even when entered into the multivariate model. Second, most of the explanatory variables included in the table have the same relationship (or lack thereof) with attitudes toward both Fords. Education, visible minority status, geography, age, and all four attitudinal factors have the same relationship with attitudes toward the two brothers. Two variables included in the models, however, reveal a statistically significant relationship with attitudes toward Rob, but not Doug: immigrant status and gender.

Comparing these two models is insufficient to discern whether these factors are differentially associated with ratings of the two brothers (statistical significance cannot readily be inferred from two separate models). To do so, we refer to the third and final model, where the dependent variable is the difference between ratings of Rob and Doug. This also brings us to the third pattern of note in the table: three factors are associated with rating the two brothers differently.[7] Respondents born outside of Canada gave Rob Ford an average rating four points higher than their Canadian-born counterparts did, and women were relatively more likely to give Doug a higher rating than Rob. Finally, a result that was not evident from the separate models is that economic conservatives favoured Doug over Rob, rating the mayoral candidate higher than the incumbent mayor. For some segments of Ford Nation, therefore, the "leader" mattered. While most factors associated with support for Rob are also associated with support for Doug, not all segments of Ford Nation are equally supportive of the two brothers.

What If Rob Had Run?

So far, we have identified the bases of Ford Nation and shown which segments of the Nation held different attitudes toward Rob and Doug. Three factors have been identified that point to differential support for the two brothers (immigrant status, gender, and economic ideology), and it is very likely that others exist. Such differences make inevitable the question of whether the result of the 2014 mayoral election would have differed had Rob not dropped out of the race. If Ford Nation alone was loyal to their new banner carrier, then we should expect the outcome of a hypothetical election contested by Rob to be the same as that of the actual contest. If some segments of the nation were disloyal, or if Doug was able to attract voters that Rob would not have, then the outcome of an election including Rob might have been different. Which possibility is correct?

We begin to assess the effects of the Ford swap on vote choice by considering whether Torontonians, as a whole, saw Rob and Doug Ford similarly. Were the two viewed as interchangeable? While there are limitations to such hypothetical questions (there is no way to determine whether Rob would have campaigned differently than his brother, for example), there is nevertheless value in probing these issues. Among other things, the answers to these questions provide additional information about the existence of Ford Nation.

Some basic measures provide very strong evidence that Torontonians were overwhelmingly of the opinion that Rob and Doug had very similar policy preferences. TES respondents were asked, "In your opinion, how similar are Doug Ford's policies to those of his brother, Rob?" A meagre 3.1 per cent of interviewees responded that the brothers were either "mostly" or "all" different. In contrast, 52.1 per cent and 35.8 per cent believed that their policies were mostly or all the same, respectively (the remaining 8.9 per cent of respondents were unsure).[8] There was therefore a broad consensus that the Ford brothers shared a common set of policy preferences.

Furthermore, an analysis of feeling thermometer ratings shows that the two received nearly identical likability scores among Torontonians. On a scale from 0 to 100, TES respondents assigned Doug a score of 38.3, while Rob managed a value of 38.2. These values are (perhaps obviously) statistically indistinguishable from each other (for their parts, Tory and Chow received scores of 57.2 and 47.0, respectively).[9] In addition to this, there is a very strong relationship between the two feeling thermometer ratings: the Pearson correlation between the two measures is an impressive 0.90.

For the sake of comparison, we can turn to the federal election of 2004, the last example at the federal level where an incumbent party contested an election under a new leader. Although Jean Chrétien and Paul Martin were very different politicians (and indeed, there was some animosity between them), Martin, as finance minister, had been a prominent member of Chrétien's cabinet. When Martin ran as the new leader of the incumbent Liberal Party in 2004, there was a similar situation of change in leadership for an established brand. Canadian Election Study data reveal that the average ratings of the two politicians were quite different. Martin received an average feeling thermometer value of 47.0, and Chrétien a value of 40.5.[10] Moreover, the Pearson correlation between the ratings for the two party leaders was only 0.47.[11] In comparison, then, the Ford results from Toronto are particularly compelling, and suggest strongly that overall, the citizens of Toronto saw the brothers as virtually interchangeable.

Given this perceived similarity, one might assume that had Rob contested the 2014 election instead of Doug, the election outcome would have been precisely the same. However, we saw earlier that certain groups in society viewed the two brothers differently. Considering attitudes among the population as a whole can be misleading if such analyses mask differences among specific segments of the electorate. Might those differences mean that Rob would have either over- or under-performed Doug had he remained on the ballot in 2014?

TES data allow us to speculate, with some precision, about how the mayoral contest would have ended had Rob stayed in the race. In addition to feeling thermometer measures and the aforementioned questions about policy similarity, the survey included pre- and post-election measures that provide insight into voter preferences regarding a hypothetical election in which Rob was a candidate. The two waves of the TES included measures of pre-election vote intention and post-election vote choice recall. During both survey waves, respondents were also asked whether they would have voted for Rob Ford had he been running. The answers to these questions about Rob can be compared to vote intention/recall to allow us to speculate as to the impact of the last-minute sibling switch on the election outcome. Conducting this analysis at two points in time (pre- and post-election) improves the certainty with which conclusions can be drawn from the data.

The first two columns in Table 5.4 show the share of respondents who indicated they planned to vote for Doug and the share that would have supported Rob had he been running, measured in the pre-election questionnaire. The last two columns compare the reported and hypothetical vote shares for Doug and Rob respectively, measured during the post-election questionnaire.

Both sets of comparisons suggest that Rob might well have *outperformed* his brother. In the pre-election questionnaire, 26.8 per cent of respondents indicated that they planned to support Doug, as compared to 31.7 per cent who asserted that they would have voted for Rob (this difference is significant at $p < 0.01$). Though fewer respondents were undecided when asked about Rob, the difference of 6.3 percentage points in the "undecided" category is not much bigger than the 4.9-point gap between the support levels of the two brothers, indicating that Doug would have needed to win a large majority of the undecided group to catch up to Rob's level of support.

The post-election results paint a similar picture, though strictly speaking, Rob did not outperform his brother in the post-election

Table 5.4. Vote intention and recall – actual and hypothetical (%)

	Pre-election (n = 2,843)		Post-election (n = 1,677)	
	Doug	Rob	Doug	Rob
Vote for Ford	26.8	31.7	32.7	32.6
Vote for other candidate	54.4	55.8	66.4	58.8
Undecided/don't know	18.8	12.5	0.9	8.6

questionnaire. There is no statistically significant difference between reported support for Doug and hypothetical support for Rob. Particularly important here, however, is that 8.6 per cent of voters were not sure who they would have supported if Rob had run. If even a fraction of this group of voters had supported him, Rob would have fared better in the election than his brother.

Thus both pre- and post-election data suggest that Rob would have received a higher vote share than his older brother. Importantly, however, it is very unlikely that Rob would have defeated John Tory, who received 40.3 per cent of the vote in the actual election. To defeat Tory, Rob would have needed to capture almost all of the 8.6 per cent of post-election respondents who were undecided in the hypothetical election. Rob would have received a higher vote share than his brother, but he would still have finished second in the race.

The aggregate data in Table 5.4 speak to (hypothetical) differences in overall results, but they lack information on how individual Rob supporters or detractors actually voted in the 2014 election. What share of Rob's supporters voted for Doug, and how many voted for other candidates? How did those who did not support Doug vote? Was he able to win over electors who would not have backed his brother? To answer these questions, we present Table 5.5, which shows vote choice, with respondents grouped on the basis of whether they would have voted for Rob, had he contested the election.

Table 5.5 considers not only voters but also TES respondents who abstained from the mayoral election. Focusing on non-voters is important, for it is conceivable that the replacement of Rob had an impact on turnout rates (and thus, indirectly, also on vote shares). Both Fords were highly polarizing figures, but only Rob had a mayoral record, which invariably brings with it loyal supporters and vocal opponents. As was noted in a previous chapter, attitudes toward Rob were bimodal; a great many electors had either strongly positive or strongly negative attitudes toward him (attitudes toward Tory and Chow were more normally

Table 5.5. Vote choice and hypothetical support for Rob Ford (%)

| | | If Rob Ford had been a mayoral candidate, would you have voted for him? | | |
		Yes (n = 685)	No (n = 1,223)	Don't know (n = 169)
Reported vote choice	Doug Ford	74.7	3.0	28.0
	Olivia Chow	2.8	31.2	10.7
	John Tory	8.5	51.7	28.0
	Other	1.0	2.5	9.4
	Abstain	13.1	11.6	24.0

distributed). These strong feelings may have had an effect on turnout: Rob's supporters may have been less inclined to vote in his absence, while his opponents may have felt less urgency to vote against him (though it is possible that on both fronts, Doug's entry into the race cancelled out these potential effects). If those respondents who claimed they would have supported Rob had different turnout rates than those who claimed they would not, it would suggest that the outgoing mayor's decision to drop out of the race affected both turnout and candidate vote shares. The purpose of Table 5.5 is thus to speculate about how vote shares and voter turnout were affected by the Rob/Doug switch. Note that entries report column percentages.[12]

There are several findings of note in Table 5.5. To begin with, as one might expect, there is strong overlap in support for the two Ford brothers. Nearly 75 per cent of survey respondents who would have voted for Rob ended up voting for Doug. If we ignore those respondents who abstained from the election, we find that 85.9 per cent of voters who would have backed Rob ended up voting for Doug. Such high values suggest that the ballot swap functioned in very much the same way as a change in leadership of a political party. Most voters saw the brothers as nearly interchangeable.

With respect to the impact of the change on candidate vote shares, Table 5.5 provides two key findings. First, the rate of abstention among individuals who claimed they would have voted for Rob (13.1 per cent) is statistically indistinguishable from the rate for those who said they would not have backed him (11.6 per cent). Though both rates are lower than the abstention rate of those individuals who are unsure whether they would have supported Rob ($p < 0.01$ in both instances), there is no evidence here that Doug replacing his brother on the ballot affected turnout in the 2014 mayoral election.

Second, the data suggest that Doug received very little support from those individuals who would not have voted for Rob. Only 3.0 per cent of electors who said they would not have backed Rob ended up supporting Doug. In contrast, among those individuals who would have voted for Rob, 12.3 per cent eventually supported candidates other than Doug. This difference of 9.3 percentage points reveals that the switch from Rob to Doug attracted fewer voters to the "Ford Nation" banner than it lost to other candidates.

The evidence thus strongly suggests that in a hypothetical election, Rob would have received a higher vote share in the 2014 Toronto municipal election than Doug did in the actual election. Though the switch had no discernible impact on turnout rates, TES data indicate that Rob's support was higher among voters, and a significant number of Rob's supporters abandoned Doug for other candidates. So, while the last-minute swap of the Ford brothers had an undeniable effect on the decisions of voters, it remains unlikely that Rob would have defeated John Tory. In this sense, with respect to the outcome of the election, a Ford by any other name would not have smelled any sweeter to the electorate.

Conclusion

It is impossible to predict with absolute certainty what the outcome of the 2014 Toronto mayoral election would have been had Doug not replaced Rob on the ballot. In the absence of a time machine that would enable us to rerun the election with a different representative of Ford Nation, TES data provide the best possible method for predicting the outcome of a hypothetical election. By comparing answers to questions about vote intention, vote recall, and whether electors would have supported Rob had he been a candidate, we are able to speculate as to the outcome of a fictitious election. In brief, TES data suggest that Rob would have received a higher vote share than Doug. Though we hesitate to speculate as to the exact size of this difference, we are confident that Rob would not have been able to surpass the vote share received by the winner of the election, John Tory.

Besides serving as an interesting thought exercise, our analysis sheds light on the much-discussed composition of Ford Nation. Several of the characteristics that pundits have suggested identify this group have been confirmed. Both Rob and Doug performed best among individuals without a university education, visible minorities, residents of the periphery of the city, and voters under fifty. There are also attitudinal components to Ford Nation. The group is politically disaffected with respect to provincial and federal politics, though the opposite is true when asked about municipal politics (presumably since the incumbent mayor was a Ford). Finally, Ford supporters are also economically conservative and relatively likely to vote on the basis of the candidates' policies, as opposed to their personalities. These factors constitute the core of Ford Nation, regardless of which Ford is on the ballot.

Of course, our results leave us with a fascinating question: why did certain groups have different attitudes toward the brothers? We are unable to answer this using available data. What is it about Doug that made immigrants, men, and the economically liberal less fond of him than of his brother? This combination of factors is interesting given that two of these characteristics are negatively related to each other. According to TES data, men are, on average, less economically liberal than women ($p < 0.01$) (in contrast, immigration status is not correlated with either of the other two factors). The fact that Rob outperformed his brother among these groups, when these characteristics might be pulling electors in different directions, speaks to the varied interests of the groups that fall under the Ford Nation banner.

One final point to stress is that Ford Nation remains committed to the brand, despite the scandals that plagued Rob's tenure as mayor; support for Rob carried very strongly forward to Doug. TES respondents were asked a series of three questions in the pre-election period meant to tap into attitudes toward Rob's problematic behaviour: whether they agreed that the private behaviour of politicians is relevant to professional performance; whether people who make mistakes in their private lives should be given a second chance; and whether the media had given Rob a harder time than he deserved. There is no doubt that these questions are highly endogenous to vote intention – in fact, it is almost certain that attitudes toward the Fords affected responses to these questions. Not surprisingly, the differences between Ford and non-Ford supporters was striking: 77 per cent of respondents who stated that they would have voted for Rob agreed that the private behaviour of politicians is irrelevant (this figure was only 24 per cent among those who would not have supported him). Among Doug supporters, this value was comparable, at 73.8 per cent. We see a similar pattern in responses to the question about whether people who make mistakes in their private lives should be given a second chance: 90.9 per cent of Rob's hypothetical supporters agreed with the statement (as compared to only 66.2 per cent of those who would not have voted for him). This value barely changed when Doug was the candidate: 90.1 per cent of his supporters agreed with this position. Finally, it seems that there was a considerable amount of motivated reasoning affecting attitudes toward the media: 87.7 per cent of those who would have voted for Rob agreed that the media had given him a harder time than he deserved, compared to only 23.9 per cent of non-Rob supporters. Again, this attitude carried over well to Doug, for whom the comparable figure was 85.4 per cent. Ford Nation is therefore made up of a loyal group of individuals quite committed to seeing their candidates in a positive light.

Chapter 6

A New Mayor, a New Dawn for Toronto?

On 22 March 2016, Robert Bruce Ford, the sixty-fourth mayor of Toronto, passed away. Though he initially beat the cancer that had led him to drop out of the 2014 mayoral race, the illness returned in late October 2015, taking his life only six months later (Hopper, 2015, 29 October). For better or worse, Ford left a lasting impression on politics in Toronto. He served as Ward 2 councillor for nearly twelve years. As mayor, he drew unprecedented international attention to the City of Toronto, and even though he eventually dropped out of the 2014 mayoral race, that contest had been very much influenced by his past, his policies, and his personality.

Rob Ford remained a presence on City Council for the first year and a half of John Tory's tenure as mayor – and a thorn in the new mayor's side (Spurr, 2015, 11 March) until his death. For many of Ford's detractors, John Tory's election no doubt reflected a welcome return to normalcy in the mayor's office. News coverage of politics in the city two years after Tory's victory certainly suggests that City Hall was turning away from Ford-style melodrama. On 27 October 2016, two years after the highest-profile municipal election in Canadian history, newspapers and other media outlets covering City Hall rang out with riveting headlines about the city's new road safety plan (Simcoe, 2016, 27 October; Spurr, 2016, 27 October) and Toronto's decision not to go forward with a bid for Expo 2025 (Shum, 2016, 27 October). Politics in the city had changed sharply from just two years earlier, when Ford sat in the mayor's chair.

However, while many residents no doubt applauded the apparent return of decorum to City Hall, Tory's first few years in office continued to be dominated by many of the issues that had plagued both Rob Ford and his predecessor, David Miller, such as mass transit and garbage collection. As in most large cities in Canada, and in sharp contrast to many major American cities like New York and Chicago, Toronto's mayor is institutionally weak. Although Toronto's mayor acquired the authority to appoint the chairs of council committees and form a twelve-member executive committee in 2007, City Council remains the final decision-maker in Toronto. With no party system, and with an executive accounting for only 29 per cent of the votes on a forty-five-member council, the city's mayor must carefully navigate and build coalitions – often fragile and short-lived – to achieve any success in realizing his or her policy priorities. (How the mayor's authority and the executive committee will be affected by the recent reduction in the size of council from forty-four councillors to twenty-five remains to be seen.) So John Tory's first term as mayor followed the same bumpy road of his predecessors, sans the personal issues that had overshadowed Ford's tenure as mayor.

Transit and transportation have been the defining issues in Toronto politics for at least the last decade, ever since David Miller unveiled his Transit City plan in 2007. Not surprisingly, Tory's 2014 election platform focused heavily on both issues. After many years of conflict in council between proponents of LRT and subways, Tory proposed a new transit system called SmartTrack, which would make use of the rail lines used by the existing Greater Toronto Area commuter rail system, GO Transit. He also took a stand against levying tolls on city-owned highways and supported replacing the eastern section of the Gardiner Expressway, a city-owned highway that runs along the waterfront.

Despite his electoral success, his plans for transit and the city's highways caused him headaches, just as it did his predecessors. During the election, his SmartTrack proposal had come under fire from numerous directions, and over the course of his first term in office questions about the feasibility and utility of the plan remained (Moore, 2017, 16 March; Spurr, 2018, 4 August). In fact, a report from the province's transit body, Metrolinx, seemed to suggest that Tory's SmartTrack could actually reduce transit ridership in the city (Metrolinx, 2017; 2016; Moore, 2017, 16 March). Tory's decision as mayor to change his tune on road tolls by asking the province for the power to put tolls on city-owned highways angered his base in the suburbs (Pelley, 2016, 1 December; Powell, 2016, 4 December) and put him at odds with Ontario's then-premier Kathleen Wynne, undermining their otherwise affable relationship (Rider, 2017, 29 January).

Efforts to move forward with his position on the Gardiner Expressway and his plan to privatize garbage collection east of Yonge Street (Ford having privatized it in the west) revealed his limited control of City Council. While he won City Council support for his preferred option, which was to replace the eastern portion of the Gardiner Expressway and provide a new connection between the two city-owned highways, the margin of victory was very slim (24–21), with suburban councillors just beating opposition from downtown wards. His position also put him at odds with the city's Chief Planner and Medical Officer of Health (CBC News, 2015, 11 June). Council's later decision to support the costliest version of the new connection undermined Tory's image as a fiscally conservative mayor (CBC News, 2016, 31 March). Tory also came very close to defeat in council when he tried to push through his plan for garbage privatization. In the end, to stave off defeat, he had council refer the issue back to city staff indefinitely (Gray, 2017, 31 January).

All things considered, Tory's first term as mayor was less a radical departure from his predecessor's than a continuation of pre–Ford era city politics. Conflict remained on City Council, but the city's politics were no longer overshadowed by the mayor's behaviour. In 2014, voters returned 97 per cent of the incumbent city councillors who had sought re-election, and the composition of City Council has remained largely unchanged over the past decade. Thus, it should not be surprising that city politics under John Tory has followed the same old script.

This chapter goes behind the stories to examine how Torontonians have viewed the performance of Mayor Tory and the city in the post-Ford era. Setting aside feelings (positive or negative) related to ridding themselves of a scandal-ridden mayor, it is unclear how voters have viewed politics in the city since the 2014 election. Given that Torontonians have shown that they prioritize policy over personality (see chapter 4), it stands to reason that, especially in the absence of a mayor with a domineering personality, policy considerations should become even more prominent in the minds of voters.

Our "midterm" survey of nearly 1,500 Torontonians, conducted in the fall of 2016, found that evaluations of the city's policy performance in the two years following the 2014 election were generally negative. Yet at the same time, levels of satisfaction with elected city officials were overwhelmingly positive. This disconnect raises questions about the degree to which municipal politicians are held accountable for local policy outcomes; it also casts doubt on the extent to which Torontonians really do privilege policy considerations when evaluating politicians.

Accountability in the Inter-Election Period

So far in this book we have examined how Torontonians view municipal politics and politicians in general (chapter 1), observed how they viewed specific politicians during the 2014 mayoral campaign (chapter 2), looked at the dynamics of the 2014 campaign (chapter 3), attempted to explain the outcome of the 2014 contest (chapter 4), and examined the basis of support for Ford Nation (chapter 5). We hope these chapters have helped the reader better understand voters and municipal elections in a big city. However, findings and analyses based solely on data collected during or immediately after an election almost always have limitations.

Democracy does not end with each election, but too many studies of electoral behaviour do. Elections, particularly when news coverage is plentiful and the race is competitive, as was the case in the 2014 Toronto mayoral election, focus people's attention on the world of politics and governance. But what happens during the years *between* elections? Scholars have developed a strong theoretical and empirical understanding of political attitudes and voting behaviour in Canada. Despite its depth and breadth, however, there is one major limitation to this literature: most of this research is based on data collected during or just after election campaigns. Little is known about how voters reason about politics *between* elections. This failure to adequately study citizens between elections is noteworthy. Our system of representative democracy places important demands on both citizens and their representatives, and these obligations do not end once votes have been cast and tallied. Democratic theory suggests that citizens have a duty to be attentive to politics between elections, and the legitimacy of a representative democracy rests on the public's willingness and ability to monitor the performance of their elected representatives (Adsera et al., 2003). Put another way, electors' ability to hold politicians accountable come election time depends on political engagement between elections, not simply in the months leading up to them.

So why is it important for the study of accountability to consider political orientations between elections? The inter-election period is integral to the relationship between representatives and the governed, as it is performance during this period of governing that voters must assess if they are to hold representatives accountable. During election campaigns, politicians inform voters about the policies they intend to pursue. According to the "mandate" view of representation (Manin et al., 1999), voters choose the candidate who best reflects their policy preferences. Elected politicians thus have an interest in implementing this platform, for their performance will be measured against their promises. Whether a politician's policies stem from an election platform or not, an important function of elections is to allow voters to retrospectively reward or punish incumbents for good or bad performance (Achen & Bartels, 2004; Golder & Stramski, 2010; Klingemann et al., 1994; Miller et al., 1999; Miller & Stokes, 1963; Naurin, 2011). Elections can hold governments responsible for their past actions (Przeworski & Stokes, 1999), and they can better perform this function if voters are aware of the inter-election behaviour of politicians.

What then do Torontonians think about politics, the governance of their city, and their elected officials, if anything, when political news is less prominent and the stakes seem so much lower? Are electors satisfied with the city's policy performance, and with the performance of elected officials? Importantly, are government officials held accountable for the city's direction? This chapter seeks to answer such questions, which had important implications for the 2018 Toronto election, as well as, more generally, for our understanding of whether voters hold local politicians accountable, and if so, how.

Attributions of Responsibility

Away from the glare of an election and the accompanying news media spectacle, how do residents perceive their elected officials and the direction of the city? In many ways, Toronto residents' perceptions of their councillor and of City Council as a whole resemble how American voters view Congress and their respective representatives. The incumbency rate for city councillors in Toronto is very high, just as it is for representatives and senators in the United States. We also know that most voters in Toronto approve of their individual councillor but disapprove of City Council as a whole (Moore et al., 2017), just as Americans tend to approve of their own congresspersons but disapprove of Congress (Cook, 1979).

As in the United States, this dichotomy poses a problem for voters in Toronto. How can we reasonably expect the performance of City Council to improve if voters continue to re-elect the same councillors? Given the disproportionate focus on the race for mayor in the 2014 election, it may be that the electorate views the office of mayor as the institution that defines politics and governance in the city. If so, by replacing the incumbent mayor with a new one, voters may have felt that they were voting for change. However, as the discussion that opened this chapter suggests, the new mayor has done little to change the direction of the city. Given the institutional weakness of the mayor, this is hardly surprising.

Though we cannot directly test the contention using available data, there is some evidence that voters misunderstand authority and misplace credit and blame when evaluating local politicians. For instance, though municipal governments have little influence on the economy, voters' perception of the local economy have been shown to shape whether they will vote for the incumbent in municipal elections (Anderson et al., 2017; Cutler & Matthews, 2005). If voters are inaccurately attributing credit and blame for policy outcomes, how can they be expected to hold elected officials accountable for performance in areas that they *can* reasonably affect? Even when voters know little about the candidates or the issues in an election, it is commonly believed that voters should be able to draw on their experience with incumbent elected officials to form a judgment about whether they wish to "throw the rascals out" (vote for a new candidate) or stay with "the devil they know" (the incumbent). This type of limited information is vital to promoting democratic accountability.

An obvious impediment to such accountability would be if voters do not pay enough attention to politics during the inter-election period. If residents are not paying attention, then one can assume that they lack the information necessary to hold politicians to account. However, lack of attention cannot entirely explain election outcomes in the city. A voter who has failed to follow the city's direction over the four years between elections will still have an opinion about whether the city is getting better, or worse, or staying the same, and can use this opinion to determine whether to support the incumbent candidate, thus maintaining the status quo, or vote for an alternative. As Key (1966) suggests, voters can use this information to make such an assessment and thus to hold officials to account.

But what if voters are using evaluations of the direction of the city as information when voting, but are misplacing blame and credit when doing so? TES data suggest that voters have a limited understanding of the powers of the various orders of government in this country. Respondents were presented with a series of policy areas and asked which order of government was responsible for them. While at least a plurality of survey respondents understood that the municipal government (rather than provincial or federal) is primarily responsible for social housing (44.1 per cent), public transit (59.9 per cent), sewage and water (71.5 per cent), and police and fire services (67.9 per cent), a substantial share of the electorate held another level of government accountable for these policy areas. It seems reasonable to conjecture, therefore, that some voters hold local politicians accountable for policy outcomes outside of their control.

Further complicating attributions of responsibility and accountability is the fact that even *within* local government, city governance is complex. The mayor and councillors play a role, but so too do the provincial and federal governments, along with a host of government agencies. Throughout Canada, provincial governments, through legislation empowering or disempowering municipalities, significantly affect the latter's ability to address various policy issues. In Ontario, the province has become the *de facto* regional planner for the Greater Toronto Area through legislation such as the *Places to Grow Act, 2005*, and for subsequent growth plans for the Greater Golden Horseshoe, a larger region encompassing the GTA. There have also been calls for the province's regional transit authority, Metrolinx, to take over the TTC and other municipal transit systems in the GTA (Spurr, 2017, 27 November).

Within the city, the Mayor of Toronto and the executive committee (appointed by the mayor) are supposed to set policy direction in the city, through budgets and other mechanisms. However, while Toronto's mayor does typically attempt to set the agenda for City Council, institutionally and in practice it is with council that the authority to govern and implement policy lies. Mayor Tory's inability to pass his plan to privatize garbage collection in the city's east end is just one example of council's pre-eminence. Rob Ford, more than any other mayor, witnessed the might of council when it stripped him of most of his authority, placing it instead in the deputy mayor, at the end of his third year as mayor (Church & Hui, 2013, 24 May). The weakness of the mayor's office, for all the publicity surrounding the mayoral election, may lead to particularly low "clarity of responsibility" in Toronto, which in turn may prevent voters from identifying who is responsible for the state of the city.

The rest of this chapter asks whether Torontonians attribute responsibility for policy outcomes to municipal politicians, including the mayor and individual councillors, or to council as a whole, during non-election times. To that end, we examine whether there is a relationship between assessments of policy performance in a variety of policy areas, and those of a politician's performance (working under the assumption that, come election time, evaluations of performance are strongly correlated with vote choice). Our data reveal a complex and somewhat surprising relationship between assessments of policy outcomes and the performance of Toronto's politicians.

Results

All data for this chapter are based on responses to a "mid-term" survey of electors, conducted in late fall 2016 (at the halfway point of Tory's first term as mayor). Measuring attitudes at this point in time provides insight into how voters view politics outside of the campaign setting, when media coverage is less exhaustive and the average Torontonian will almost certainly be paying less attention to politics and politicians. Even without the constant glare of the electorate's attention, elected officials are busy governing during this period, making decisions (or not) that can have important effects on Torontonians' lives. By two years into their mandate, politicians have had ample opportunity to make their mark on local government. So it is important to investigate how voters view municipal politics and politicians during this period.

Before considering how satisfied electors are with the city's policy performance, and whether or not they attribute this performance to elected officials, it is worth briefly considering how electors view local politics itself. How interested are Torontonians in local politics, and what type of impact do they imagine municipal government has upon their lives? The results of the 2016 mid-term survey point to an interesting contradiction on this front. In short, Torontonians are less interested in local politics than in either federal or provincial politics, but respondents nevertheless tend to believe that the municipal government has a relatively significant impact on their lives. The average level of interest (on a scale from 0 to 10) was 6.6 for municipal politics, compared to 6.9 and 7.3[1] for provincial and federal politics, respectively (all differences are significant at $p < 0.05$).[2] Of the three levels of government, therefore, the average Torontonian shows the least interest in the municipal one.

One conceivable explanation for this relatively low level of interest may spring from the belief that municipal politics simply *matters* less to electors. Are Torontonians relatively uninterested in municipal politics because they believe it has less impact on their lives than the other orders of government? Such an explanation does not square with 2016 survey data.

Survey respondents were asked to rank the orders of government with respect to how much of an impact those governments had on their lives. The data suggest that respondents believe Toronto's government to be relatively influential: 31.2 per cent of those interviewed were of the opinion that the city had a greater impact than either of the other two levels of government (41.4 per cent selected the federal government as most impactful, while only 27.4 per cent said the same of the province). A sizable majority (58.6 per cent) believed that Toronto had a greater impact on their lives than at least one of the constitutionally recognized orders of government. Such a pattern points to an interesting contradiction: even though Torontonians tend to believe that local politics matter, they are relatively uninterested in local affairs.

It is against this backdrop that we turn to consider the matter of accountability, and whether voters are assigning local politicians credit or blame for the performance of the city. Though most Torontonians believe the local government has a relatively big impact on their lives, they show, on average, less interest in this level of government than any other. Low levels of interest may translate into low levels of understanding of the performance of municipal officials. Nevertheless, on the assumption that they view the Toronto government as relatively important, we expect that Torontonians will hold their elected officials responsible for the city's performance.

Performance of the City and Politicians

Before considering whether local politicians are assigned credit or blame for the city's policy performance, we must first consider how electors view the city's direction on a number of policy fronts. Survey respondents were asked a standard retrospective question on whether they thought the situation in Toronto had improved since the 2014 election, in five policy areas: public transit, property taxes, traffic and congestion, housing affordability, and managing Toronto's finances. (These issues were chosen because they mirrored those included in the 2014 survey.) The results of these questions are represented in Figure 6.1, which shows the share of respondents who thought things had gotten better, gotten worse, or stayed about the same in the two years since the election. If the public holds positive views of the city's performance, and voters assign credit or blame to their elected officials for that performance, it would seem to bode well for incumbents seeking re-election.

The single most important takeaway from Figure 6.1 is that very few Torontonians believed that the city had seen improvement on *any* policy front since 2014.[3] In all five policy areas, no more than one in six respondents believed that things had gotten better; on average across the policies, only 8.3 per cent of electors were of the view that the situation had improved. By contrast, the modal view for all but one policy area (city finances) was that things had worsened. Views on property taxes, traffic and congestion, and housing affordability were particularly abysmal, with a majority believing that things had gotten worse for all three.

Given that most electors saw the policy situation as deteriorating (or at least as not improving), and the fact that they viewed Toronto's government as relatively influential, one might expect levels of satisfaction with city politicians to be as negative as assessments of the city's policy performance. If politicians were blamed for this poor performance, it could bode poorly for their re-election prospects. Is there a relationship between evaluations of policy direction and assessments of the decision-makers themselves? Before answering this question, we must consider how politicians were judged by the electorate. To that end, Figure 6.2 shows levels of satisfaction with the performance of the mayor, City Council as a whole, and respondents' individual councillors.

In light of the poor assessments of the city's policy performance observed in Figure 6.1, Figure 6.2 reveals astonishingly positive attitudes toward municipal politicians. Fewer than one in five Torontonians

Figure 6.1. Policy directions since 2014

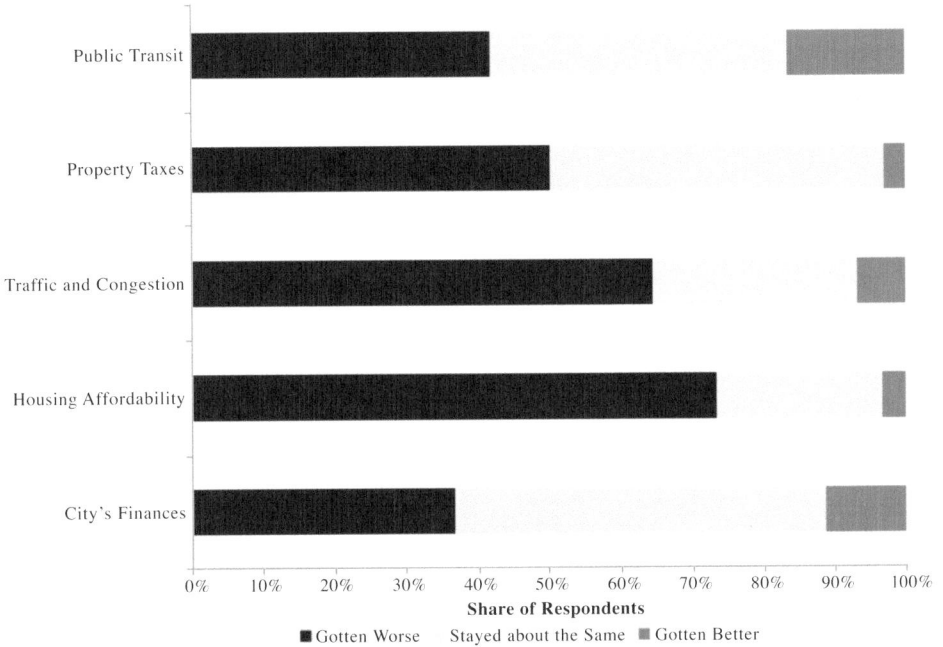

Figure 6.2. Satisfaction with elected officials

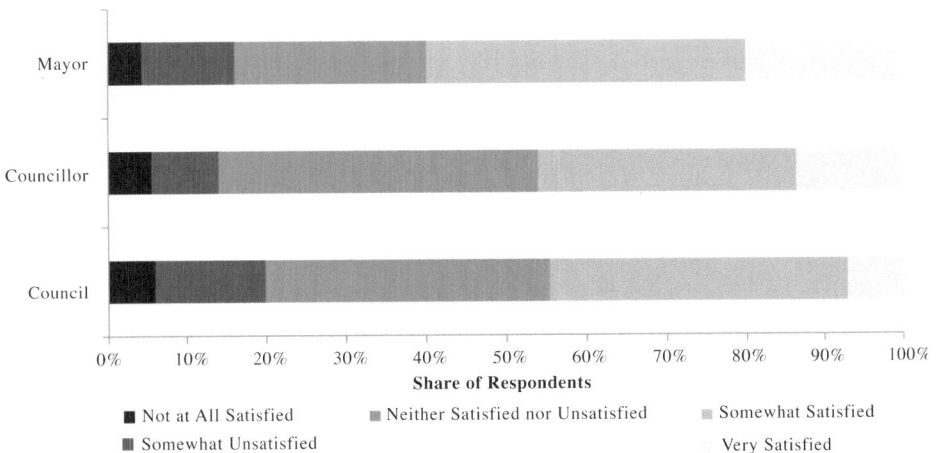

were dissatisfied with the mayor, their councillor, or council as a whole. Indeed, levels of satisfaction were very high: 44.6 per cent of respondents were satisfied (very or somewhat) with City Council, as were 46.0 per cent with their individual councillor. Though a noteworthy segment of the population is on the fence regarding all three types of elected officials (being neither satisfied nor dissatisfied), positive assessments were considerably more common than negative ones.

Mayor Tory, in particular, was viewed positively by Torontonians: 59.9 per cent of respondents were either somewhat or very satisfied with his performance. At 20.0 per cent, Tory also received the highest level of "very satisfied" respondents. Slightly more respondents (15.9 per cent) were dissatisfied with him (very or somewhat) than were dissatisfied with their local councillor (13.8 per cent), so he did have his fair share of detractors. Respondents had modestly more positive assessments of their city councillors than they did of council as a whole. Such a finding is consistent with American research, which suggests that people's levels of satisfaction with Congress are lower than they are toward their individual congresspersons (Cook, 1979).

The big takeaway from Figures 6.1 and 6.2 is the apparent disconnect between assessments of policy performance and satisfaction with the performance of elected officials. Despite overwhelmingly negative assessments of policy performance, the politicians elected to influence those policy areas tended to be viewed in a positive light. These contrasting results are all the more confounding given that local government was widely seen as comparatively influential. Such a finding leads one to ask whether there is any relationship between evaluations of policy performance and satisfaction with the performance of those elected in 2014. It is to this question that we now turn.

Policy Performance and Satisfaction with Politicians

In any system of government in which power is shared by more than one person, lines of accountability will inevitably be blurred. For voters to hold decision-makers accountable (either punishing or rewarding them for their track record), they must consider the government's performance, but also the extent to which each politician influenced that performance. Torontonians perceived that the city was going in the "wrong" direction on the policy fronts considered in Figure 6.1. Were Toronto's politicians not being held accountable for this? Alternatively, were they being held accountable for some policy areas but not others? And was the mayor being credited/blamed for different things than council or councillors?

To consider these questions, in Table 6.1 we present the results of a series of ordinary least squares regression models. In each instance, the outcome variables (the ones we are seeking to explain) are the above-mentioned indicators of levels of satisfaction with the mayor, council,

Table 6.1. Policy performance and satisfaction with elected officials

	Mayor		Councillor		Council	
Public transit	0.07 (0.02)**	0.09 (0.02)**	0.02 (0.02)	0.02 (0.02)	0.05 (0.02)*	0.05 (0.02)*
Property taxes	0.05 (0.03)	0.04 (0.03)	0.00 (0.03)	0.01 (0.03)	0.02 (0.03)	0.02 (0.03)
Traffic and congestion	0.00 (0.03)	0.02 (0.03)	−0.01 (0.03)	0.00 (0.03)	0.05 (0.03)	0.05 (0.03)
Housing affordability	0.00 (0.03)	0.00 (0.03)	0.13 (0.03)**	0.11 (0.03)**	0.09 (0.03)**	0.07 (0.03)*
City finances	0.25 (0.02)**	0.25 (0.02)**	0.12 (0.02)**	0.12 (0.02)**	0.18 (0.02)**	0.17 (0.02)**
18–34	–	−0.03 (0.02)	–	0.01 (0.02)	–	−0.02 (0.02)
Over 55	–	0.04 (0.02)*	–	0.04 (0.02)*	–	−0.02 (0.02)
Female	–	0.02 (0.02)	–	0.04 (0.02)**	–	0.05 (0.01)**
University education	–	0.00 (0.02)	–	−0.01 (0.02)	–	−0.02 (0.01)
Home owner	–	0.03 (0.02)	–	0.05 (0.02)**	–	0.03 (0.02)
Interest in municipal politics	–	0.07 (0.03)*	–	0.12 (0.03)**	–	0.10 (0.03)**
Political knowledge	–	0.05 (0.03)*	–	−0.06 (0.02)*	–	−0.05 (0.02)*
Ideology	–	0.01 (0.00)	–	0.00 (0.00)	–	0.00 (0.00)
Constant	0.53 (0.02)**	0.38 (0.04)**	0.54 (0.02)**	0.41 (0.04)**	0.46 (0.02)**	0.40 (0.04)**
R-squared	0.133	0.167	0.056	0.093	0.106	0.132

Entries report coefficients and standard errors (in parentheses).

* $p < 0.05$
** $p < 0.01$
n = 1,288

and councillors. The variables have been coded from 0 (not at all satisfied) to 1 (very satisfied). The primary explanatory variables in the models are the measures of policy performance for the five policy areas considered above. If the mayor, council, or councillors are being credited with the city's policy performance, then these factors should have positive and statistically significant relationships with levels of satisfaction.[4] Such findings would suggest that the better the city is perceived as performing, the more satisfied respondents are with politicians.

For each outcome variable, we run two models. The first includes the five policy variables alone, while the second adds variables to control for socio-demographic and attitudinal factors (these allow us to account for the possibility that attitudes toward policy may be affected by such characteristics). Socio-demographic variables include age (dummies for under 35 and over 55, with 35–55 as the baseline), gender, education (university education versus none), and homeownership (versus renting). Attitudinal variables include a measure of interest in municipal politics (the same one considered above), an index of political knowledge, and an indicator of political ideology (0 = left, 1 = right). All explanatory variables are coded from 0 to 1, so entries in the table can be interpreted as the effect on satisfaction of going from minimum to maximum values of the independent variables (a one-unit change).

Table 6.1 tells a complex but intriguing story about how municipal electors attribute responsibility to elected officials for policy performance. Assessments of policy performance were negative, and levels of satisfaction with elected officials were generally positive, but several policy variables in the table are statistically significant. This finding suggests that politicians are being assigned credit/blame for policy performance in some fields but not in others. At the same time, there are differences between the models with respect to which policy variables are significant.[5] This pattern suggests that electors hold different politicians accountable for different policy areas.

Satisfaction with the mayor is linked to evaluations of public transit and the city's finances (but not property taxes, traffic, or affordability). Those who view the situation on either of these fronts as having improved in the previous two years are more likely to report being satisfied with Tory than are those who think the policy situation has deteriorated. Tory's link to the city's finances is particularly strong: the coefficient of 0.25 is the largest of any in the table. His fate in the 2018 election may thus have been influenced by the city's performance on transit, but even more so the financial health of the municipal government.

Levels of satisfaction with local councillors and council as a whole are also associated with the city's financial performance. However, evaluations of these politicians are also affected by housing affordability, an issue from which Tory seems to be insulated (such a finding is interesting in light of the fact that respondent attitudes toward performance on this policy are more negative than for any other issue). It seems that City Council as a whole is being held accountable for public transit, but individual councillors are not.

Electors thus assign credit and blame for different policy areas to different politicians. While all groups are held accountable for the state of the city's finances, Tory is viewed as being responsible for transit, while support for councillors is affected by evaluations of housing affordability. Short of explaining why such differences exist (or whether they might apply to other settings and times or are unique to this particular set of elected officials and this setting), the finding that politicians of the same level of government are held differentially responsible for policy performance is an important one.[6] Politicians might do well to recognize this fact and focus on the issues on which they are judged.

Turning to the specific results, the fact that the public seems to hold the mayor responsible for the city's finances is not surprising. After all, it is the mayor and his Executive Committee who are largely responsible for creating the budget. However, council as whole has the authority to pass or alter the budget, and the process of creating the budget requires the mayor to work with council to ensure that a majority of councillors support it; thus, the public is correct to attribute the state of the City's finances to all parties.

That both the mayor and the council are held accountable, to varying degrees, for transit is also reasonable, given the ongoing saga of transit in the city. It seems that with each new mayor, a new plan for city transit materializes, and Tory has been no exception. His SmartTrack proposal was a new and significant departure from past plans for transit in the city, and therefore, transit is an issue that the public is likely to associate with him. Setting aside various mayors' plans, council as whole bears much of the responsibility for the continued flip-flopping on new and improved transit, however. Council under both Ford and Tory has repeatedly changed its mind when it comes to the direction of transit in the city, and this has led to delays and repeated backtracking. Given that transit is an important policy area that continues to receive significant media attention, voters in Toronto are largely correct to attribute the state of transit to City Council. However, given that many of the problems surrounding transit seem to arise from the ever-changing whims of city councillors, that electors do not associate transit with individual councillors may explain why they are not held responsible for the actions of council on the transit file.

Our results suggest that Toronto voters attribute responsibility on some important policy issues to the appropriate individuals or body. However, voters' attribution of affordable housing first to individual councillors and then to council as whole, but not to the mayor, is somewhat mystifying, as is the lack of attribution of traffic and congestion and property tax issues to any elected official or body in the city. The city is responsible for subsidized housing but has few tools at its disposal to address housing affordability in general. Though the recent addition of inclusionary zoning – a tool allowing municipalities to require that a share of new housing development be set aside for affordable housing – to the city's repertoire of planning tools may change this somewhat, the province and the federal government are much better situated to address the broader issue of affordability. More importantly, since his election in 2014, John Tory has been the most vocal elected official in Toronto on the issue of affordability, and he has actively lobbied the province to address the issue. Thus, if any municipal official should be associated with the issue, it should be the mayor.

In contrast, and despite holding the mayor and council accountable for transit, electors apparently believe that neither influence traffic and congestion, despite their mutual responsibility for the city's roads and two city highways. Last, and most perplexing, respondents to our survey made no connection between any city official and the issue of property taxes. Given that the mayor and council set the property tax rate each year, and how negatively voters respond to property tax hikes, this last finding seems to defy all logic.

Conclusion

While Torontonians seem to correctly assign some policy issues to the mayor and council, many voters apparently lack the ability, or willingness, to draw a link between the city's policy performance and the politicians they have elected. There is a stark contrast between voters' largely positive assessment of elected officials in Figure 6.2 and their assessment of the direction of the city on policy issues in Figure 6.1. Moreover, the results of Table 6.1 show that attributions for responsibility are somewhat unpredictable and vary according to position.

Though there are multiple policy areas in each model that are related to evaluations of politicians' performance, the explanatory power of the models in Table 6.1 is relatively limited. The pseudo-R^2 values in the models with policy variables only range from 0.056 (for councillor) to

0.133 (for the mayor), and these values increase only slightly with the addition of controls. The policy performance variables thus account for only a small fraction of the variation in the outcome variables. Given the obvious disconnect between aggregate-level attitudes toward policy outcomes and politicians, this is perhaps not surprising. Substantively, this suggests that when our survey respondents evaluate incumbents, policy performance plays a small role.

These findings do not bode well for the accountability function of future elections in Toronto. The lack of a link between policy outcomes and evaluations of politicians is of obvious relevance to vote choice. There is little reason to think that voters will be able to do a better job of linking policy and politicians when formulating vote decisions in the future. This disconnect is likely to be good news for incumbents.

Though perhaps a bit disheartening, these results are in keeping with the observations from chapter 4 and suggest that policy considerations (either promises or outcomes) have a limited impact on evaluations of politicians. In chapter 4, we found that the majority of Torontonians claimed to prioritize policy over personality when making their vote decisions in the 2014 election. Despite such attestations, we also found that most voters did not support the mayoral candidate whose policies most closely resembled their own (which in most cases was Doug Ford). While, strictly speaking, there was no incumbent to evaluate in the 2014 election, Ford can certainly be viewed as a pseudo-incumbent, and his policy positions, as well as those of the other candidates, were widely circulated in the news media. Nevertheless, most voters seemed unable, or unwilling, to make their vote decisions by comparing candidate policy positions to their own policy preferences. Given the failure of voters to make such connections in one of the highest-profile elections in recent Canadian history, it is not surprising that they have a hard time attributing responsibility for policy outcomes away from the high-information environment of the election period. These findings also largely explain the high rate of incumbency among Toronto city councillors. Given that voters are unable to assess the performance of incumbents, and given that elections for council face far less media scrutiny than the mayoral election, it is hardly surprising that voters continue to elect the same representatives despite their negative assessment of the direction of the city on important policy issues.

These results raise an important question about the vibrancy of local democracy in Toronto. For many, elections are a means for the public to punish or reward incumbents based on past performance. In fact, the ability to "throw the bums out" is of vital importance to any democracy. For elections to serve this purpose, however, the public must be able to assess the performance of their elected officials in light of policy out-comes, something voters in Toronto seem largely incapable of doing.

The reasons for our findings are unclear and certainly call for future research. It may be that electors fundamentally misunderstand the power and responsibilities of those whom they elect to local office. And it may be that the media focuses so much on topics other than policy (such as sensational stories about the private behaviour of politicians) that policy considerations are not central in evaluations of government officials. It may therefore be the case that electors simply do not care much about municipal public policy, and thus they hold incumbents accountable for factors other than policy outcomes. Whatever the explanation for this pattern, the results in this chapter suggest there is a significant demo-cratic deficit in Canada's largest city. It remains to be seen whether this has changed for the better since 2014.

Chapter 7

Portrait of a Municipal Voter

The Toronto Election Study is the first large-scale municipal election study ever conducted in Canada. With information gathered from 3,000 electors in 2014, and a follow-up study of another 1,500 individuals in 2016, we have been able to paint a comprehensive portrait of the Toronto voter. The numerous and varied findings of this study represent a sizable addition to the underdeveloped though developing literature in the field of Canadian municipal political behaviour. This in-depth examination of an exceptionally high-profile election in the country's biggest city should be of significant interest to both observers and practitioners of Toronto politics, who may be keen to understand local elections in the country's most powerful and important city.

As noted in previous chapters, the 2014 Toronto mayoral election was exceptional for a multitude of reasons. Drawing media attention from around the world and boasting a number of well-known candidates for mayor, it was perhaps the most high-profile municipal election in the country's history. With an outgoing mayor who had done both the American talk show circuit and a stint in rehab, the election captured the attention of Torontonians and non-Torontonians alike. The substantial media coverage of the election, even if often focused on Rob Ford, provided Toronto voters with unusually high levels of information about the campaign and the candidates.

The City of Toronto itself is quite distinct in ways that also suggest that residents should be among the best-informed in the country. With a population of over 2.7 million, Toronto is 60 per cent larger than Canada's second-largest municipality (Montreal). Its constituency is the sixth-largest of all governments in Canada, after only the federal government and four provinces (Ontario, Quebec, Alberta, and British Columbia). Toronto being Canada's largest city and media market, its municipal elections receive a disproportionate amount of media coverage, even in years when the mayoral election is less contentious than it was in 2014. Torontonians, therefore, should be among the most informed and knowledgeable municipal voters in Canada. Despite the unique nature of Toronto in general, and of its 2014 election in particular, however, we expect that many of the lessons from the Toronto Election Study are applicable to other Canadian cities.

This concluding chapter reflects on what our findings from a single election in one city tell us about municipal electors elsewhere in Canada, as well as in Toronto more generally. Though the data presented here are from only two points in time (2014 and 2016), they nevertheless allow us to make a series of comments about voters and non-voters in other places on other occasions. The fact that the 2014 election was, in many ways, an "extreme case" enables us to draw more general inferences about how electors might reason about and behave during local elections.

Of course, each election is unique in terms of candidates, issues, and (sometimes) scandals. We would be remiss if we did not also acknowledge that there is a noteworthy amount of institutional variation between Canadian municipalities. While most local elections are non-partisan, parties do contest elections in some cities, such as Vancouver and Montreal. Some communities have an additional upper-tier municipality, such as the regional and county municipalities in Ontario, and some municipalities are subdivided into community-level entities, such as the borough councils in Quebec.[1] There are also variations in terms of electoral systems. For instance, Vancouver employs an at-large electoral system to elect councillors, and London, Ontario, used a ranked-ballot system in 2018. Finally, cities can differ substantially in terms of population, geographic size, and ethnic and linguistic diversity. In short, Canadian cities differ from one another in various and numerous ways.

However, local governments and the populations they serve also share many foundational and defining features. Municipalities provide more or less the same services across the country. They are all creatures of the provinces, subject to the whims of provincial governments, and they are all made up of politicians concerned with a very limited geographic area. Municipal voters are also similar to one another in that they are all members of three "political worlds" (federal, provincial, and local) and thus inhabit a multi-level context in which decision-making authority is divided and accountability can be blurry.

Perhaps paradoxically, then, the exceptional nature of the 2014 Toronto mayoral election enables us to use TES data to draw conclusions about other municipalities. The city's sheer size, the high-profile candidates, and the extraordinarily high levels of media attention made Toronto in 2014 an extreme case – a most likely case, if you will, on several dimensions. Considering the low-information context typical of municipal elections, the 2014 election is most likely to demonstrate the maximums on several dimensions. Importantly, the case represents a minimum level of difference from elections at other levels of government; the 2014 contest had more in common with provincial and federal elections than almost all other local elections. The vast attention the media paid to the campaign, and the high levels of public interest and attention (based on indicators from survey data, and assuming that voter turnout was related to these factors), coupled with the obvious partisan ties of the three major candidates, meant that electors were more likely to be engaged in and informed about this local election than they would have been in almost any other local context.

Thus, the unique features of this election, coupled with the fundamental similarities between Toronto and the country's other cities, allow us to infer that many of the lessons from the TES can indeed be applied elsewhere in the country. In short, we are able to generalize several of our findings to other contexts *because of* the exceptional nature of this case.

We consider what the 2014 Toronto Election Study can tell us about other Canadian cities by focusing on two questions, first introduced in chapter 1 of this work. First, how do Canadian municipal voters reason and make decisions in a non-partisan setting–or at least a setting where parties do not structure the campaigns? Again, the vast majority of local elections in this country are contested by individuals rather than political parties. At the federal and provincial levels, parties structure campaigns and government, and they also provide a vital information shortcut for voters during elections. Though the 2014 mayoral candidates had ties to parties at other orders of government, other research on this election shows that voters were far from unanimous with respect to the links they perceived between the candidates and their respective parties (McGregor et al., 2016). At the same time, the lack of institutionalized parties, and the structure they bring to campaigns, means that despite the partisan histories of the candidates, the 2014 election was far from a partisan campaign; it was, perhaps, a quasi-partisan election. Still, it was not *formally* partisan, and lessons from 2014 provide valuable insight into how electors in Canadian cities operate in the absence of familiar and important party cues.

Second, we consider the more fundamental question of how much (or little) municipal elections and politics actual matter to Canadians. Voter turnout in municipal elections tends to be significantly lower than in federal or provincial elections, despite the many important responsibilities of this order of government. If levels of interest and engagement are low in the largest city and media market in the country, it is hard to imagine that electors elsewhere would be more interested and engaged. Similarly, if the population in a city with an operating budget of roughly $10 billion does not believe that municipal government matters to them, then there is little reason to expect this not to be the case elsewhere.

The next pages of this chapter provide answers to these questions based on our findings from the Toronto Election Study. We conclude by making the case that local elections represent a vast and relatively untapped resource for scholars of political behaviour and Canadian politics.

Non-Partisan Municipal Elections and Voters

The very existence of non-partisan elections at the municipal level disproves Schattschneider's (1942) famous decree that democracy cannot be imagined without political parties. Parties do indeed dominate at the federal and provincial levels, and scholars have conducted a great deal of research into how Canadians formulate attitudes and behave in a partisan setting. Relatively little is known, however, about how those same electors reason and make choices in the absence of parties, as is the case in the vast majority of Canadian municipalities, including Toronto. How, then, do voters make decisions when partisan information is either scarce (where candidates have past partisan ties) or completely lacking (where they have no such ties)?

Given that parties and partisanship are such important staples of provincial and federal elections, we might expect the absence of such factors at the local level to have dramatic effects on the decision-making calculus of electors. Without party labels as a shortcut, voters must base their decisions on other factors. In such a scenario, it is likely that policy considerations and evaluations of candidates will, *ceteris paribus*, be of heightened importance, as voters seek out different types of information on which to base their vote choices. A corollary of such a statement is that campaigns should also be of relatively greater importance to election outcomes, as campaigns enable electors to gather and synthesize information about the candidates and their policies. In Canada at the local level, the absence of parties compels voters to reason in a unique manner.

Yet TES data suggest that the last five and a half weeks of the 2014 Toronto mayoral campaign (a period of comparable length to federal and provincial campaigns, which corresponded with the period after the candidate nomination deadline) did not have a discernible impact on the election outcome. At the same time, despite claims by Torontonians that policy considerations were central to their mayoral vote choices, there is evidence that voters did a poor job of selecting the candidate they might have had they based their decisions solely on policy (and had perfect knowledge of the policy positions of the candidates). Such results are of relevance for other local elections in Canada.

Again, given the absence of official party cues, we might expect an electoral campaign to play a relatively major role in shaping voter decisions. It has long been recognized that voter partisanship is one of the best predictors of an early voting decision (see Campbell et al., 1960). If individuals with a partisan attachment tend to finalize their vote decisions well in advance of a campaign, then the opposite situation – an absence of party cues – should lead to later vote decisions, making the campaign period more important. For many candidates, the campaign is their first and only opportunity to convey themselves and their platform to the public.

Yet we found that in Toronto in 2014 the absence of political parties did not necessarily mean that the campaign period was more important to the election outcome. In the absence of prejudices that inevitably exist in partisan elections, one might expect voters to be more responsive to information transmitted and received during the course of a local campaign. Information transfer can begin happening as soon as candidates announce their intentions, but the actual campaign period is far more intense and filled with specific announcements that might make a difference. Scholars of federal and provincial politics have moved past the "minimal effects" thesis to conclude that campaigns can indeed have important effects in partisan elections, whereas we, in fact, found very little evidence of attitudinal change during the (intense) final five and a half weeks of the 2014 Toronto campaign (see chapter 3). TES data reveal that most voters made their decisions well in advance of election day and that they stuck to those decisions through the final weeks of the campaign.

If the campaign did not affect vote choices in Toronto in 2014, then it is possible that campaigns have a limited effect on outcomes in other non-partisan elections. Even in the media-saturated, information-rich context of Toronto in 2014, we found no evidence that the final weeks of the campaign affected the election outcome. Of course, an important countervailing force to consider in this discussion is the quasi-partisan nature of the race. Partisan ties may have conceivably had a dampening effect on attitudinal change. At the same time, however, there was no incumbent in 2014, and the race was much more competitive than most local elections. Both of these factors suggest that the 2014 race should have had the potential for significant attitudinal change (compared to other elections in Toronto and elsewhere where an incumbent may be present). Still, the absence of formal political parties does not necessarily bring with it a great deal of attitudinal fluctuation in the closing stages of local electoral contests. Future research is required to more fully understand campaign effects in local elections.[2]

Regardless of when vote decisions are made, voters must determine which factors to base their decisions on. In the absence of formal party cues, one might expect policy considerations to be more important for voters' decisions. The personal characteristics of candidates are another feature that some voters may choose to base their decisions on, particularly in a context in which one of the contenders is a personally divisive figure (like Rob Ford). In terms of information on both policy and personality, there was certainly no shortage provided to Torontonians in 2014. On the policy front, there is evidence that voters were able to discern clear ideological differences between the three major contenders (McGregor et al., 2016). So it seems highly likely that messages about policy were being received by Torontonians, and given the significant media coverage afforded the election, there is reason to believe that Torontonians were as informed as any electorate in a Canadian city is ever likely to be.

Despite the widespread availability of policy information, we discovered in chapter 4 that policy promises were perhaps less important to vote decisions than many Torontonians would care to admit. In that chapter we considered the phenomenon of "correct" voting (or voting for the candidate with policy positions most closely matching one's own). In the case of the 2014 mayoral election, Torontonians arguably did a poor job of voting in such a manner. The rate of correct voting was estimated at 57.5 per cent, and it was determined that, had all voters cast their ballots "correctly," Doug Ford would have won the mayoralty.

This, despite the fact that a significant majority of Torontonians claimed to have prioritized policy over the personal characteristics of the candidates when making vote decisions: 73 per cent of TES respondents reported that their vote decisions were driven by policy rather than the personalities of the contenders. There are at least two possible reasons for this apparent disconnect between stated behaviour and rates of correct voting: either Torontonians were unable to identify the candidate with policy positions that most closely matched their own, or they chose not to base their decisions on this knowledge (and potentially answered the TES survey question about the basis of their decision wrongfully). The reason for this disconnect is less important, however, than the fact that it exists.

There is good reason to believe that the non-partisan nature of the Toronto election negatively affected the ability of Torontonians to vote correctly. In their work on correct voting in the United States, Lau & Redlawsk (1997) suggest that the availability of partisan labels significantly improves the ability of voters to identify the candidate who best reflects their personal preferences. Their logic is that knowledge of party ideology and general policy orientations can be learned over time and that, provided the party does not make a sudden and dramatic shift, this past information can provide insight into the policy stances of current candidates.

We therefore expect that the absence of political parties (and the informational shortcuts they provide) had a negative effect on rates of correct voting in Toronto in 2014, and that a similar effect will be present in other non-partisan local elections in Canada. That is, without the vital informational shortcut provided by party labels, the ability of voters to identify and support the candidate who best reflects their own policy preferences is diminished. Moreover, it is highly conceivable that the lack of parties will have a stronger effect in other settings. If this is the case in information-rich Toronto, in an election in which two of the major candidates had past affiliations with parties at other levels of government (even if these associations were not universally understood by voters), there is little reason to suspect that voters in other non-partisan municipalities will be any better at identifying which candidate's policies closely match their own. Again, the extreme nature of Toronto 2014 allows us to speculate as to how voters might reason in other settings, where partisan cues are weaker. Though such a contention is no doubt worth testing, TES results suggest very strongly that non-partisan local elections may present a challenge for voters who wish to base their decisions on policy. Indeed, the absence of party cues makes the local level a particularly interesting one for future study of the concept of correct voting.

TES data, and the exceptional nature of the 2014 Toronto mayoral election, together allow us to make two claims about how voters in Canadian cities make their vote decisions in a non-partisan setting. First, the absence of parties does not necessarily suggest that the campaign period will be of substantial importance to an election outcome. Second, absent the informational shortcut provided by formal party cues, voters in Canadian local elections face a particularly difficult challenge when attempting to identify the candidate who best reflects their policy preferences. If this was true in the information rich-context of the 2014 Toronto mayoral election, there is little reason not to expect at least the same in other Canadian cities. We invite further research that tests these contentions.

Voter Engagement at the Municipal Level

The finding that Torontonians did a poor job of voting correctly in the 2014 election is perhaps indicative of a lack of public interest or engagement. In fact, possibly the most important result from Toronto that we can generalize to electors in other Canadian cities relates to orientations toward municipal government. In short, even in a city where turnout is very high by municipal standards, where the candidates are well known and media coverage is intense, and where the municipal budget and bureaucracy are both immense, we find evidence that local elections and politics are viewed as relatively unimportant and uninteresting.

Indeed, chapter 1 provides ample evidence that Torontonians attach relatively little importance to local government. Roughly 50 per cent of respondents are of the opinion that the city has less impact on their lives than the federal and provincial governments. Even during the height of a municipal election campaign, Torontonians were less interested in local than in federal politics (though there was no observed difference in interest with the provincial level). They were also less likely to believe that voting in municipal elections is a duty (as opposed to a choice).

If such findings are observed with respect to an extreme case such as Toronto in 2014, it is hard to argue that they cannot be generalized to the municipal electorate in more conventional times, or to other Canadian cities. If electors are uninterested and unengaged in local politics in Toronto, when attitudes were measured in the midst of an exceptionally sensationalized election, we cannot reasonably expect them to be interested and engaged elsewhere, all other things being equal. TES data suggest strongly, therefore, that Canadian municipal voters seem to attach little importance to local politics. Comparatively low rates of voter turnout at the municipal level across the country seem to confirm this assessment. Turnout in Toronto in 2014 was just shy of 55 per cent, while voter participation in local elections across the country is nearer to 40 per cent. If one assumes that turnout is associated with the belief that local politics matters, our results paint a dreary picture of attitudes toward local government outside of Toronto.

Perhaps related to the seeming lack of interest in local politics is our finding, based on the "midterm" survey of Torontonians in 2016, that there is a significant disconnect between evaluations of the city's performance (which were overwhelmingly negative) and evaluations of the performance of politicians themselves (overwhelmingly positive). Though in some policy areas we found a modest relationship between assessments of policy and politicians, overall policy considerations had very little impact on evaluations of elected officials. Our findings suggest that voters either do not or cannot track the behaviour of their elected municipal officials and their policy decisions between elections. Such a result is perhaps not surprising: if Torontonians are disengaged and uninterested in local politics at campaign time, it is unlikely that they will be more attentive *between* elections. This lack of attentiveness could signal that Torontonians have a diminished capacity to hold their local officials accountable for local conditions.

If the relationship between attitudes toward performance and evaluations of politicians is weak in Toronto, we see no reason to expect it to be otherwise in other municipalities. Given the extensive media attention paid to local politics in Toronto, we suspect that voters in this context have a better understanding than voters elsewhere of the performance and influence of their local officials. It is certainly true that policy outcomes in the city are shaped by factors other than the municipal government, but this is true of all Canadian municipalities that are similarly affected by the actions of two other orders of government, not to mention non-governmental and international factors. As an exceptionally large municipality with a budget larger than that of many provincial governments in Canada, however, the City of Toronto's policies should, *ceteris paribus*, be expected to have a relatively large impact on policy outcomes. As such, if voters in Toronto do not hold elected officials responsible for local policy outcomes, there is little reason to expect it of voters elsewhere.

We should stress that we make our claims about the generalizability of TES results with some degree of modesty. Though the extreme nature of the 2014 Toronto election gives us some confidence in our assertions about how Canadian electors respond to the non-partisan nature of local elections, as well as how they view local politics more generally, we do recognize that all elections and municipalities have idiosyncrasies. We see no reason to expect that our observations will not hold elsewhere; even so, we welcome future research that tests the applicability of findings from the 2014 Toronto municipal election in other times and settings.

Going Forward

In *Electing a Mega-Mayor*, we have sought to provide a detailed understanding of the outcome of the 2014 Toronto election, to paint a comprehensive portrait of Toronto's voters, and to draw some conclusions about Canadian municipal voters more generally. We conclude here with a brief call for scholars to significantly increase the intensity with which they study local political behaviour in this country.

As noted earlier, future work that tests our findings in other settings is welcome and needed. More than this, however, we encourage the study of important questions about political behaviour at the local level. The reason for this is simple: local elections represent a vast, untapped resource for scholars of political behaviour. As noted in the introductory chapter of this work, local governments account for 99.6 per cent of governments in this country. When scholars focus almost exclusively on national and provincial elections, they are missing a big piece of the puzzle that is the Canadian voter (and non-voter). In fact, they are missing many more pieces than they are not.

Local elections are a potentially invaluable resource in part because they offer variation that simply does not exist in elections at the other levels of government. That is, there are important differences not only between local, provincial, and federal elections but also between municipalities. As noted earlier, Canadian municipalities vary with respect to many features worthy of study, including the presence and type of party system, the strength of the mayor, government structure (regional governments or borough councils, for example), population density, immigration levels, language, ethnicity patterns, and even historical differences, such as experiences with municipal amalgamation. Local elections in cities that vary in these ways can be studied to determine the effects of these types of variation on voters, elections, politicians, and policies.

Another noteworthy way in which municipalities differ from one another is with respect to the density of representation experienced by residents. Niagara Region, for example, with a population of 450,000, is represented by a total of 125 elected municipal officials (this includes the mayors and councillors of twelve municipalities, as well as regional councillors). Just down the road, Hamilton (with a population of over 550,000) is represented by just fifteen councillors and a mayor. In Niagara, there is one local politician for roughly 3,600 inhabitants, while this ratio is roughly one to 34,000 in Hamilton. Residents in these two nearby communities almost certainly have vastly different experiences with, and views toward, municipal government, and comparing electors in these two settings could speak to many important debates on representation and the quality of democracy, among other topics.

There are countless other ways in which municipalities differ from one another. Each difference represents an opportunity for scholars to learn about how Canadian electors respond to institutional, historical, cultural, and other contextual dissimilarities. This variation can be leveraged to answer a variety of questions about political behaviour that are simply impossible to answer by focusing on elections at other levels of government, where far less variation exists.

The study of municipal elections is also of significant value because these contests are so very different from those fought at the national and provincial levels. In many respects, municipalities are the laboratories of electoral reform in this country. This is the only order of government in Canada where elections employ internet voting (hundreds of municipalities, mainly in Ontario and Nova Scotia, do so) or telephone voting. As well, municipalities are the only places where a simple single-member-plurality system is not always in place. Notable variations include an at-large system to elect councillors (Vancouver), multi-member council districts (many municipalities), and a ranked ballot electoral system for mayor and councillor positions (London in 2018). The results of adopting these novel electoral features can be studied in these relatively small settings, and findings can contribute to debates on electoral modernization and reform at higher orders of government.

There is no doubt that local elections represent the next great frontier in the field of Canadian political voting behaviour. The sheer number of municipal contests that take place around the country each year, as well as the variations provided by these cases mean there is an almost limitless potential to learn various important lessons from the study of local elections. We have covered a great deal of ground in this book, but there remains much to be learned about many features of local elections, such as the importance of campaigns, how financing works, and how candidates organize and canvass, in addition to much more about turnout and vote choice. We hope that *Electing a Mega-Mayor* encourages researchers to take up our call to scholarly arms and helps usher in a golden age for the study of local political behaviour.

Epilogue

Election cycles pause for no one, not even academics. Since this book was first drafted, the City of Toronto has held another mayoral election, one that was very different from, though certainly not independent of, the 2014 contest. In the fall of 2018, John Tory cruised to a comfortable re-election victory over a field that included only one credible challenger, former chief city planner Jennifer Keesmaat. Tory saw his vote share climb from 40.3 per cent in 2014 to 63.5 per cent in 2018. Neither Olivia Chow nor Doug Ford returned to challenge the mayor, although, in his new role as Premier of Ontario, Ford nevertheless had a substantial impact on the election (a topic to which we will return). The 2018 election also differed in that voter turnout declined significantly, down to 40.9 per cent from a high of 54.7 per cent in 2014.

In this epilogue we discuss some of the major features of the 2018 mayoral election, paying particular attention to characteristics that are applicable to the content of this book. This will enable us to consider what the results from 2014 and 2018 tell us about elections in Toronto more generally. We discuss three related themes: the drop in voter turnout, John Tory's re-election, and Doug Ford's continuing impact on Toronto's politics. This will provide additional evidence of the exceptional nature of the 2014 Toronto mayoral election, while at the same time showing that some key findings from 2014 continue to be applicable, which in turn suggests that they are regularities in Toronto politics.

Turnout

In many respects, the 2018 election represented a return to normalcy in Toronto. The antics of Rob Ford were but a distant memory, and the incumbent mayor was re-elected. As part of this return to normalcy, voter turnout declined by nearly 14 percentage points, to just over 40 per cent – nearly 225,000 fewer Torontonians participated in 2018. That turnout was actually much more typical of elections in Toronto (the average prior to 2014 was 41.8 per cent) as well in other Canadian municipalities.

One of this book's findings has been that electors care relatively little about municipal politics. We have argued that if this is true in a high-profile contest such as the 2014 race, it is likely to be true in other times and places. The sharp decrease in turnout in 2018 is compatible with these claims. Even in 2014, in the most high-profile of elections, many Torontonians viewed local government and politics as relatively unimportant and uninteresting (see chapters 1 and 6). Conversely, one would be hard-pressed to design a mayoral election that would elicit less interest than was the case in 2018. The mayor was not involved in any scandals, and the public was largely satisfied with his performance. The challenger (Keesmaat) had nowhere near the profile Tory's opponents did in 2014. She also had no obvious partisan ties to any other level of government (a cue that might decrease information-seeking costs for voters, perhaps making them more likely to vote). Polls also suggested that the race was uncompetitive (a point to which we return below), a factor that is known to decrease turnout (Blais, 2006). Given that public interest and engagement are undeniably related to each other, it is not at all surprising that turnout declined as it did. We therefore interpret the decline in voter turnout as supporting our claim that voters place relatively little importance on local politics and elections.

For further evidence of the comparatively low public interest in the 2018 election, we turn to data from Google Trends (see trends.google.com). That tool allows us to compare the number of Web searches for key terms related to the two contests, across time.[1] A strong argument can be made that, all else equal, an electorate interested in a mayoral election should be expected to conduct more searches on related terms. It follows that we can use search volume as a proxy (albeit an imperfect one) for public interest.

We can compare search volume in Ontario in the week prior to (and excluding) election day in 2014 and 2018 on several relevant terms. The results overwhelmingly indicate that the public was less interested in the 2018 election than they were in the 2014 contest. The term "Toronto election" was searched only 80 per cent as much in the week prior to the election in 2018 as it was in 2014 (Google provides data in "normalized" format, rather than in terms of the absolute number of searches). Google reports the same pattern for other, related search terms, such as "Toronto mayoral election" (37 per cent), "Toronto mayor" (61 per cent), and "Toronto mayoral race" (15 per cent). We conducted a similar search on candidate names and observed similar trends. "John Tory" was searched only 31 per cent as much in 2018 as it was in 2014. Also, Tory's competitors received more attention in 2014. "Jennifer Keesmaat" was searched only 28 per cent as much during election week as "Doug Ford" was in 2014, and 52 per cent as much as "Olivia Chow" was that same year. So it seems that voters were much less interested in both the mayor and his competitors in 2018 than they were in 2014. Even though some of the decline could be attributed to Tory being the incumbent, it is particularly telling that there were fewer searches for his main competitor, Keesmaat. Thus, along with the significant decline in voter turnout, the observed search trends provide further evidence of an electorate that was much less interested in the mayoral election in 2018. These findings reinforce our view that 2014 was indeed an extreme case.

Tory's Re-election

John Tory received nearly two thirds of the popular vote in 2018 and won a plurality of votes in every ward (and a majority in every ward but one). His dominance can be attributed to several factors, many of which can be traced back to his victory in 2014. Perhaps most importantly, Tory's first term as mayor provided him with an opportunity to make a positive impression on voters. Our data from 2016 show that Torontonians were, on the whole, very satisfied with the mayor (59.9 per cent of respondents reported being satisfied; only 15.9 per cent were not – a ratio of nearly 4:1).

By themselves, these high levels of satisfaction might have made it difficult for Tory to lose even if he had faced a strong challenger. Such a challenger did not emerge, which further explains Tory's dominance in the race. Incumbents have a well-documented advantage in local elections. Besides being able to run on their records, they enjoy name recognition (something that challengers can struggle with, particularly in a non-partisan setting) and fundraising advantages. At the same time, the presence of an incumbent (and a popular one at that), "scares off" high-quality challengers, providing incumbents with an indirect advantage (Krebs, 1998; Kushner, Siegel, & Stanwick, 1997). In all likelihood, Tory's popularity and status as incumbent served to dissuade many strong candidates from running who might otherwise have considered it.

Though popular in some circles, former Toronto City Planner Jennifer Keesmaat never represented a serious threat to Tory. Polling data from Forum Research reveal that at no point was she able to close the gap with Tory significantly (see Figure E.1). There was little movement in the polls during the campaign, and, as was the case in 2014, Tory had a healthy lead for months leading up to the election. The dip in the mayor's support after the second poll was a result of the fact that Forum did not allow respondents to select a candidate other than the two front-runners in the first two polls.

On election day, Keesmaat won 23.6 per cent of the vote, enough to secure her runner-up status. However, that meant she received almost 50,000 fewer votes than did the third-place finisher in 2014, Olivia Chow. High levels of public satisfaction with his performance, combined with the advantages of incumbency, served John Tory well in 2018.

Figure E.1. 2018 polling data – vote intentions

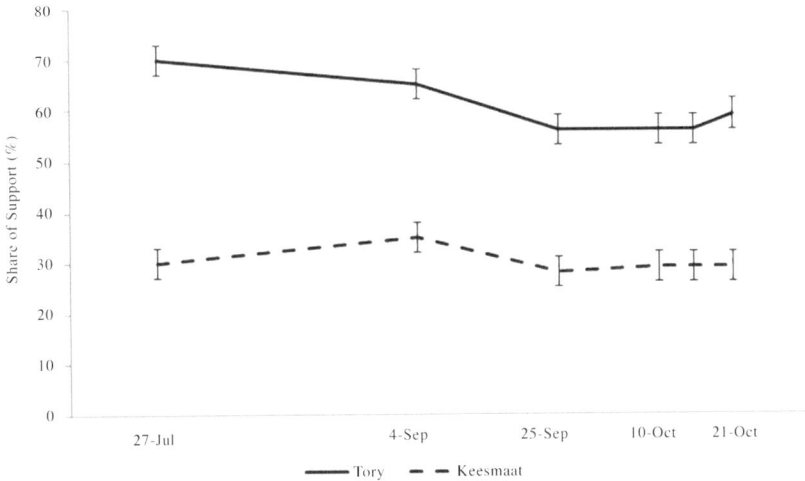

Note: These data were compiled using Forum Research's "TO Horserace" news releases from 27 July 2018 through 21 October 2018, inclusive. The news releases are available online at http://poll.forumresearch.com/category/3/toronto.

A look at the geographic distribution of Tory's support adds to our understanding of his dominance in 2018. As has been shown in this book (and by previous scholars, such as Walks, 2004, 2005), geography – the urban–suburban divide in particular – is a significant factor in Toronto politics. Tory outperformed Keesmaat in every ward in the city, but was there a geographic dimension to his dominance, and did his support shift between the two elections?

The 2014 and 2018 elections offered different constellations of candidates. In 2014, Tory faced a major candidate on both his right (Ford) and his left (Chow), but in 2018 there was no strong candidate on the right (Faith Goldy, a controversial right-wing political commentator, received a mere 3.4 per cent of the vote). Figure 5.2 in this book shows that in 2014, Doug Ford performed well on the edges of the city, in the northeast and northwest more specifically. Given that he did not participate in the 2018 election, a question arises: to whom did "Ford Nation" (at least as it can be described in geographic terms) shift its support? The more general question of whether the relationship between vote choice and geography persisted across elections also is worth considering. We consider both matters in the aggregate by investigating ward-level election results. As a first step, Figure E.2 shows the level of support enjoyed by the three major candidates in 2014.

Figure E.2. Candidate vote share by ward – 2014

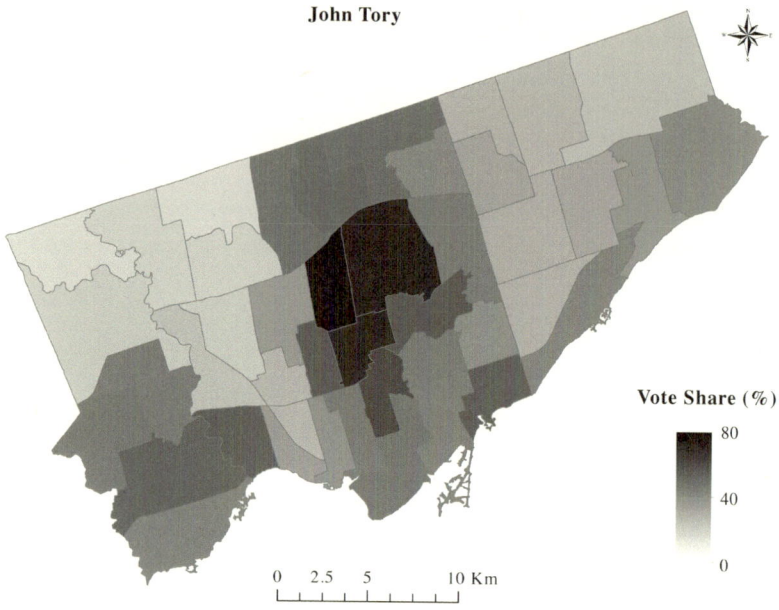

John Tory

Vote Share (%)

80

40

0

0   2.5   5   10 Km

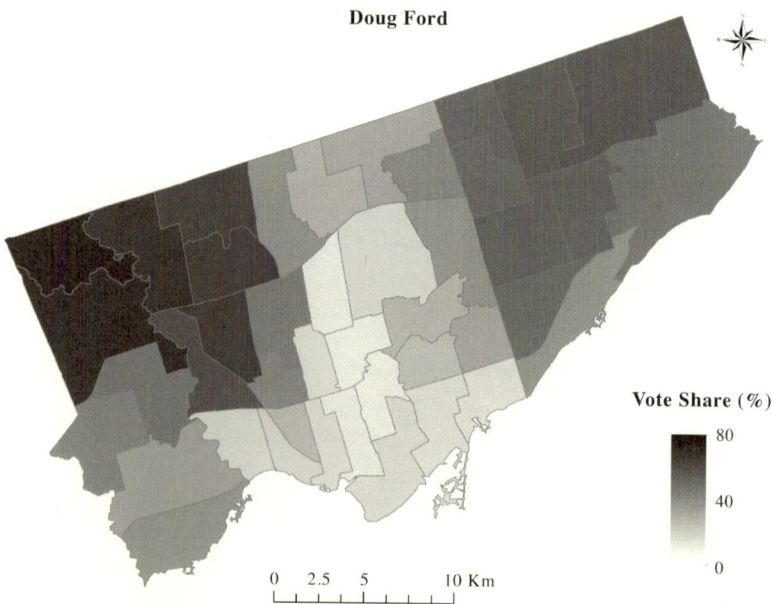

Doug Ford

Vote Share (%)

80

40

0

0   2.5   5   10 Km

Figure E.2. (Continued)

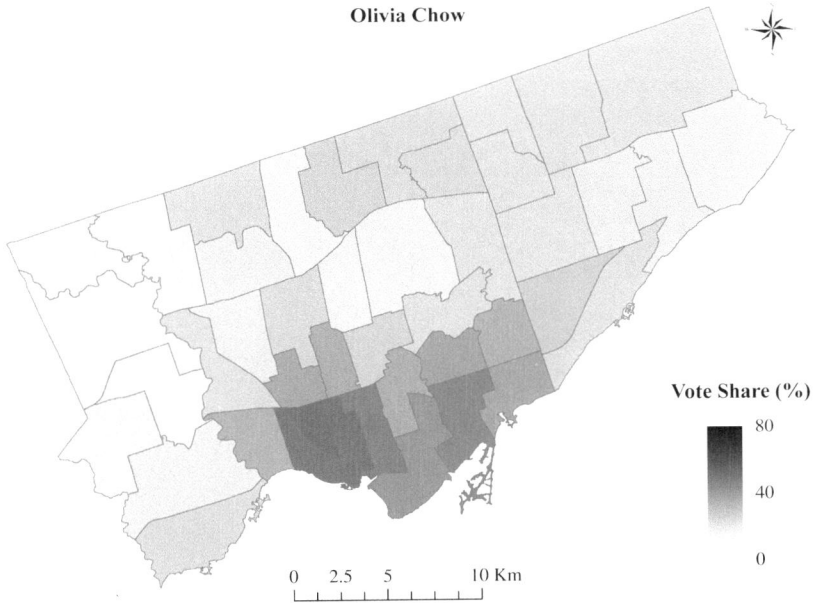

The patterns in Figure E.2 are clear: Ford performed well in the northeast and northwest, and Chow's base was in the downtown core. The distribution of Tory's 2014 support is somewhat more complex. He did best in the north-central part of the city, but he also had pockets of strength downtown and in the southeast and southwest. The areas he fared worst in were those won by Ford – the northern corners of the city.

Without Ford (or any viable right-wing candidate) running in 2018, the relationship between geography and vote choice comes into question. If the northern corners of the city can be viewed as the geographic bases of "Ford Nation," to whom did they turn in 2018? Was Tory able to retain his existing geographic bases, did he expand them, or, when voters were presented with a different set of options, did the relationship between vote choice and geography shift? To consider this, in Figure E.3 we show the geographic distribution of John Tory's support in 2018.[2]

Given Tory's dominance in 2018, it is not surprising that the shading in Figure E.3 is much darker that it was on that same candidate's map in E.2.

Figure E.3. John Tory vote share by ward – 2018

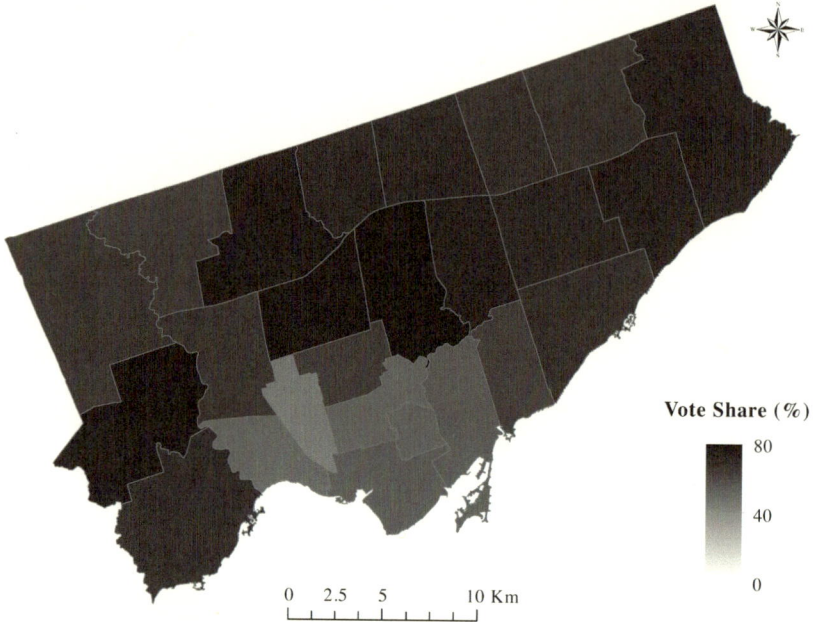

Nevertheless, there is important geographic variation. The mayor had strengths in the same areas as he did in 2014, including the north-central parts of the city and the southern corners. However, the most striking observation from the figure is that he also performed extremely well in areas where Ford dominated in 2018 (the northern corners). In ideological terms, such a finding makes sense – the right-wing support-ers of Ford moved to Tory, the furthest right of the two major candidates in 2018.

Still, a shift from Ford to Tory cannot be assumed. Recall that Ford Nation is/was not a typical right-wing coalition. As was shown in chapter 5, several groups that are not generally associated with support for par-ties or candidates of the right, including younger voters, immigrants, and visible minorities, tended to back the Fords. Still, at least in terms of geography, voters in the regions that supported Ford (and where Tory performed very poorly) in 2014 turned to Tory in large numbers in 2018. Across both elections, then, we see evidence that geography (in particular, the divide between the downtown and the periphery) is strongly related to vote choice in Toronto. As is the case with federal and provincial elections (see chapter 5), urban and suburban voters have very different preferences in municipal elections.

The Ford Factor

Though not a mayoral candidate, Doug Ford once again played a significant role in a Toronto election. After Patrick Brown was forced to step down as provincial Progressive Conservative leader in January 2018 following accusations of sexual impropriety, Doug Ford was elected to replace him. Shortly after that, he led the party to victory in the 2018 provincial election. His new role as premier precluded the possibility of a rematch between him and his old rival, Tory, for the position of mayor. It seemed as though the 2018 election would be the first since 2006 where a Ford would not be a factor in the mayoral race.

These assumptions were proven incorrect when, the day before the candidate nomination deadline, Ford announced that his government would be introducing the *Better Local Government Act*. That act would, without input or permission from the city itself, redistrict the council boundaries and reduce the number of city councillors from forty-four to twenty-five. The putative rationale for the change was "smaller government," though some viewed the decision as a way for Ford to exact revenge on councillors who had opposed him and his brother in the past, by eliminating their positions (Ferguson, 2018, 14 August; Jeffords & Loriggio, 2018, 27 July). The provincially imposed redistricting was shocking for a number of reasons. Toronto had functioned under the forty-four-ward system since 2000, and in 2005 the provincial government had revised the City of Toronto Act to grant the city the authority to establish its own electoral boundaries. In 2014, the Toronto Ward Boundary Review Commission (an ad hoc municipal body tasked with revisiting the city's boundaries) had actually recommended an *increase* in the size of council to forty-seven to account for population changes. Toronto City Council accordingly adopted the forty-seven-seat system in time for the 2018 election (Pagliaro, 2020, 26 March). A final striking feature of the provincial government's announcement was the timing – Ford made the announcement on 26 June, the day before the official candidate nomination deadline (though this date was later revised for council elections to account for boundary changes). The change was extraordinary both in substance and in implementation.

Though the provincial government's imposition of new boundaries primarily affected elections for City Council, it also had a significant, though indirect, impact on the mayoral election. Jennifer Keesmaat, who entered the mayoral race on 27 July (the nomination deadline), credited her decision to enter the race to the surprising change (Gray, 2018, 5 October). At first, her position (via Twitter) was that the boundary changes, and the manner in which they were being implemented, were so intolerable that the City of Toronto should seek to become its own province. On 26 July, she tweeted, simply, "Secession," and the next day she followed up with "Now I have had a chance to sleep on it. Secession. Why should a city of 2.8 million not have self governance?" Keesmaat eventually distanced herself from the notion of turning Toronto into the county's eleventh province (Maloney, 2018, 31 July). However, according to Keesmaat, it was Ford's actions that had led her to run for mayor. She soon became Tory's strongest challenger.

The issue of redistricting dominated news coverage of the election for most of the campaign. There were several legal challenges to the *Better Local Government Act*. In one of these, an Ontario Superior Court ruled that the act was unconstitutional on the grounds that the sudden reduction in the number of City wards infringed on the freedom of expression of both candidates and voters, and ordered that the election move forward under a forty-seven-ward system (*City of Toronto et al. v. Ontario (Attorney General)*, 2018). Responding to this judicial setback, Ford announced that he would invoke the notwithstanding clause of the Charter, which has never before been used in Ontario. In the end, however, both the original judicial decision and Ford's threat were moot, as the Ontario Court of Appeal stayed the Superior Court's decision, arguing that the reasoning used by the original judge was flawed (*Toronto (City) v. Ontario (Attorney General), 2018*). The 2018 election went forward under Ford's preferred boundaries (though in early 2020, the Supreme Court agreed to hear the city's appeal of the cuts to City Council; Pagliaro, 2020, 9 November).

Despite the significant levels of attention paid to the redistricting issue, it seemingly did little to help Keesmaat's chances. Both she and Tory publicly opposed the reduction in the size of City Council (though there is little doubt that she was more vocal in her opposition), meaning that the issue that prompted her entry into the race could not be used as a wedge to differentiate herself from the mayor. As shown by the poll results discussed earlier, she was never a serious threat to Tory's re-election.

For better or worse, the Ford family has left an indelible mark on the city and on the government of Toronto. As councillors, mayor, mayoral candidates, and premier, their actions continue to be felt by Torontonians. Moreover, the brothers are not the only standard-bearers of Ford Nation. Michael Ford, a nephew of Doug and Rob, continues to serve on City Council, having won Doug's old seat in a 2016 by-election and in the newly created Etobicoke North ward in 2018. Rob's widow, Renata Ford, was a candidate in the 2019 federal election (in Etobicoke North) for the fledgling People's Party of Canada, itself a right-wing populist movement. Even after Rob's passing, Ford Nation continues to be an enduring and powerful movement in Toronto politics.

Concluding Thoughts

In many ways, the events of the 2018 election contribute to our understanding of municipal politics in Toronto. They also confirm that the 2014 election was an extreme case on several dimensions, including voter interest and turnout. Using voter turnout and Google search histories as indicators, Torontonians were significantly less interested and engaged with the mayoral election in 2018. This is likely for a number of reasons, including the uncompetitive nature of the race, generally high levels of satisfaction with the mayor, and the absence of a high-profile candidate named Ford.

So, what does this information from 2018 tell us about elections in Toronto more generally? First, it is not the case that elections in the city will always elicit high levels of interest and attention, despite the size and profile of the city and its government. Torontonians react to the forces of incumbency and non-competitiveness in much the same way as local voters elsewhere – by turning their attention away from the election. Another noteworthy observation from this epilogue is that of the enduring relationship between geography and vote choice. At least in the aggregate, Torontonians behaved as one would expect on ideological grounds, given the change in the constellation of candidates. Absent a right-wing challenger in 2018, Tory dominated not only the areas he captured in 2014 but also the regions of Toronto dominated by Ford in 2014 (the northern corners of the city). In both elections, he performed relatively poorly in the downtown core.

All elections have their quirks, but the 2014 Toronto mayoral race stands out as particularly distinct. It is unlikely that we will see a contest quite like it again. At the same time, many of the findings in this book are consistent with the 2018 experience, and a large part of the analysis contained here speaks to elections in Toronto more generally. As a whole, the results of this book show the value of studying local elections and point to many relevant points of inquiry for analyses of future contests in Toronto, elsewhere in Canada, and even beyond.

Appendix I

Survey Questions

Note that questions are listed in the order they appeared in surveys.

2014 Toronto Election Study

Pre-Election Questionnaire

In what year were you born?

○ Years listed in dropdown menu

In which part of the city do you live?

○ North York
○ Scarborough
○ Toronto & East York
○ Etobicoke

Please rank the following characteristics in terms of how important you think they are for municipal politicians. You can drag and drop the characteristics from the first column into the second column or use the arrows:

○ Intelligent
○ Honest and trustworthy
○ Gets things done
○ Really cares about people
○ Shares my political beliefs
○ Approachable

○ Central African (for example, Chadian, Congolese etc.)
○ Eastern African (for example, Somali, Kenyan, etc.)
○ Western African (for example, Nigerian, Ghanaian, etc.)
○ Southern African (for example, South African, Namibian, etc.)
○ Mainland Chinese
○ Hong Kong Chinese
○ Korean
○ Other East Asian (for example, Japanese, Taiwanese etc.)
○ Indian
○ Tamil
○ Pakistani
○ Other South Asian (for example, Nepalese, Bangladeshi, etc.)
○ Filipino
○ Other South East Asian (for example, Vietnamese, Cambodian, etc.)
○ Persian/Iranian
○ Other Middle-eastern/Southwest Asian (for example, Arabian, Israeli, Afghani, etc.)
○ British (English, Irish, Scottish, Welsh)
○ French
○ Other Northern European (for example, German, Dutch, etc.)
○ Italian
○ Portuguese
○ Other Southern European (for example, Spanish, Greek, etc.)
○ Russian
○ Polish
○ Other Eastern European (for example, Czech, Romanian, etc.)
○ Australian / New Zealander
○ Other Oceanian (for example, Papua New Guinean)
○ Other ethnic or cultural group
○ Prefer not to say/Don't know

What is your gender?

○ Male
○ Female
○ Other
○ Prefer not to say

Which mayoral candidate do you think you will vote for?

○ Doug Ford
○ Olivia Chow
○ John Tory
○ Other
○ Don't know or haven't decided

Is there a mayoral candidate you would absolutely not vote for?

○ No
○ Doug Ford
○ Olivia Chow
○ John Tory
○ Other
○ Don't know or haven't decided

What is the main reason that you would not vote for that candidate?

○ Dislike him/her personally
○ Dislike his/her policy ideas
○ Other, please specify: _____
○ Don't know

Do you think you would vote for Rob Ford if he were running for mayor?

○ Yes
○ No
○ Don't know

Recently the province passed legislation that will allow Toronto to use ranked ballots for elections. This means that voters will be able to rank candidates in terms of their preferences on a single ballot. If such a ballot was going to be used in the upcoming election, how would you rank the mayoral candidates? You don't have to rank all of the candidates.

○ Doug Ford
○ Olivia Chow
○ John Tory
○ Other

In FEDERAL politics, do you usually think of yourself as a:

- ○ Liberal
- ○ Conservative
- ○ NDP
- ○ Green
- ○ Other
- ○ None of the above
- ○ Don't know

How strongly do you associate with that party?

- ○ Very strongly
- ○ Fairly strongly
- ○ Not very strongly
- ○ Don't know

Governments at all levels make decisions that impact the lives of citizens. Please rank each level of government in terms of the amount of impact its decisions have upon your quality of life. You can drag and drop the options from the first column into the second column or use the arrows.

- ○ Federal
- ○ Provincial
- ○ Municipal

How do you feel about each of the following mayoral candidates? Please use the sliders to indicate your feelings on a scale from 0 to 100, where zero means you REALLY DISLIKE the candidate and one hundred means you REALLY LIKE the candidate.

Doug Ford

- ○ 0–100
- ○ Don't know

Olivia Chow

- ○ 0–100
- ○ Don't know

John Tory

- ○ 0–100
- ○ Don't know

Finally, how do you feel about the current mayor, Rob Ford?

○ 0–100
○ Don't know

What are the following candidates' chances of winning the mayoral race? Please use the sliders to indicate your expectations on a scale from 0 to 100, where zero means the candidate has NO CHANCE of winning, and one hundred means the candidate is CERTAIN TO WIN.

Doug Ford

○ 0–100
○ Don't know

Olivia Chow

○ 0–100
○ Don't know

John Tory

○ 0–100
○ Don't know

In politics people sometimes talk of left and right. Where would you place yourself on a scale from 0 to 10, where 0 means left and 10 means right?

○ 0–10
○ Don't know

How important are each of the following issues to you in this election? Please indicate each issue's importance on a 0–10 scale, where 0 means not at all important and 10 means extremely important.

○ Public transit
○ Property taxes
○ Traffic and congestion
○ Housing affordability
○ Managing Toronto's finances

On the issue of PUBLIC TRANSIT, which policy idea do you prefer?

○ Build subways instead of planned light rail transit on Sheppard and Finch.
○ Build planned light rail transit routes on Sheppard and Finch.
○ Electrify GO transit lines, add more stops along them, and increase frequency of service.
○ Don't know

On the issue of PROPERTY TAXES, which policy idea do you prefer?

○ Keep taxes below inflation.
○ Reduce small business taxes and keep property taxes "around" inflation.
○ Reduce commercial taxes and keep overall taxes near or below inflation.
○ Don't know

On the issue of TRAFFIC AND CONGESTION, which policy idea do you prefer?

○ Oppose policies that will negatively affect drivers.
○ Create 200km of new bike lanes.
○ Don't know

Which candidate do you think would be best at managing the City of Toronto's finances?

○ Doug Ford
○ Olivia Chow
○ John Tory
○ Don't know

In your opinion, how similar are Doug Ford's policies to those of his brother, Rob?

○ All the same
○ Mostly the same
○ Mostly different
○ All different
○ Don't know

Do you strongly agree, agree, disagree or strongly disagree with the following statement: Behaviour in private lives is irrelevant to the capabilities of politicians.

- ○ Strongly agree
- ○ Agree
- ○ Disagree
- ○ Strongly disagree
- ○ Don't know

Do you strongly agree, agree, disagree or strongly disagree with the following statement: The media has given Rob Ford a harder time than he deserves.

- ○ Strongly agree
- ○ Agree
- ○ Disagree
- ○ Strongly disagree
- ○ Don't know

Do you strongly agree, agree, disagree or strongly disagree with the following statement: People who make mistakes in their private lives should be given a second chance.

- ○ Strongly agree
- ○ Agree
- ○ Disagree
- ○ Strongly disagree
- ○ Don't know

How interested are you in (Municipal/Provincial/Federal) politics?

- ○ 0–10
- ○ Don't know

Do politicians keep their promises most of the time, some of the time, or hardly ever? (At municipal/provincial/federal levels)

- ○ Most of the time
- ○ Some of the time
- ○ Hardly ever
- ○ Don't know

For you personally, is voting first and foremost a duty or a choice at the Municipal, Provincial and Federal levels?

○ Duty
○ Choice
○ Don't know

What is the highest level of education that you have completed?

○ No schooling
○ Some elementary school
○ Completed elementary school
○ Some secondary/high school
○ Completed secondary/high school
○ Some technical, community college
○ Completed technical, community college
○ Some university
○ Bachelor's degree
○ Master's degree
○ Professional degree or doctorate
○ Prefer not to say/Don't know

Were you born in Canada?

○ Yes
○ No
○ Prefer not to say/Don't know

To what ethnic or cultural group or groups do you belong? Please select up to two options.

○ Canadian
○ American
○ Mexican
○ Caribbean (for example, Jamaican, Haitian, etc.)
○ Aboriginal (for example, Cree, Métis, etc.)
○ Other North American
○ Central American (for example, Nicaraguan, Panamanian, etc.)
○ Brazilian
○ Argentinian
○ Other South American (for example, Chilean)
○ Northern African (for example, Egyptian, Algerian, etc.)

Which of the following best indicates your annual household income before taxes?

○ Less than $20,000
○ $20,000–$29,999
○ $30,000–$39,999
○ $40,000–$49,999
○ $50,000–$59,999
○ $60,000–$69,999
○ $70,000–$79,999
○ $80,000–$89,999
○ $90,000–$99,999
○ $100,000–$109,999
○ $110,000–$119,999
○ $120,000 or more
○ Prefer not to say/Don't know

Post-Election Questionnaire

In each election we find that a lot of people were not able to vote because they were not registered, they were sick, or they did not have time.

Did you vote in this election?

○ Yes
○ No
○ Don't know/Don't remember

Which mayoral candidate did you vote for?

○ Doug Ford
○ Olivia Chow
○ John Tory
○ Other
○ Did not vote for a mayoral candidate
○ Don't know/Don't remember

What is the main reason that you voted for that mayoral candidate?

○ Liked him/her personally
○ Liked his/her policy ideas
○ Other, please specify _____
○ Don't know

If Rob Ford had been a mayoral candidate, would you have voted for him?

○ Yes
○ No
○ Don't know

On the issue of AFFORDABILITY, which policy idea do you prefer?

○ Press federal and provincial governments for more funding for affordable housing
○ Require 20% of new residential units to be affordable
○ Explore tax incentives for affordable private sector housing
○ Don't know

For each statement below, please indicate if you strongly agree, agree, disagree, or strongly disagree.

Government should leave it entirely up to the private sector to create jobs.
Government should see to it that everyone has a decent standard of living.
Same-sex marriage rights are a good thing.
More should be done to reduce the gap between the rich and poor in Canada.

○ Strong agree
○ Agree
○ Disagree
○ Strongly disagree
○ Don't know

How much do you think the following care about what people like you think: a lot, some, a little or none? (Federal government, provincial government, municipal government):

○ A lot
○ Some
○ A little
○ None

Which level of government is primarily responsible for the following policy areas?

Employment Insurance
Social Housing
Health Care

Primary and Secondary Education
Defence Policy
Transit and Transportation
Sewage and Water
Police and Fire Services

○ Federal
○ Provincial
○ Municipal
○ Don't know

Do you recall which mayoral candidate promised to ...?

Build a surface rail subway called SmartTrack.
Phase out the Land Transfer Tax.
Consolidate economic development responsibilities into one new body called
  Global Toronto.

○ Doug Ford
○ Olivia Chow
○ John Tory
○ None of these candidates

Do you know the name of the Mayor of Toronto prior to Rob Ford?

○ John Tory
○ Barbara Hall
○ Dalton McGuinty
○ David Miller
○ Don't know

Do you know the name of the Governor General of Canada?

○ Preston Manning
○ David Johnston
○ Michaëlle Jean
○ David Onley
○ Don't know

Do you know the name of the Finance Minister of Canada?

○ Joe Oliver
○ Jim Flaherty

7 These findings are consistent with those observed in Figure 5.1, which suggests that the brothers are relatively unpopular downtown, but that geography has no bearing on differences in ratings of the two Fords.

8 n = 2,844.

9 n = 2,598. The differences in ratings between all candidates (other than the Fords) are significant at $p < 0.01$.

10 The difference between these values is significant at $p < 0.01$.

11 n = 3,727.

12 Due to rounding, columns do not all sum to 100. Results are weighted for age, gender, education, vote choice, and turnout.

6. A New Mayor, a New Dawn for Toronto?

1 The observant reader will notice that levels of interest reported in the 2016 survey are slightly higher than those from 2014 (reported in chapter 1). We find it highly surprising that levels of interest would actually increase outside of election time (especially given the relatively demure manner of the new mayor in comparison to his predecessor). Though such a pattern is not of direct relevance to the current discussion, we believe it worthwhile to briefly speculate as to the reasons for such a difference; we can think of at least two. First, we suspect that such a difference may be due to the opt-in nature of the 2014 and 2016 surveys. For both, survey respondents were recruited by a survey firm and invited to fill out a survey on municipal politics. In both, only a fraction of those invited actually completed the survey. Given the survey topic, we suspect that there was some self-selection on the basis of interest in municipal politics, and our intuition is that the self-selection effect may be stronger outside of election time (in 2016). If this is the case, then interested individuals were less likely to complete the 2016 survey, and thus the reported levels of interest among those who did were higher in the mid-term survey. Though we do not have the data to test that supposition, we nevertheless believe this to be very likely. The second potential reason assumes that levels of interest in politics did, indeed, increase after the election. Between 2014 and 2016 we saw the election of a new Canadian prime minister and a new American president, both of whom were arguably high-profile individuals. Such changes may have led to a general increase in public interest in politics, including at the municipal level. Whatever the reason(s) for the observed differences in levels of interest, we are hesitant to place too much value on comparisons of results from the 2014 and 2016 surveys. Instead, we focus on comparisons between levels of government, at each survey time point.

2 n = 1,477.

○ Paul Martin
○ Peter MacKay
○ Don't know

Do you know the name of the leader of the New Democratic Party of Ontario?

○ Bob Rae
○ Thomas Mulcair
○ Andrea Horwath
○ Howard Hampton
○ Don't know

2016 "Midterm" Survey

In what year were you born?

○ Years listed in dropdown menu

What is your gender?

○ Male
○ Female
○ Other
○ Prefer not to say

What is the highest level of education that you have completed?

○ High school or less
○ College or technical school
○ Bachelor's degree
○ Master's degree or professional/doctorate degree
○ Prefer not to say/Don't know

How interested are you in (Municipal/Provincial/Federal) politics?

○ 0–10
○ Don't know

How satisfied are you with the performance of:

Mayor John Tory
Toronto City Council

Your City Councillor

○ Not at all satisfied
○ Somewhat unsatisfied
○ Neither satisfied nor unsatisfied
○ Somewhat satisfied
○ Very satisfied
○ Don't know

Governments at all levels make decisions that impact the lives of citizens. Please rank each level of government in terms of the amount of impact its decisions have upon your quality of life. You can drag and drop the options from the first column into the second column or use the arrows.

○ Federal
○ Provincial
○ Municipal

For each of the following issues, has the situation in Toronto gotten better, gotten worse, or stayed about the same since the 2014 election?

Public transit
Property taxes
Traffic and congestion
Housing affordability
Managing Toronto's finances.

○ Gotten better
○ Gotten worse
○ Stayed about the same
○ Don't know

In politics people sometimes talk of left and right. Where would you place yourself on a scale from 0 to 10, where 0 means left and 10 means right?

○ 0–10
○ Don't know

Which level of government is primarily responsible for

Employment insurance
Social housing

Health Care
Primary and Secondary education

O Federal
O Provincial
O Municipal
O Don't know

Do you know the name of the Mayor of Toronto prior to Rob Ford?

O John Tory
O Barbara Hall
O Dalton McGuinty
O David Miller
O Don't know

Do you know the name of the Governor General of Canada?

O Preston Manning
O David Johnston
O Michaëlle Jean
O David Onley
O Don't know

Do you know the name of the Finance Minister of Canada?

O Joe Oliver
O Jim Flaherty
O Paul Martin
O Bill Morneau
O Don't know

Do you know the name of the leader of the New Democratic Party of Ontario?

O Bob Rae
O Thomas Mulcair
O Andrea Horwath
O Howard Hampton
O Don't know

Do you or someone else in your household own your home?

O Yes
O No
O Prefer not to say/Don't know

Canadian Election Study
2004 Canadian Election Study

Pre-Election Questionnaire

How do you feel about Paul Martin? Use any number from zero to one hundred. Zero means you really DISLIKE him and one hundred means you really LIKE him.

- ○ 0–100
- ○ Don't know any of the leaders
- ○ Don't know who he is
- ○ Don't know/don't know how to rate him

How do you feel about Jean Chretien? Use any number from zero to one hundred. Zero means you really DISLIKE him and one hundred means you really LIKE him.

- ○ 0–100
- ○ Don't know any of the leaders
- ○ Don't know who he is
- ○ Don't know/don't know how to rate him

2008/2011/2015 Canadian Election Study

Pre-Election Questionnaire

Which party do you think you will vote for?

- ○ Liberal
- ○ Conservatives
- ○ NDP
- ○ Bloc Quebecois
- ○ Green Party
- ○ Other
- ○ Will not vote
- ○ None

Post-Election Questionnaire

Which party did you vote for?

- ○ Liberal
- ○ Conservatives

○ NDP
○ Bloc Quebecois
○ Green Party
○ Other
○ Did not vote
○ None

Notes

1. The Study of Local Elections

1 For information on the number of elections, see Quesnel (2007) and Sancton (2015). Information on the number of elected official in municipalities is from the Federation of Canadian Municipalities (2013).

2 Indigenous self-governments also function without parties.

3 Many cities in BC and Quebec have political parties that contest municipal elections, although they are not the same as the parties that exist at the provincial and federal levels.

4 All analyses based upon survey data are weighted for age, gender, and education to match census data. The TES also included a question to ensure that respondents were paying attention and answering seriously. 3.1 per cent of respondents "failed" this question and were consequently excluded from our analyses.

5 The survey was administered to a large sample in order to make the dataset sensitive to relatively minor relationships in our analyses. The reader should be mindful of both statistical and substantive significance when interpreting the results that follow.

6 n = 2,907.

7 n = 2,727.

8 n = 2,802.

2. The Contenders

1 Without significant data examining the public's perception of Soknacki and Stintz, it is impossible to conclusively determine why their campaigns failed. Certainly, the greater news coverage and higher profiles of Chow and Tory likely played a role. However, Chow and Tory also benefited from clear partisan ties from their past lives as federal NDP and provincial PC

politicians, respectively. Soknacki and Stintz, despite their leanings, had no explicit ties to parties at the federal or provincial level. For less politically-engaged voters, the absence of an easy voting cue such as a party label may have made it difficult to assess each candidate. In fact, as discussed in Chapter 3, Olivia Chow's ties to the NDP may have been her undoing in the election.

2 David Soknacki's position as a centre-right candidate was not as apparent in the mayoral election as Stintz's, in part because of his choice to back light rail over subways. While not really a left/right issue, support for light rail versus subways seemed to cleave left and right, besides dividing downtown Torontonians from suburban residents.

3 There are many instances where multiple candidates are assigned the same score, and these individuals are excluded from this value.

4 All mean estimates are different from one another at $p < 0.01$.

5 Note that all analyses in this chapter are based upon questions from the pre-election survey.

6 n = 2,713 for all histograms.

7 Ford's distribution has a skewness of 0.51. The comparable values for Chow and Tory are –0.04 and –0.57, respectively.

8 During the 2018 election, two other cities (Kingston and Cambridge) voted in favour of using ranked ballots in future elections.

9 Results change very little if the electorate as a whole is considered.

10 5.2 per cent of voters responded "don't know" to the ranking question and are excluded here.

11 McGregor et al. (2016) report that, on a scale from 0 (left) to 10 (right), Chow received a mean score of 2.96, while Tory and Ford had values of 6.53 and 7.38, respectively.

12 Chow was the second choice of those who favoured an "other" candidate, but since there are relatively few voters in this category, such a pattern would have very little effect upon the election outcome.

13 As we pool all "other" candidates here, we only require one round of counting to "drop" them all. In reality, many more rounds of counting would have been necessary to drop these candidates, as the 2014 contest included sixty-five contenders. In all, sixty-four rounds would have been required.

14 Counting in the second round is straightforward, as we simply need to consider the second-place votes among "other" supporters. Round three calculations are somewhat more complex, however. In this round, the third-place preferences of those who ranked "other" first and Chow second would need to be counted (among this group, 13.6 per cent ranked Ford third, while the remaining 86.4 per cent assigned Tory a third-place ranking). The third-place preferences of those who ranked Chow first and

an "other" candidate second must also be counted (in this instance 82.0 per cent and 18.0 per cent ranked Tory and Ford third, respectively).

15 As an example of how support for a candidate can affect attitudes that seemingly bear little relationship to vote choice, TES respondents were asked whether they agreed with the following statement: "Behaviour in private lives is irrelevant to the capabilities of politicians." Such a statement was clearly related to Rob Ford and the problematic behaviours he exhibited while in office. Among Doug Ford supporters, 20.8 per cent disagreed with the statement, while 73.8 per cent agreed (the remaining 5.5 per cent did not know how to answer the question). In contrast, only 28.7 per cent of respondents who voted for Chow or Tory agreed that the private lives of politicians are irrelevant to their public roles. While there is a clear relationship between vote choice and this attitude, the direction of causality is unclear. On the one hand, one would expect that those individuals who believe that one's public life is irrelevant to performance in office should be relatively likely to support Doug Ford (given that the two brothers were so closely linked with each other). However, the direction of causality might go the other way: being a Ford supporter might bias one's attitude as to the relevance of private behaviour to the public performance of politicians. In other words, knowing that one is planning to support Doug Ford might lead some voters to respond differently than they otherwise would to the agree/ disagree statement. As with attitudes toward policy and candidate traits, causality almost certainly goes both ways.

16 n = 502 for Ford, 337 for Chow and 745 for Tory.

17 n = 499 for Ford, 337 for Chow and 747 for Tory.

3. In the Thick of Things: The 2014 Campaign

1 Once nominated, candidates are allowed to raise and spend money on their campaigns.

2 Forum uses interactive voice response (IVR) for all of its polls. Sample sizes for each poll varied from a high of 1,945 on 25–26 August to a low of 634 on 27 March. While differences in sample size affect confidence intervals, methodological consistency ensures that estimates are unbiased with respect to one another.

3 Note that there is some variation in the number of respondents interviewed during each week of the campaign. These differences, however, should have no effect on the patterns observed here, as the figures presented here indicate confidence intervals, which are a function of sample size. The sample sizes are as follows: September 19–28 = 1,000, September 29–October 5 = 598, October 6–12 = 529, October 13–19 = 392, October 20–26 = 480. Note also that all data have been weighted to the

population average for age, gender, and education for each week/group represented in all figures, to maximize representativeness of the sample and comparability between groups.

4 Ideally, each group would cover the same period of time (one week). Given that the TES has data on 38 days (a number that cannot be divided evenly by 7), respondents from the first 10 days (19–28 September) were grouped together.

5 Though Chow was a former federal NDP MP, the federal party is fully integrated with the provincial wing and has a unitary membership structure (Pruysers, 2014). More so than for any other party, therefore, the federal and provincial wings are one and the same.

6 The data for Horwath's approval rating were taken from Forum Research's "ON Horserace" news releases from 3 May 2014 through 11 June 2014, inclusive, and Forum Research's "ON Political Issues" news release from 3 July 2014. The news releases are available online at http://poll.forumresearch.com/category/2/ontario.

7 See Forum Research's "TO Horserace" news release for 6 October 2014: http://poll.forumresearch.com/post/163/doug-ford-surges–tory-falters.

8 As noted above, our study relies on responses from a sample of the population and is thus subject to possible error. So it is conceivable that the temporary dip in Tory's support seen in Figure 3.6 might reflect differences in the subsample of respondents interviewed at various points, rather than actual changes in the preferences of the public. Put another way, it may simply be the case that, by fluke, those respondents interviewed during the period from 13–19 October were less supportive of Tory than participants interviewed at other times. We can safely rule out this possibility, however, and state with confidence that the TES data suggest a real change in voter attitudes. An analysis of post-election vote choice reveals that TES respondents interviewed during this period supported Tory (and the other candidates) at the same rate as individuals interviewed at other points during the campaign.

9 CES data are available through the Canadian Opinion Research Archive at queensu.ca/cora.

10 We focus here upon those individuals who voted, but recognize that campaigns may also have an effect on turnout decisions. For our purposes, however, an examination of voters is sufficient to compare the magnitude of campaign effects between the two types of elections.

4. Policy versus Personality: Correct Voting and the Outcome of the 2014 Toronto Mayoral Election

1 The concept originated with Lau and Redlawsk (1997; 2001), who included factors other than policy in their operationalization of a correct

vote. Such factors, including partisanship, for example, are not considered here as they are not directly linked to policy, particularly in a non-partisan setting such as this. See McGregor (2013) for a fuller justification of the policy-only focus.

2 Ford and Tory shared the same position on traffic and congestion (which was simply to oppose policies that would negatively affect drivers, or the "war on the car").

3 While Tory's policy was officially titled "SmartTrack," the label was avoided as it would make it very easy for supporters to identify their candidate's policy without considering the policy itself.

4 This approach is consistent with Canadian Election Studies, which ask respondents an analogous question about the ability of each party to manage the national economy. While not strictly ideal for studying correct voting, we altered the question format so that we could incorporate this important issue into our calculations. Policy specifics on managing the city's finances were sparse, but we judged the issue to be important, and this was confirmed by TES data: 15.3 per cent of respondents selected that issue as the single most important in the election, and when respondents were asked to assign salience scores to the five issues we consider, municipal finances had the highest average value of any of the five policy areas (8.3 out of 10). If anything, this introduces an upward bias in the estimated rate of correct voting, following the assumption that survey respondents are more likely to select a candidate on this question because they already have a positive inclination toward that candidate. On the basis of the other four policy issues, the estimated rate of correct voting drops to 50.4 per cent. We have no reason to expect that this bias influenced the relationship between correct voting and whether voters emphasized policy or personality. In our view, therefore, any potential bias is less problematic than omitting this policy dimension altogether. That said, we should note that if all analyses below are conducted without factoring the "finances" issue into correct voting calculations the substantive conclusions remain unchanged.

5 Most policy questions (position and salience) were included in the pre-election wave of the survey. However, the "affordability" policy question was asked in the post-election wave, as candidate positions on this issue shifted during the campaign (after the survey was already in the field).

6 n = 1,154.

7 n = 1,709 for this analysis.

8 For the sake of parsimony, we do not include socio-demographic controls. The substantive conclusions of this analysis remain unchanged, however, when controls for age, gender, and education are included in the models.

9 One possibility is that voters will find some politicians more trustworthy than others. While we are unable to control for this possibility here,

this subject is certainly worthy of attention in the future. For instance, researchers might determine how such trust differentials affect rates of correct voting and whether they benefit or harm particular candidates.

10 In keeping with other research, we code weak identifiers as non-partisans.

11 We use a one-tailed test of significance, as all variables have directional expectations.

12 The interactions of the two types of policy variables were insignificant, suggesting that the effect of each does not depend upon the presence of the other.

5. Understanding Ford Nation

1 Analyses of this type suffer from ecological (causal) concerns, and using aggregate-level data to draw conclusions about individuals is widely frowned upon by academics and pollsters alike. Given the nature of his data, Cain is able to draw conclusions about neighbourhoods but not individual electors.

2 The urban wards are 14, 18, 19, 20, 21, 26, 27, 28, 29, 30, 31, and 32. All other wards are considered suburban. The urban ridings (for the federal and provincial analysis) are: Beaches East York, Davenport, Parkdale High Park, St Paul's, Toronto Centre, Toronto Danforth, and Trinity Spadina. The suburban ridings are: Don Valley East, Done Valley West, Eglinton Lawrence, Etobicoke Centre, Etobicoke Lakeshore, Etobicoke North, Pickering Scarborough East, Scarborough Agincourt, Scarborough Centre, Scarborough Guildwood, Scarborough Rouge River, Scarborough Southwest, Willowdale, York Centre, York South-Weston, and York West.

3 Cain also suggests that single parents form part of Ford Nation, but the TES does not have a question that operationalizes this variable.

4 We employ feeling thermometer values as our dependent variable, rather than vote choice, because the former is a much more sensitive measure; instead of having two values (a vote for Ford or not), it has 101 potential options. It also allows for a relatively sensitive measure of *differences* in attitudes toward the Ford brothers, a comparison we take up in Table 5.4.

5 All results are weighted for age, gender, and education.

6 We are hesitant to make causal claims about this relationship, particularly given the unique nature of the controversies surrounding the Ford brothers. It may indeed be the case that electors who support the Fords prioritize policy considerations over the personal characteristics of politicians. We recognize, however, that some of those who support the Fords may be hesitant to state that they support the brothers on the basis of personality, given these controversies. For the purposes of this chapter, however, the goal is to determine simply whether there is a relationship between policy importance and attitudes toward the Fords.

3 A correlation matrix reveals that all five measures are positively related to one another, with Pearson coefficients ranging from 0.11 (transit vs taxes) to 0.37 (affordability vs traffic and congestion). This pattern suggests that respondents who were satisfied on some fronts also tended to be relatively satisfied on others. Pearson values are low enough, however, to indicate that these variables maintain considerable independence from one another.

4 We recognize that the relationship between policy evaluations and satisfaction with politicians is a complex one. Specifically, we suspect that the causal relationship between these two types of variables may not be unidirectional. Though evaluations of policy performance surely affect satisfaction with incumbent performance, it is possible that evaluations of politicians may also bias evaluations of policy performance. For our purposes, we are interested in determining which policy areas are related to satisfaction with performance and whether this varies by position. The direction of causality (if it is not unidirectional) is thus less important than establishing that such relationships do or do not exist.

5 The socio-demographic and attitudinal variables are comparatively unimportant when explaining satisfaction with elected officials. Though several of these variables do exhibit a statistically significant relationship with satisfaction, the policy variables make up the majority of variation (as indicated by R-squared values) in each set of models. Furthermore, the results remain similar even after the control variables are included in the models.

6 Policy performance displays a statistically significant relationship with evaluations of elected officials but does not go very far towards explaining that satisfaction. While the R-squared values in the table (which range from 0.056 to 0.133 in the policy-only models) are not negligible, they do indicate that other factors are important when explaining satisfaction with politicians.

7. Portrait of a Municipal Voter

1 Though the boroughs in Montreal have their own councils, they are not municipalities.
2 The epilogue of this book shows that there was no evidence of campaign effects in 2018 either.

Epilogue

1 Values are based on searches in the entire Province of Ontario, for that is the smallest geographic area possible using the Google Trends tool.
2 Toronto's ward boundaries were changed between elections, but the maps nevertheless allow for a useful comparison of the geographic distribution of the vote.

References

Abramowitz, A., & Webster, S. (2016). The rise of negative partisanship and the nationalization of U.S. elections in the 21st century. *Electoral Studies, 41*: 12–22. https://doi.org/10.1016/j.electstud.2015.11.001

Achen, C. H., & Bartels, L. M. (2004). Blind retrospection: Electoral responses to drought, flu, and shark attacks. Estudio, Working Paper 199. Instituto Juan March de Estudios e Investigaciones.

Adams, B. E., & Schreiber, R. (2011). Gender, campaign finance, and electoral success in municipal elections. *Journal of Urban Affairs, 33*(1): 83–97. https://doi.org/10.1111/j.1467-9906.2010.00508.x

Adsera, A., Boix, C., & Payne, M. (2003). Are you being served? Political accountability and quality of government. *Journal of Law, Economics, and Organization, 19*(2): 445–90. https://doi.org/10.1093/jleo/ewg017

AMO (Association of Municipalities of Ontario). (2014). *2014 municipal election stats.* http://www.amo.on.ca/AMO-Content/Elections/Municipal/2014/Counts-are-in-for-this-year%E2%80%99s-municipal-election.aspx

Anderson, C. D., McGregor, R. M., Moore, A. A., & Stephenson, L. B. (2017). Economic voting and multilevel governance: The case of Toronto. *Urban Affairs Review, 53*(1): 71–101. https://doi.org/10.1177/1078087415617302

Arceneaux, K. T. (2008). Can partisan cues diminish democratic accountability? *Political Behavior, 30*(2): 139–60. https://doi.org/10.1007/s11109-007-9044-7

Asako, Y., Iida, T., Matsubayashi, T., & Ueda, M. (2015). Dynastic politicians: Theory and evidence from Japan. *Japanese Journal of Political Science, 16*(1): 5–32. https://doi.org/10.1017/S146810991400036X

Barreto, M. A. (2007). ¡Si se Puede! Latino candidates and the mobilization of Latino voters. *American Political Science Review, 101*(3): 425–41. https://doi.org/10.1017/S0003055407070293

Barreto, M. A., Villarreal, M, & Woods, N. D. (2005). Metropolitan Latino political behavior: Voter turnout and candidate preference in Los Angeles. *Journal of Urban Affairs, 27*(1): 71–91. https://doi.org/10.1111/j.0735-2166.2005.00225.x

Bastien, F., Bélanger, E., & Gélineau, F. (Eds.). (2013). *Les Québécois aux urnes: Les partis, les médias et les citoyens en campagne.* Presses de l'Université de Montréal.

Baumeister, R. F., Bratslavsky, E., Finkenauer, C., & Vohs, K D. (2001). Bad is stronger than good. *Review of General Psychology, 5*(4): 323–70. https://doi.org/10.1037/1089-2680.5.4.323

Beasley, R., & Joslyn, M. (2001). Cognitive dissonance and post-decision attitude change in six presidential elections. *Political Psychology, 22*(3): 521–40. https://doi.org/10.1111/0162-895X.00252

Bélanger, E. (2003). Issue ownership by Canadian political parties, 1953–2001. *Canadian Journal of Political Science, 36*(3): 539–58. https://doi.org/10.1017/S0008423903778755

Bélanger, E., & Meguid, B. (2008). Issue salience, issue ownership, and issue-based vote choice. *Electoral Studies, 27*(3): 477–91. https://doi.org/10.1016/j.electstud.2008.01.001

Berelson, B., Lazarsfeld P. F., & McPhee, W. N. (1954). *Voting.* University of Chicago Press.

Berry, C. R., & Howell, W. G. (2007). Accountability and local elections: Rethinking voting. *The Journal of Politics, 69*(3): 844–58. https://doi.org/10.1111/j.1468-2508.2007.00579.x

Bird, K., Jackson, S. D., McGregor, R. M., Moore, A. A. & Stephenson, L. B. (2016). "Sex (and ethnicity) in the city: Affinity voting in the 2014 Toronto Mayoral election." *Canadian Journal of Political Science, 49*(2): 359–83. https://doi.org/10.1017/S0008423916000536

Blais, A. (2000). *To vote or not to vote: The merits and limits of rational choice theory.* University of Pittsburgh Press.

Blais, A. (2006). What affects voter turnout? *Annual Review of Political Science, 9*(1): 11–25.

Blais, A., Gidengil, E., Nadeau, R., & Nevitte, N. (2002). *Anatomy of a Liberal victory: Making sense of the vote in the 2000 Canadian Election.* University of Toronto Press.

Blais, A., Gidengil, E., Nadeau, R., & Nevitte, N. (2003). Campaign dynamics in the 2000 Canadian election: How the leader debates salvaged the Conservative Party. *PS: Political Science and Politics, 36*(1): 45–50. https://doi.org/10.1017/S1049096503001677

Blais, A., Gidengil, E., & Nevitte, N. (2006). Do polls influence the vote? In H. E. Brady & R. Johnston (Eds.), *Capturing campaign effects.* University of Michigan Press.

Blais, A., & Kilibarda, A. (2016). Correct voting and post-election regret. *PS: Political Science and Politics, 49*(4): 761–5. https://doi.org/10.1017/S1049096516001372

Bohlken, A., & Chandra, K. (2012). Dynastic politics and party organizations: Why family ties improve electoral performance in India. Mimeo.

Bonneau, C. & Cann, D. (2015). Party identification and vote choice in partisan and nonpartisan elections. *Political Behavior*, *37*(1): 43–66. https://doi.org/10.1007/s11109-013-9260-2

Breux, S., & Bherer, L. (2011). *Les élections municipales au Québec: Enjeux et perspectives*. Presses de l'Université Laval, Collection Études Urbaines.

Brockington, D., Donovan, T., Bowler, S., & Brischetto, R. (1998). Minority representation under cumulative and limited voting. *The Journal of Politics*, *60*(4): 1108–25. https://doi.org/10.2307/2647733

Buchanan, W. (1977). American institutions and political behavior. In D. M. Freeman (Ed.), *Foundations of political science*. Free Press.

Camp, R. A. (1995). *Political recruitment across two centuries: Mexico, 1884–1991*. University of Texas Press.

Campbell, A, Converse, P., Miller, W. & Stokes, D. (1960). *The American voter*. University of Chicago Press.

Caruana, N., McGregor, R. M., Moore, A. A., & Stephenson, L. B. (2018). Voting "Ford" or against: Understanding strategic voting in the 2014 Toronto Municipal Election. *Social Science Quarterly*, *99*(1): 231–45. https://doi.org/10.1111/ssqu.12359

Caruana, N., McGregor, R. M., & Stephenson, L. B. (2015). The power of the dark side: Negative partisanship and political behaviour. *Canadian Journal of Political Science*, *48*(4): 771–89. https://doi.org/10.1017/S0008423914000882

Chiasson, G., Gauthier, M., Andrew, C. (2014). Municipal political parties and politicization: The case of the 2013 Gatineau elections. *Canadian Journal of Urban Research*, *23*(2): 79–99.

Chiasson, G, & Mévellec, A. (2013). The 2013 Quebec municipal elections: What is specific to Quebec? *Canadian Journal of Urban Research*, *23*(2): 1–8.

City of Toronto. (2014). Declaration of results: 2014 Municipal General Election. Monday, 27 October 2014. City Clerk's Office, City of Toronto.

City of Toronto v. Ontario (Attorney General). (2018). ONSC 5151. http://www.ontariocourts.ca/scj/decisions/

Clarkson, S. (1972). *City Lib: Parties and reform*. A. M. Hakkert.

Cook, T. E. (1979). Legislature vs legislator: A note on the paradox of congressional support. *Legislative Studies Quarterly*, *4*(1): 43–52. https://doi.org/10.2307/439602

Cross, W. P., Malloy, J., Small, T. A., & Stephenson, L. B. 2015. *Fighting for votes: Parties, the media, and voters in an Ontario election*. UBC Press.

Cutler, F. (2002). The simplest shortcut of all: Sociodemographic characteristics and electoral choice. *The Journal of Politics*, *64*(2): 466–90.

Cutler, F. (2008). One voter, two first-order elections? *Electoral Studies*, *27*(3): 492–504.

Cutler, F., & Matthews, J. S. (2005). The challenge of municipal voting: Vancouver 2002. *Canadian Journal of Political Science*, *38*(2): 359–82. https://doi.org/10.1017/S0008423905040151

Dahl, R. A. (1967). *Pluralist democracy in the United States: Conflict and consent.* Rand McNally.

Dalton, R. J. (2002). *Citizen politics* (3rd ed.). Chatham House Publishers of Seven Bridges Press.

Dancey, L., & Sheagley, G. (2013). Heuristics behaving badly: Party cues and voter knowledge. *American Journal of Political Science, 57*(2): 312–25. https://doi.org/10.1111/j.1540-5907.2012.00621.x

Delli Carpini, M. X., & Keeter, S. (1996). *What Americans know about politics and why it matters.* Yale University Press.

Doolittle, R. (2014). *Crazy town: The Rob Ford story.* Viking Canada

Dornan, C., & Pammett, J. H. (2016). *The Canadian federal election of 2015.* Dundurn.

Downs, A. (1957). *An economic theory of democracy.* Harper and Row.

Duch, R. M., Palmer, H. D., & Anderson, C. J. (2000). Heterogeneity in perceptions of national economic conditions. *American Journal of Political Science, 44*(4): 635–52. https://doi.org/10.2307/2669272

FDM (Federation of Canadian Municipalities). (2013). *2013 – Municipal statistics: Elected officials gender statistics.* http://www.fcm.ca/Documents/reports/Women/2013_municipal_statistics_elected_official_gender_EN.pdf

Feinstein, B. D. (2010). The dynasty advantage: Family ties in congressional elections. *Legislative Studies Quarterly, 35*(4): 571–98.

Ferguson, R. (2018). Bill to slash the size of Toronto city council passes. *Toronto Star.* https://www.thestar.com/news/queenspark/2018/08/14/bill-to-slash-the-size-of-toronto-city-council-passes.html

Festinger, L. (1957). *A theory of cognitive dissonance.* Row, Peterson, & Company.

Fey, M. (1997). Stability and coordination in Duverger's law: A formal model of pre-election polls and strategic voting. *American Political Science Review, 91*(1): 135–47. https://doi.org/10.2307/2952264

Fischel, W. A. (2001). *The homevoter hypothesis: How home values influence local government taxation, school finance, and land-use policies.* Harvard University Press.

Fournier, P. (2002). The uninformed Canadian voter. In J. Everitt & B O'Neill (Eds.), *Citizen politics: Research and theory in Canadian political behaviour.* Oxford University Press.

Fournier, P., Cutler, F., Soroka, S., Stolle, D., & Bélanger, E. (2013). Riding the orange wave: Leadership, values, issues, and the 2011 Canadian Election. *Canadian Journal of Political Science, 46*(4): 863–97. https://doi.org/10.1017/S0008423913000875

Fournier, P., Nadeau, R., Blais, A., Gidengil, E., & Nevitte, N. (2004). Time-of-voting decision and susceptibility to campaigns. *Electoral Studies, 23*(4): 661–81. https://doi.org/10.1016/j.electstud.2003.09.001

Gidengil, E., Nevitte, N., Blais, A., Everitt, J., & Fournier, P. (2012). *Dominance and decline: Making sense of recent Canadian elections.* University of Toronto Press.

Gidengil, E., & Vengroff, R. (1997). Representational gains of Canadian women or token growth? The case of Québec's municipal politics. *Canadian Journal of Political Science, 30*(3): 513–37. https://doi.org/10.1017/S0008423900015997

Gierzynski, A., Kleppner, P., & Lewis, J. (1998). Money or the machine: Money and votes in Chicago aldermanic elections. *American Politics Quarterly, 26*(2): 160–73. https://doi.org/10.1177/1532673X9802600202

Golder, M., & Stramski, J. (2010). Ideological congruence and electoral institutions. *American Journal of Political Science, 54*(1): 90–106. https://doi.org/10.1111/j.1540-5907.2009.00420.x

Golder, S., Lago, I., Blais, A., Gidengil, E., & Gschwend, T. (2017). *Multi-level electoral politics: Beyond the second-order election model.* Oxford University Press.

Green, D. P., Gerber, A. S., & Nickerson, D. W. (2003). Getting out the vote in local elections: results from six door-to-door canvassing experiments. *Journal of Politics, 65*(4): 1083–96.

Ha, S. E., & Lau, R.R. (2015). Personality traits and correct voting. *American Politics Research, 43*(6): 975–98. https://doi.org/10.1177/1532673X14568551

Hajnal, Z. L., & Lewis, P. G. (2003). Municipal institutions and voter turnout in local elections. *Urban Affairs Review, 38*(5): 645–68. https://doi.org/10.1177/1078087403038005002

Hamilton, H. D. (1971). The municipal voter: Voting and nonvoting in city elections. *American Political Science Review, 65*(4): 1135–40. https://doi.org/10.2307/1953505

Heath, A., McLean, I., Taylor, B. & Curtice, J. (1999). Between first and second order: A comparison of voting behaviour in European and local elections in Britain. *European Journal of Political Research, 35*: 389–414. https://doi.org/10.1111/1475-6765.00454

Hobolt, S. B. (2005). When Europe matters: The impact of political information on voting in EU referendums. *Journal of Elections, Public Opinion, and Parties, 15*(1): 85–109. https://doi.org/10.1080/13689880500064635

Jacobson, G. (1983). *The politics of congressional elections.* Little, Brown.

Johnston, R., Blais, A., Brady, H. E, & Crête, J. (1992). *Letting the people decide: Dynamics of a Canadian election.* McGill–Queen's University Press.

Kahneman, D., & Tversky, A. (1979). Prospect theory: An analysis of decision under risk. *Econometrica: Journal of the Econometric Society, 47*: 263–91. https://doi.org/10.2307/1914185

Key, Jr., V. O. (1966). *The responsible electorate: Rationality in presidential voting, 1936–1960.* The Belknap Press of Harvard University Press.

Klingemann, H-D., Hofferbert, R. I., & Budge, I. (1994). *Parties, policies, and democracy.* Westview Press.

Krebs, T. B. (1998). The determinants of candidates' vote share and the advantages of incumbency in city council elections. *American Journal of Political Science, 42*(3): 921–35. https://doi.org/10.2307/2991735

Kushner, J. (2001). Canadian mayors: A profile and determinants of electoral success. *Canadian Journal of Urban Research*, *10*(1): 5–22.

Kushner, J., Siegel, D., & Stanwick, H. (1997). Ontario municipal elections: Voting trends and determinants of electoral success in a Canadian province. *Canadian Journal of Political Science*, *30*(3): 539–53. https://doi.org/10.1017/S0008423900016000

Lassen, D. D. (2005). The effect of information on voter turnout: Evidence from a natural experiment. *American Journal of Political Science*, *49*(1): 103–18. https://doi.org/10.2307/3647716

Lau, R. R. (2013). Correct voting in the 2008 U.S. presidential nominating elections. *Political Behavior*, *35*(2): 331–55. https://doi.org/10.1007/s11109-012-9198-9

Lau, R. R., Andersen, D. J., & Redlawsk, D. P. (2008). An exploration of correct voting in recent U.S. Presidential Elections. *American Journal of Political Science*, *52*(2): 395–411.

Lau, R. R., Patel, P., Fahmy, D. F., & Kaufman, R. R. (2014). Correct voting across thirty-three democracies: A preliminary analysis. *British Journal of Political Science*, *44*(2): 239–59. https://doi.org/10.1017/S0007123412000610

Lau, R. R., & Redlawsk, D. P. (1997). Voting correctly. *American Political Science Review*, *91*(3): 585–98. https://doi.org/10.2307/2952076

Lau, R. R., & Redlawsk, D. P. (2001). Advantages and disadvantages of cognitive heuristics in political decision making. *American Journal of Political Science*, *45*(4): 951–71. https://doi.org/10.2307/2669334

Lazarsfeld, P. F., Berelson, B., & Gaudet, H. (1948). *The people's choice: How the voter makes up his mind in a presidential campaign*. Columbia University Press.

Lieske, J. (1989). The political dynamics of urban voting behavior. *American Journal of Political Science*, *33*(1): 150–74. https://doi.org/10.2307/2111257

Locke, J. (2003). *Two treatises of government and a letter concerning toleration*. Yale University Press.

Lupia, A. (1994). Shortcuts versus encyclopedias: Information and voting behavior in California insurance reform elections. *American Political Science Review*, *88*(1): 63–76. https://doi.org/10.2307/2944882

Manin, B., Przeworski, A., & Stokes S. C. (1999). Elections and representation. In A. Przeworski, S. C. Stokes, & B. Manin (Eds.), *Democracy, accountability, and representation*. Cambridge University Press.

Marschall, M., Shah, P, & Ruhil, A. (2011). The study of local elections: Editors' introduction: A looking glass into the future. *PS: Political Science and Politics*, *44*(1): 97–100. https://doi.org/10.1017/S1049096510001940

Marsh, M. (1998). Testing the second-order election model after four European elections. *British Journal of Political Science*, *28*(4): 591–607. https://doi.org/10.1017/S000712349800026X

McGregor, R. M. (2013a). Cognitive dissonance and political attitudes: The case of Canada. *Social Science Journal, 50*(2): 168–76. https://doi.org/10.1016/j.soscij.2013.01.004

McGregor, R. M. (2013b). Measuring "correct voting" using comparative manifestos project data. *Journal of Elections, Public Opinion, and Parties, 23*(1): 1–26. https://doi.org/10.1080/17457289.2012.691883

McGregor, R. M. (2018). Voters who abstain: Explaining abstention and ballot roll-off in the 2014 Toronto municipal election. *Urban Affairs Review, 54*(6): 1081–106. https://doi.org/10.1177/1078087416688960

McGregor, R. M., Moore, A. A., & Stephenson, L. B. (2016). Political attitudes and behaviour in a non-partisan environment: Toronto 2014. *Canadian Journal of Political Science, 49*(2): 311–33. https://doi.org/10.1017/S0008423916000573

McGregor, R. M., & Spicer, Z. (2016). The Canadian homevoter: Property values and municipal politics in Canada. *Journal of Urban Affairs, 38*(1): 123–39. https://doi.org/10.1111/juaf.12178

Mendoza, R. U., Beja Jr., E. L., Venida, V. S., & Yap, D. B. (2012). Inequality in democracy: Insights from an empirical analysis of political dynasties in the 15th Philippine congress. *Philippine Political Science Journal, 33*(2): 132–45. https://doi.org/10.1080/01154451.2012.734094

Merolla, J. L., Stephenson, L. B., & Zechmeister, E. J. (2016). Deciding correctly: Variance in the effective use of party cues. In A. Blais, J-F. Laslier, & K. Van der Straeten (Eds.), *Voting experiments.* Springer International.

Metrolinx. (2016). GO Regional Express Rail Update. Staff Report. Metrolinx. June 28.

Metrolinx. (2017). New Stations. http://www.metrolinx.com/en/regionalplanning/newstations/default.aspx

Milic, T. (2012). Correct voting in direct legislation. *Swiss Political Science Review, 18*(4): 399–427. https://doi.org/10.1111/spsr.12000

Miller, W. E., Pierce, R., Thomassen, J., Herrera, R., Holmberg, S., Esaisson, P., & Wessels, B. (1999). *Policy representation in Western democracies.* Oxford University Press.

Miller, W. E., & Stokes, D. E. (1963). Constituency influence in Congress. *American Political Science Review, 57*(1): 45–57. https://doi.org/10.2307/1952717

Moore, A. A. (2017). The potential and consequences of municipal reform. IMFG Perspectives, no. 20. Institute on Municipal Finance and Governance, Munk School of Global Affairs, University of Toronto.

Moore, A. A., McGregor, R. M., & Stephenson, L. B. (2017). Paying attention and the incumbency effect: Voting behaviour in the 2014 Toronto municipal election. *International Political Science Review, 38*(1): 85–98. https://doi.org/10.1177/0192512115616268

Morlan, R. L. (1984). Municipal vs national election voter turnout: Europe and the United States. *Political Science Quarterly, 99*(3): 457–70. https://doi.org/10.2307/2149943

Mullainathan, S., & Washington, E. (2009). Sticking with your vote: Cognitive dissonance and political attitudes. *American Economic Journal: Applied Economics, 1*(1): 86–111. https://doi.org/10.1257/app.1.1.86

Nadeau, R., Cloutie, E., & Guay, J. H. (1993). New evidence about the existence of a bandwagon effect in the opinion formation process. *International Political Science Review, 14*(2): 235–46.

Naurin, E. (2011). *Election promises, party behaviour, and voter perceptions.* Palgrave Macmillan.

Niven, D. (2004). The mobilization solution? Face-to-face contact and voter turnout in a municipal election. *Journal of Politics, 66*(3): 868–84. https://doi.org/10.1111/j.1468-2508.2004.00280.x

Niven, D. (2006). A field experiment on the effects of negative campaign mail on voter turnout in a municipal election. *Political Research Quarterly, 59*(2): 203–10. https://doi.org/10.1177/106591290605900203

Oliver, J. E., & Ha, S. E. (2007). Vote choice in suburban elections. *American Political Science Review, 101*(3): 393–408. https://doi.org/10.1017/S0003055407070323

Olson, M. (1969). The principle of "fiscal equivalence": The division of responsibilities among different levels of government. *The American Economic Review, 59*(2): 479–87.

Ontario. Ministry of Municipal Affairs and Housing. (2016). Ontario passes legislation to allow ranked ballot option for municipal elections [press release]. https://news.ontario.ca/mma/en/2016/06/ontario-passes-legislation-to-allow-ranked-ballot-option-for-municipal-elections.html.

Ostrom, V., Tiebout, C. M., & Warren, R. (1961). The organization of government in metropolitan areas: A theoretical inquiry. *American Political Science Review, 55*(4): 831–42. https://doi.org/10.2307/1952530

Pomper, G. (1966). Ethnic and group voting in nonpartisan municipal elections. *Public Opinion Quarterly, 30*(1): 79–97. https://doi.org/10.1086/267383

Popkin, S. L. (1994). *The reasoning voter* (2nd ed). University of Chicago Press.

Pruysers, S. (2014). Reconsidering vertical integration: An examination of national political parties and their counterparts in Ontario. *Canadian Journal of Political Science, 47*(2): 237–58. https://doi.org/10.1017/S0008423914000407

Przeworski, A., & Stokes, S. C. (1999). Introduction. In A. Przeworski, S. C. Stokes, & B. Manin (Eds.), *Democracy, accountability, and representation.* Cambridge University Press.

Quesnel, L., with Hamel, S. (2007). *Your guide to municipal institutions in Canada.* Federation of Canadian Municipalities, International Centre for Municipal Development.

RaBIT (Ranked Ballot Initiative of Toronto). (n.d.). Benefits of ranked ballots [website]. http://www.rabit.ca/benefits

Rahn, W. M. (1993). The role of partisan stereotypes in information processing about political candidates. *American Journal of Political Science, 37*(2): 472–96. https://doi.org/10.2307/2111381

Reif, K., & Schmitt, H. (1980). Nine second-order national elections: A conceptual framework for the analysis of European election results. *European Journal of Political Research, 8*(1): 3–44. https://doi.org/10.1111/j.1475-6765.1980.tb00737.x

Ryan, J. B. (2011). Social networks as a shortcut to correct voting. *American Journal of Political Science, 55*(4): 753–66. https://doi.org/10.1111/j.1540-5907.2011.00528.x

Sancton, A. (2015). *Canadian local government: An urban perspective* (2nd ed). Oxford University Press.

Schaffner, B. F., & Streb, M. J. (2002). The partisan heuristic in low-information elections. *Public Opinion Quarterly, 66*(4): 559–81. https://doi.org/10.1086/343755

Schattschneider, E. E. (1942). *Party government.* Rinehart.

Schmidt, G. D., & Saunders, K. L. (2004). Effective quotas, relative party magnitude, and the success of female candidates: Peruvian municipal elections in comparative perspective. *Comparative Political Studies, 37*(6): 704–24. https://doi.org/10.1177/0010414004265884

Schmitt, H. (2005). The European Parliament elections of June 2004: Still second-order? *West European Politics, 28*(3): 650–79. https://doi.org/10.1080/01402380500085962

Selokela, T. (2014). The representation of female councilors in South African municipal elections. *Journal of Peacebuilding and Development, 9*(3): 95–101. https://doi.org/10.1080/15423166.2014.983368

Sheffield, J. F., & Hadley, C. D. (1984). Racial voting in a biracial city: A reexamination of some hypotheses. *American Politics Research, 12*(4): 449–64. https://doi.org/10.1177/1532673X8401200404

Siemiatycki, M., & Marshall, S. (2014). Who votes in Toronto municipal elections? Report. Maytree.

Smith, D. M. (2012). *Succeeding in politics: Dynasties in democracies.* PhD dissertation. University of California, San Diego.

Sniderman, P. M., Brody, R. A., & Tetlock, P. E. (1991). *Reasoning and choice: Explorations in political psychology.* Cambridge University Press.

Squire, P., & Smith, E. R. A. N. (1988). The effect of partisan information on voters in nonpartisan elections. *The Journal of Politics, 50*(1): 169–79. https://doi.org/10.2307/2131046

Stanwick, H. (2000). A megamayor for all people? Voting behaviour and electoral success in the 1997 Toronto municipal election. *Canadian Journal of Political Science, 33*(3): 549–68. https://doi.org/10.1017/S0008423900000196

Stephenson, L. B., McGregor, R. M., & Moore, A. A. (2018). Sins of the brother: Partisanship and accountability in Toronto 2014. In S. Breaux & J. Couture (Eds.), *Accountability and responsiveness at the local level: Views from Canada*. McGill–Queen's University Press.

Stokes, D. E. (1963). Spatial models of party competition. *American Political Science Review, 57*(2), 368–77. https://doi.org/10.2307/1952828

Sussmann, C. (2006). Vancouver's 2002 municipal election: Growth coalition defeated. *Studies in Political Economy, 77*(1): 157–74. https://doi.org/10.1080/19187033.2006.11675116

Taylor, Z. (2011). Who elected Rob Ford, and why? An ecological analysis of the 2010 Toronto election. Paper presented at the annual meeting of the Canadian Political Science Association. Waterloo, ON, 2011.

Thompson, M. R. (2012). Asia's hybrid dynasties. *Asian Affairs, 43*(2): 204–20.

Tolley, E. (2011). Do women "do better" in municipal politics? Electoral representation across three levels of government. *Canadian Journal of Political Science, 44*(3): 573–94. https://doi.org/10.1017/S0008423911000503

Toronto (City) v. Ontario (Attorney General). (2018). ONCA 761. http://www.ontariocourts.ca/decisions/2018/2018ONCA0761.pdf

Tremblay, M., and Mévellec, A. (2013). Truly more accessible to women than the legislature? Women in municipal politics. In L. Trimble, J. Arscott, & M. Tremblay (Eds.), *Stalled: The representation of women in Canadian governments*. UBC Press.

Walks, A. (2015). Stopping the "war on the car": Neoliberalism, Fordism, and the politics of automobility in Toronto. *Mobilities, 10*(3): 402–22. https://doi.org/10.1080/17450101.2014.880563

Walks, R. A. (2004). Place of residence, party preferences, and political attitudes in Canadian cities and suburbs. *Journal of Urban Affairs, 26*(3): 269–95. https://doi.org/10.1111/j.0735-2166.2004.00200.x

Walks, R. A. (2005). The city-suburban cleavage in Canadian federal politics. *Canadian Journal of Political Science, 38*(2): 383–413. https://doi.org/10.1017/S0008423905030842

Walks, R. A. (2007) The boundaries of suburban discontent? Urban definitions and neighbourhood political effects. *The Canadian Geographer, 51*(2): 160–85. https://doi.org/10.1111/j.1541-0064.2007.00172.x

Walks, R. A. (2013). Metropolitan political ecology and contextual effects in Canada. In J. M. Sellers, D. Kübler, M. Walter-Rogg, & R. A. Walks (Eds.), *The political ecology of the metropolis*. ECPR Press.

Wesley, J. J. (Ed.). (2015). *Big worlds: Politics and elections in the Canadian provinces and territories*. University of Toronto Press.

Zaller, J. (1992). *The nature and origins of mass opinion*. Cambridge University Press.

News Articles

Alamenciak, T. (2014, 3 May). Support for mayor is waning, poll shows. *Toronto Star*, p. GT4.

Al Jazeera. (2014, 1 May). Toronto mayor in new crack video scandal. *Al Jazeera*. http://www.aljazeera.com/news/americas/2014/05/toronto-mayor-new -crack-video-scandal-2014511477859150.html

Benzie, R. (2014, 28 June). Wynne warns next mayor against nixing transit. *Toronto Star*, p. A6.

Boesveld, S. (2014, 9 September). David Soknacki drops out of mayoral race, citing voters' desire to keep Rob Ford from re-election. *National Post*. http:// nationalpost.com/posted-toronto/david-soknacki-drops-out-of-mayoral-race -citing-voters-desire-to-keep-rob-ford-from-re-election

Boesveld, S. (2014, 10 September). Rob Ford in "good spirits" after checking into hospital for tumour on his abdomen. *National Post*. http://nationalpost .com/news/canada/rob-ford-admitted-to-hospital-with-a-tumour-on-his -abdomen

Cain, P. (2014, 8 September). 11 things demographic data tells us about Ford Nation. *Global News*. https://globalnews.ca/news/1546074/11-things -demographic-data-tells-us-about-ford-nation/

Canadian Press. (2014, 12 September). Facts about the other Ford: A look at mayoral candidate Doug Ford. *CP24*. https://www.cp24.com/news/facts -about-the-other-ford-a-look-at-mayoral-candidate-doug-ford-1.2005035

Canadian Press. (2016, 26 July). Rob Ford's nephew wins former Toronto mayor's council seat. *CTV News*. https://www.ctvnews.ca/canada/rob-ford -s-nephew-wins-former-toronto-mayor-s-council-seat-1.3002359

Carlson, K. B. (2010, 25 October). Election wrap-up: Ford thanks Toronto for "vote of confidence." *National Post*. http://nationalpost.com/news/polls -almost-closed-in-toronto-election

CBC News. (2014, 12 September). Rob Ford pulls out of mayoral race, Doug Ford steps in. *CBC News*. http://www.cbc.ca/news/canada/toronto/doug -ford-makes-gains-in-toronto-mayor-s-race-poll-suggests-1.2790005

CBC News. (2014, 7 October). Doug Ford makes gains in Toronto mayor's race, poll suggests. *CBC News*. http://www.cbc.ca/news/canada/toronto/doug -ford-makes-gains-in-toronto-mayor-s-race-poll-suggests-1.2790005

CBC News. (2015, 11 June). Gardiner Expressway vote: Toronto council backs "hybrid" plan. *CBC News*. http://www.cbc.ca/news/canada/toronto /gardiner-expressway-vote-toronto-council-backs-hybrid-plan-1.3109935

CBC News. (2016, 31 March). Eastern Gardiner redevelopment plan chosen by city council also the priciest. *CBC News*. http://www.cbc.ca/news/canada /toronto/gardiner-hybrid-vote-1.3515566

Chabas, C. (2014, 2 May). Rob Ford, un genou à terre. *Le Monde.* http://www
.lemonde.fr/ameriques/article/2014/05/01/rob-ford-un-politicien-en
-pleine-descente-aux-enfers_4410256_3222.html

Church, E. (2014, 22 February). Karen Stintz steps into ring. As of Monday,
the former TTC chair will be the first high-profile challenger to Rob Ford
officially registered to run. *The Globe and Mail,* p. M4.

Church, E. (2014, 18 June). $168-million surplus aided by Toronto real estate
fees. *The Globe and Mail,* p. A7.

Church, E., & Hui, A. (2013, 24 May). Mayor's allies prepare to run city. *The
Globe and Mail,* p. A1.

Church, E., & Hui, A. (2014, 13 March). Chow makes candidacy official. *The
Globe and Mail,* p. A10.

Church, E., & Hui, A. (2014, 2 May). Calls grow for Ford to resign in wake of
new video, audio. *The Globe and Mail,* p. A1.

Church, E., & Hui, A. (2014, 12 September). Doug Ford running for mayor was
a long-time back-up plan: sources. *The Globe and Mail.* https://www
.theglobeandmail.com/news/toronto/passing-the-political-torch-from-one
-ford-brother-to-the-other/article20592615/

Cohn, M. R. (2018, 29 January). PCs wanted a leadership race and Doug Ford
gave them one. *Toronto Star.* https://www.thestar.com/opinion/star
-columnists/2018/01/29/pcs-wanted-a-leadership-race-and-doug-ford
-gave-them-one.html

Dale, D. (2013, 5 November). Rob Ford: "Yes, I have smoked crack cocaine."
Toronto Star. https://www.thestar.com/news/crime/2013/11/05/rob_ford
_yes_i_have_smoked_crack_cocaine.html

Dale, D. (2014, 26 February). Toronto mayoral election poll shows tight early
race among Chow, Ford, Tory. *Toronto Star.* https://www.thestar.com/news
/city_hall/toronto2014election/2014/02/26/toronto_mayoral_election
_poll_shows_tight_early_race_among_chow_ford_tory.html

Dale, D. (2014, 30 June). Ford's back, but power remains with Kelly. *Toronto
Star,* p. A6.

Dale, D. (2014, 16 July). Tory sharpens attack on Ford record. *Toronto Star,*
p. GT1.

Dale, D. (2014, 29 July). The transit wars: How John Tory, Olivia Chow are
selling their plans. *Toronto Star.* https://www.thestar.com/news/city_hall
/toronto2014election/2014/07/29/the_transit_wars_how_john_tory_olivia
_chow_are_selling_their_plans.html

Dale, D. (2014, 20 August). John Tory slams Olivia Chow's response to
operative's "segregationist" tweet. *Toronto Star.* https://www.thestar.com
/news/city_hall/toronto2014election/2014/08/20/chow_operative_warren
_kinsella_calls_torys_transit_proposal_segregationist.html

Di Ciano, J. (2017, 27 March). Ranked ballots on life support. *Toronto Sun*.
    http://www.torontosun.com/2017/03/27/ranked-ballots-on-life-support

Diebel, L. (2014, 14 June). 7 things Wynne's victory says about us. *Toronto Star*,
    p. A15.

Diebel, L. (2014, 25 October). Mayoral candidate John Tory a leader from
    childhood. *Toronto Star*. https://www.thestar.com/news/city_hall
    /toronto2014election/2014/10/25/mayoral_candidate_john_tory_a_leader
    _from_childhood.html

Doolittle, R. (2014, 15 March). Toronto mayoral election profile:
    Olivia Chow. *Toronto Star*. https://www.thestar.com/news/city_hall
    /toronto2014election/2014/03/15/toronto_mayoral_election_profile
    _olivia_chow.html

D'Souza, S. (2014, 3 October). David Soknacki claims Fords used city
    resources for mayoral campaign. *CBC News*. http://www.cbc.ca/news
    /canada/toronto/david-soknacki-claims-fords-used-city-resources-for-mayoral
    -campaign-1.2787221

Ferguson, R. (2018, 14 August). Bill to slash the size of Toronto
    city council passes. *Toronto Star*. https://www.thestar.com/news
    /queenspark/2018/08/14/bill-to-slash-the-size-of-toronto-city-council
    -passes.html

Flavelle, D. (2013, 13 May). Poll shows Chow remains strong. *Toronto Star*,
    p. GT2.

Gee, M. (2014, 27 March). Don't count Rob Ford out just yet. *The Globe and
    Mail*, p. A12.

Gee, M. (2014, 21 August). Toronto mayoral race: Chow–Tory dust-up portends
    nothing good. *The Globe and Mail*, p. A8.

Gillis, C. (2014, 7 October). Poll has Doug Ford in hunt for Toronto mayoralty.
    Maclean's. http://www.macleans.ca/politics/poll-has-doug-ford-in-hunt-for
    -toronto-mayoralty/

Gilmour, D. (2012, 23 November). The great lie of the populist politician.
    Toronto Star. https://www.thestar.com/news/insight/2012/11/23/the
    _great_lie_of_the_populist_politician.html

The Globe and Mail. (2016, 25 March). The real lessons of Rob Ford and Donald
    Trump. https://www.theglobeandmail.com/opinion/editorials/the
    -real-lessons-of-rob-ford-and-donald-trump/article29382995/

Gray, J. (2017, 31 January). Toronto Mayor John Tory backs down on
    contracting out garbage. *The Globe and Mail*. https://www.theglobeandmail
    .com/news/toronto/toronto-mayor-john-tory-backs-down-on-contracting-out
    -garbage/article33849453/

Gray, J. (2018, 5 October). Why Toronto mayoral candidate Jennifer Keesmaat
    feels she has to keep running. *The Globe and Mail*. https://www

.theglobeandmail.com/canada/ toronto/article-why-toronto-mayoral
-candidate-jennifer-keesmaat-feels-she-has-to-keep/

Grenier, E. (2015, 26 November). Change to preferential ballot would benefit
Liberals. *CBC News*.://www.cbc.ca/news/politics/grenier-preferential
-ballot-1.3332566

The Guardian. (2014, 1 May). Rob Ford admits drug problem and takes leave as
Toronto mayor. Retrieved from https://www.theguardian.com/world/2014
/may/01/rob-ford-admits-drug-problem-and-takes-leave-as-toronto-mayor

Hennessy, A. (2014, 20 August). Olivia Chow unveils her transit plan. *Toronto
Sun*. http://torontosun.com/2014/08/20/olivia-chow-unveils-her-transit
-map/wcm/45910f41-1d13-4eff-8ebd-12ca5c43ea7a

Hepburn, B. (2014, 23 January). John Tory will change dynamics of mayoral
race. *Toronto Star*, p. A21.

Hepburn, B. (2014, 8 May). Anybody-but-Chow theme emerges in Ford's
absence. *Toronto Star*, p. A25

Hepburn, B. (2014, 6 August). Three biggest blunders of John Tory's
career: Hepburn. *Toronto Star*. https://www.thestar.com/opinion
/commentary/2014/08/06/three_biggest_blunders_of_john_torys
_career_hepburn.html

Hepburn, B. (2014, 29 October). Ford Nation remains huge political
force: Hepburn. *Toronto Star*. https://www.thestar.com/opinion
/commentary/2014/10/29/ford_nation_remains_huge_political
_force_hepburn.html

Hopper, T. (2015, 29 October 29). Rob Ford acknowledges that disease
might kill him after cancer recurrence confirmed. *National Post*. http://
nationalpost.com/news/canada/new-tumour-found-on-rob-fords-bladder
-is-cancerous-will-require-extensive-chemotherapy-doug-ford

Hui, A. (2013, 22 November). New report of domestic assault while Ford
approval remains strong. *The Globe and Mail*. https://www.theglobeandmail
.com/news/toronto/fords-approval-strong-amid-new-report-of-domestic
-police-call/article15560112/

Hui, A, Church, E., & Lum, F. (2014, 12 September). Rob Ford drops out of
mayoral race, Doug Ford running in his place. *The Globe and Mail*. https://
www.theglobeandmail.com/news/toronto/ford-dropping-out-of-toronto
-mayoral-race/article20576741/

Hume, C. (2010, 18 December). The Fords and their hordes come to town.
Toronto Star, p. GT2.

The Irish Times. (2014. 1 May). Rob Ford to seek help for "substance abuse."
https://www.irishtimes.com/news/world/us/rob-ford-to-seek-help-for-substance
-abuse-1.1780013

James, R. (2010, 8 November). Miller pushes politics of surplus. *Toronto Star*, p. GT4.

James, R. (2013, 21 November). Rob Ford: Look at Ford Nation, Ford haters and the rest. *Toronto Star*. https://www.thestar.com/news/city_hall/2013/11/21/a_look_at_ford_nation_ford_haters_inc_and_the_rest_james.html

James, R. (2014, 16 January). Scrapping subway plans a risky gambit for Soknacki. *Toronto Star*, p. GT2.

James, R. (2014, 22 February). City's mayoral election is Chow's to lose. *Toronto Star*, p. GT2.

James, R. (2014, 25 February). Crowded race gains full steam: With Tory and Stintz throwing their hats in the ring, battle to become mayor heats up. *Toronto Star*, p. GT1.

James, R. (2014, 13 March). Chow well-positioned on the left to win. *Toronto Star*, p. A1.

James, R. (2014, 17 July). Pretense of playing nice vaporizes at debate. *Toronto Star*, p. GT2.

James, R. (2014, 11 October). Don't let those wild poll swings scare you. *Toronto Star*, p. GT2.

Jeffords, S., and Loriggio, P. (2018, 27 July). Ontario premier to slash size of Toronto city council nearly by half. *National Post*. https://nationalpost.com/pmn/news-pmn/canada-news-pmn/newsalert-premier-ford-to-slash-toronto-city-council-nearly-by-half-2

Johnson, R. (2014, 7 January). Mayoral hopeful Soknacki vows to serve city 24/7: Former councillor targets Scarborough subway as he registers to run in election. *Toronto Star*, p. GT2.

Kay, J. (2013, 19 November). Jonathan Kay: Sorry, but Rob Ford really does represent something bigger. *National Post*. http://nationalpost.com/opinion/jonathan-kay-sorry-kelly-mcparland-rob-ford-really-does-represent-something-bigger

Kenez, H. (2014, 5 October). Doug Ford booed at debate as he tries to distance himself from anti-Semitic slur allegedly uttered by mayor. *National Post*. http://nationalpost.com/news/doug-ford-booed-at-debate-as-he-tries-to-distance-himself-from-anti-semitic-slur-allegedly-uttered-by-mayor

Kidd, K. (2011, 6 March). Why Rob Ford might not want to ape Leafs Nation. *Toronto Star*. https://www.thestar.com/news/canada/2011/03/06/why_rob_ford_might_not_want_to_ape_leafs_nation.html

Lee, A. (2014, 15 July). Five takeaways from Toronto's mayoral debate. *Maclean's*. http://www.macleans.ca/politics/five-takeaways-from-torontos-mayoral-debate/

Loeb, V. (1998, 22 May). Barry brings halt to turbulent D.C. saga. *Washington Post*. http://www.washingtonpost.com/wp-srv/local/longterm/library/dc/barry/barryyears0522a.htm

Maloney, R. (2018, 31 July). Jennifer Keesmaat, Toronto mayoral hopeful, walks back tweets about city seceding. *Huffington Post.* https://www.huffingtonpost.ca/2018/07/31/ jennifer-keesmaat-secession_a_23493371/

McDonald, M. (2012, 15 May). The weirdest mayoralty ever – the inside story of Rob Ford's city hall. *Toronto Life.* https://torontolife.com/city/toronto-politics/rob-ford-the-weirdest-mayoralty-ever/

McParland, K. (2014, 27 October). Kelly McParland: Ford circus folds its tent as John Tory victory offers Toronto some needed calm. *National Post.* http://nationalpost.com/opinion/kelly-mcparland-ford-circus-folds-its-tent-as-john-tory-victory-offers-toronto-some-needed-calm

Mehta, D. (2014, 16 July). Rob Ford protesters, supporters in shouting match outside debate. *Global News.* https://globalnews.ca/news/1453442/cheers-and-jeers-for-rob-ford-in-toronto-mayoral-debate/

Mendleson, R., & Edwards, P. (2013, 18 November). Rob Ford stripped of power as mayor by Toronto council. *Toronto Star.* https://www.thestar.com/news/city_hall/2013/11/18/rob_ford_stripped_of_power_as_mayor_by_toronto_council.html

Moore, O. (2014, 28 March). Toronto election: Tory proposes high-frequency trains to relieve congestion. *The Globe and Mail*, p. A10.

Moore, O. (2017, 16 March). Metrolinx study finds Tory's Smart Track could spur auto commuting. *The Globe and Mail.* https://www.theglobeandmail.com/news/toronto/torys-smart-track-transit-plan-would-cause-surge-in-suburban-driving-analysis-shows/article34326461/

Morrow, A., & Hui, A. (2014, 11 March). Olivia Chow resigns seat, set to launch Toronto mayoral bid. *The Globe and Mail.* https://www.theglobeandmail.com/news/toronto/olivia-chow-jumps-into-toronto-mayoral-contest/article17449400/

Pagliaro, J. (2014, 24 September). Frontrunner Tory's strategy moves to defence. *Toronto Star*, p. A1.

Pagliaro, J. (2016, 9 November). Toronto city council approves addition of three new members. *Toronto Star.* https://www.thestar.com/news/city_hall/2016/ 11/09/ council-to-add-three-new-members-with-ward-boundary-change.html

Pagliaro, J. (2020, 26 March). Supreme Court of Canada agrees to hear Toronto's appeal of cuts to city council. *Toronto Star.* https://www.thestar.com/news/city_hall/2020/03/26/supreme-court-of-canada-agrees-to-hear-torontos-appeal-of-cut-to-city-council.html

Panetta, A. (2013, 4 December). Rob Ford saga biggest Canadian story in U.S. this century. *The Globe and Mail.* https://www.theglobeandmail.com/news/toronto/rob-ford-saga-dominated-us-headlines-in-november-analysis-suggests/article15766669/

Peat, D. (2014, 8 August). Ford's rivals attack plan to bury Eglinton Crosstown LRT. *Toronto Sun.* http://torontosun.com/2014/08/08/fords-rivals-attack-plan -to-bury-eglinton-crosstown-lrt/wcm/4f4b2614-660f-4154-866c-0d3034be1d1c

Peat, D. (2014, 23 October). Doug Ford should apologize to reporter, opponents say. *Toronto Sun.* http://torontosun.com/2014/10/23/doug -ford-should-apologize-to-reporter-opponents-say/wcm/70522b55-7b51 -44e1-b522-6eaabf9ad04d

Pelley, L. (2016, 1 December). Toronto road tolls, championed by Mayor John Tory, OK'd at executive committee. *CBC News.* http://www.cbc.ca/news /canada/toronto/tory-critics-taxes-tolls-1.3876070

Powell, B. (2014, 22 April). Meet the longshots: Mayoral candidate Ari Goldkind. *Toronto Star.* https://www.thestar.com/news/city_hall/2014/04/22/meet _the_longshots_mayoral_candidate_ari_goldkind.html

Powell, B. (2014, 28 August). Warren Kinsella no longer involved day-to-day in Olivia Chow campaign. *Toronto Star.* https://www.thestar.com/news/city _hall/2014/08/28/warren_kinsella_no_longer_involved_daytoday_in_olivia _chow_campaign.html

Powell, B. (2016, 4 December). How John Tory went from calling tolls "highway robbery" to crusading for them. *Toronto Star.* https://www.thestar.com/news /city_hall/2016/12/04/how-john-tory-went-from-calling-tolls-highway -robbery-to-crusading-for-them.html

Preville, P. (2011, 6 June). 50 reasons to love Toronto: No. 2, John Tory's not a right-wing blowhard. *Toronto Life.* https://torontolife.com/city/50-reasons -to-love-toronto-john-tory/

Rath, D. (2014, 10 October). John Tory must fight back against the Ford onslaught. *Toronto Star,* p. A17.

Rider, D. (2010, 26 October). Rob Ford elected mayor. *Toronto Star.* https:// www.thestar.com/news/gta/2010/10/26/rob_ford_elected_mayor.html

Rider, D. (2012, 18 December). Ford Nation stands by its man. *Toronto Star,* p. GT1.

Rider, D. (2014, 22 August). Stintz advisers throwing support to John Tory. *Toronto Star.* https://www.thestar.com/news/city_hall/toronto2014election/2014/08/22 /stintz_advisers_throwing_support_to_john_tory.html

Rider, D. (2014, 26 October). Father of Rob and Doug Ford a lasting influence. *Toronto Star.* https://www.thestar.com/news/city_hall/toronto2014election/2014/10/26 /father_of_rob_and_doug_ford_a_lasting_influence.html

Rider, D. (2017, 29 January). Turnabout could take toll on Kathleen Wynne's relationship with John Tory. *Toronto Star.* https://www.thestar.com/news /queenspark/2017/01/29/turnabout-could-take-toll-on-kathleen-wynnes -relationship-with-john-tory.html

Rider, D., & Dale, D. (2014, 21 August). Karen Stintz quits mayor's race, leaves politics. *Toronto Star.* https://www.thestar.com/news/city_hall

/toronto2014election/2014/08/21/karen_stintz_to_make_announcement
_after_no_comment_on_remaining_in_mayoral_race.html

Semley, J. (2014, 9 September). Jon Stewart struts the red carpet for Rosewater,
calls Canadians "upsettingly" nice. *Toronto Life.* https://torontolife.com
/culture/movies-and-tv/jon-stewart-expressed-support-olivia-chow-rosewater
-red-carpet/

Shum, D. (2016, 27 October). Toronto city executive committee rejects Expo
2025 bid. *Global News.* https://globalnews.ca/news/3028519/toronto-city
-council-executive-committee-rejects-expo-2025-bid/

Siddiqui, H. (2013, 3 November). What Stephen Harper and Rob Ford
have in common. *Toronto Star.* https://www.thestar.com/opinion/commentary
/2013/11/03/what_stephen_harper_and_rob_ford_have_in_common
_siddiqui.html

Simcoe, L. (2016, 27 October). City officials in Toronto tout new road
safety improvements. *Metro News Toronto.* http://www.metronews.ca/news
/toronto/2016/10/27/city-officials-in-toronto-tout-new-road-safety
-improvements.html

Simpson, J. (2013, 20 November). Ford Nation stands by its man. No. Matter.
What. *The Globe and Mail.* https://www.theglobeandmail.com/opinion/ford
-nation-stands-by-its-man-no-matter-what/article15519571/

Spurr, B. (2015, 11 March). Council overwhelmingly approves John Tory's
budget. *Now Toronto.* https://nowtoronto.com/news/council
-overwhelmingly-approves-john-tory%2527s-budget

Spurr, B. (2016, 27 October). Toronto councillor showcases city's progress on
road safety plan. *Toronto Star.* https://www.thestar.com/news/gta/2016/10/27
/toronto-councillor-showcases-citys-progress-on-road-safety-plan.html

Spurr, B. (2017, 27 November). Province should take over TTC and other
cities' transit systems, says Toronto Region Board of Trade. *Toronto Star.*
https://www.thestar.com/news/gta/transportation/2017/11/27/province
-should-take-over-ttc-and-other-cities-transit-systems-says-toronto-region-board
-of-trade.html

Spurr, B. (2018, 4 August). John Tory's SmartTrack plan faces uncertain fate as
PCs refuse to commit to key policy. *Toronto Star.* https://www.thestar.com
/news/gta/2018/08/03/john-torys-smarttrack-plan-faces-uncertain-fate
-as-pcs-refuse-to-commit-to-key-policy.html

Strashin, J. (2014, 2 October). Olivia Chow confronts racism, sexism in
mayoral campaign. *CBC News.* https://www.cbc.ca/news/canada/toronto
/olivia-chow-confronts-racism-sexism-in-mayoral-campaign-1.2785984

Toronto Star. (2014, 2 January). Toronto's mayoral marathon kicks off: So far,
Ford alone at the starting blocks as would-be challengers remain cautious
ahead of lengthy campaign. *Toronto Star,* p. A1.

Toronto Star. (2014, 7 January). Mayoral hopeful Soknacki vows to serve city 24/7. *Toronto Star*, p. GT2.

Toronto Star. (2014, 20 February). Stintz poised to register next week for mayoral run. *Toronto Star*, p. GT2.

Toronto Star. (2014, 24 February). Mayoral race just got more crowded: John Tory is in. *Toronto Star*, p. A1.

Toronto Star. (2014, 26 February). Mayoral poll shows tight early race. *Toronto Star*, p. GT2.

Toronto Star. (2014, 14 March). Olivia Chow's strong start. *Toronto Star*, p. A14.

Toronto Star. (2014, 15 March). Former MP leads in poll taken right after launch. *Toronto Star*, p. GT2.

Toronto Star. (2014, 17 June). Olivia Chow attacks rival John Tory over record as a Rogers exec. *Toronto Star*. https://www.thestar.com/news/city_hall /toronto2014election/2014/06/17/olivia_chow_attacks_rival_john_tory _over_record_as_a_rogers_exec.html

Toronto Star. (2014, 25 June). Toronto election poll: Rob Ford still competitive after seven-week absence. *Toronto Star*. https://www.thestar.com/news/city _hall/toronto2014election/2014/06/25/toronto_election_poll_rob_ford _still_competitive_after_sevenweek_absence.html

Visser, J. (2014, 9 August). Tory surges ahead of Chow: Survey. *National Post*, p. A11.

Wanagas, D. (2001, 10 March). Don Wanagas: The odd rantings of young Rob Ford. *National Post*. http://nationalpost.com/toronto/don-wanagas-the-odd -rantings-of-young-rob-ford/

Warnica, R. (2014, 27 October). The night that turned the tide for John Tory's fledgling mayoral campaign. *National Post*. http://nationalpost.com/news /the-night-that-turned-the-tide-for-john-torys-fledgling-mayoral-campaign

White, P. (2014, 12 September). Can Doug Ford win Toronto's mayoral race? *The Globe and Mail*. https://www.theglobeandmail.com/news/toronto/can -doug-ford-win-torontos-mayoral-race/article20591133/

Wright, J. (2013, 19 November). "Mayor voters: Just who is Ford Nation?" *Global News*. https://globalnews.ca/news/977578/mayoral-voters-just-who-is-ford -nation-2/

Index